SO-FKE-815

LATENT MEMORY

LATENT MEMORY

*Human Rights and Jewish Identity
in Pinochet's Chile*

Maxine Lowy

THE UNIVERSITY OF WISCONSIN PRESS

The University of Wisconsin Press
728 State Street, Suite 443
Madison, Wisconsin 53706
uwpress.wisc.edu

Gray's Inn House, 127 Clerkenwell Road
London ECIR 5DB, United Kingdom
eurospanbookstore.com

Originally published in Spanish as *Memoria latente: Una comunidad enfrentada por el deafío de los derechos humanos en Chile*. Published by arrangement with Lom Ediciones, copyright © 2016 by LOM Ediciones, all rights reserved.
Translation copyright © 2022 by the Board of Regents of the University of Wisconsin System
All rights reserved. Except in the case of brief quotations embedded in critical articles and reviews, no part of this publication may be reproduced, stored in a retrieval system, transmitted in any format or by any means—digital, electronic, mechanical, photocopying, recording, or otherwise—or conveyed via the internet or a website without written permission of the University of Wisconsin Press. Rights inquiries should be directed to rights@uwpress.wisc.edu.

Printed in the United States of America
This book may be available in a digital edition.

Library of Congress Cataloging-in-Publication Data

Names: Lowy, Maxine, author.
Title: Latent memory : human rights and Jewish identity in Pinochet's Chile / Maxine Lowy.
Other titles: Memoria latente. English
Description: Madison, Wisconsin : The University of Wisconsin Press, [2022] | Originally published in Spanish as Memoria latente: una comunidad enfrentada por el desafío de los derechos humanos en Chile. | Includes bibliographical references and index.
Identifiers: LCCN 2021028713 | ISBN 9780299335809 (hardcover)
Subjects: LCSH: Jews—Chile—History. | Human rights—Jews—Chile—History. | Chile—History—Coup d'état, 1973.
Classification: LCC F3285.J4 L6913 2022 | DDC 983/.004924—dc23
LC record available at https://lccn.loc.gov/2021028713

Dedicated to the memory of my cousin

Máximo Eduardo Jaroslavsky,

Argentine doctor of conscience born September 7, 1938, and
forcibly disappeared as of the evening of his abduction on
November 19, 1975, in Tucumán, Argentina

CONTENTS

ILLUSTRATIONS

ACKNOWLEDGMENTS

For their valuable contributions, I am grateful to every person who participated in this project to give voice to their personal histories, each a significant testimony that strengthens historic memory. I especially value Hanni Grunpeter and Gunter Seelmann, whose life stories form a unifying thread of this book and exemplify an ethical legacy that transcends personal tragedy, a channeling of tragedy into a lifelong commitment to justice. For her guidance and clarity throughout the process of this book, I thank Ivonne Szasz Pianta. I also sincerely appreciate the significant editing support of this English edition provided by Tracey Jaffe, Helen Hughes, Patricia Morris, and Mary Jo McConahay.

CHRONOLOGY

1970

September 4   Salvador Allende is elected president of Chile.

October 19   President Allende meets with Jewish community leaders to reassure them of his support.

November 6   President Richard Nixon convenes the National Security Council to map out a plan to destabilize the Allende government.

1971

July 11   The Chilean Congress unanimously approves constitutional amendment 17.450 to nationalize the copper mines.

1973

March 4   The Popular Unity coalition obtains 43 percent of the vote in congressional elections.

June 29   An army tank regiment headed by Lieutenant Colonel Roberto Souper attempts to carry out a military coup, known as *tanquetazo*, but fails.

August 23   President Allende appoints Augusto Pinochet army commander-in-chief after Carlos Prats resigns.

September 11   Pinochet organizes a military coup, bombing La Moneda, the presidential palace, which kills Allende. A military junta is installed that disbands Congress and suspends civil and human rights; dozens of people are assassinated and thousands are imprisoned on the first day of what will be seventeen years of dictatorial rule.

October 6   The interfaith Propeace Commission in which Rabbi Angel Kreiman participates convenes, the goal of which is to protect lives as well as to document and denounce human rights violations.

October 6–24   The Yom Kipur war, a surprise attack by a coalition of Arab forces, takes place. On the third day of the offensive, twenty-four-year-old Leo Guzmán, who had emigrated to Israel with a group of Chileans from Hashomer Hatzair, is killed.

1974

September 30   Former commander-in-chief Carlos Prats and his wife, Sofia Cuthbert, are assassinated in Buenos Aires by agents of the repressive DINA, the Chilean secret police.

November 6   The UN General Assembly adopts Resolution 3219, the first of many that urged Chile to restore human rights.

December 23   US Congress approves an amendment (known as the Kennedy Amendment) to the Foreign Assistance Act that bans providing military aid to Chile as long as it persists in violating human rights.

1975

January 27   The US Senate Select Committee on Intelligence, chaired by Senator Frank Church, begins an investigation that will culminate with documentation of CIA covert actions to undermine the Allende government.

April 16   A body falsely alleged to be that of David Silberman, a Jewish citizen of Chile who was abducted from the Santiago Penitentiary in October 1974, where he was awaiting his release, is found in Buenos Aires with a falsified ID card.

July 11, 19   The charred bodies falsely alleged to pertain to Chileans Luis Guendelman, Juan Carlos Perelman, and Jaime Robotham are found in Pilar, Argentina, with falsified ID cards. All three had been forcibly disappeared in Chile. Luis Guendelman had been abducted on September 2, 1974, Juan

Carlos Perelman on February 20, 1975, and Jaime Robotham on December 31, 1974.

July 12 and 16   In response to the growing national and international demand that the Chilean government account for the forcible disappearance of hundreds of people, the dictatorship orchestrates Operation Colombo. On these dates, fake magazines published in Argentina and Brazil as well as Chilean newspapers announce that 119 Chilean leftists killed each other in internecine battle, when in fact they had been murdered by the dictatorship in Chile.

November 25   Chile joins with the dictatorships of Argentina, Bolivia, Paraguay, and Uruguay to create Operation Condor.

1976

September 21   Orlando Letelier, a former ambassador to the United States and defense minister for the Allende administration, and Ronni Karpen Moffit, coworker at the Institute for Policy Studies, are murdered in Washington, DC, by a car bomb placed by DINA agents.

1980

September 11   A constitution drafted by military-civilian ideologues is imposed in a highly contested referendum.

1985

January 4   Boris Weisfeiller, a US mathematician and former Soviet Jewish émigré, disappears in the vicinity of Colonia Dignidad while hiking in Chile.

1988

October 5   A referendum that limits Augusto Pinochet to two more years in power and that mandates democratic elections for the first time in seventeen years wins.

1990

March 11   Patricio Aylwin takes office as the first democratically elected president of Chile since 1970. He creates the National Truth and Reconciliation Commission to document human rights violations committed by the dictatorship.

June 2   A mass grave, two meters wide, eleven meters long, and two
                meters deep, containing the remains of nineteen people
                summarily executed by the dictatorship, is discovered at
                Pisagua, in northern Chile.

September 4   A state funeral for Salvador Allende is held in Santiago,
                nearly seventeen years after his death.

December 1   The Kennedy Amendment arms sale embargo is lifted.

                                   1997
July 12   The Centro Progresista Judío (CPJ, Jewish Progressive Center)
                holds first tribute to Jewish victims of the dictatorship.

                                   1998
October 16   Augusto Pinochet is arrested in London on the orders of
                Spanish judge Baltazar Garzón. The former dictator spends
                more than five hundred days under house arrest before the
                House of Lords accepts Chile's appeal to let him return to
                Chile on humanitarian grounds.

                                   2003
September 26   The National Commission on Political Imprisonment and
                Torture headed by Monsignor Sergio Valech is created by the
                Chilean government to document cases of surviving former
                political prisoners and provide reparation.

                                   2006
December 3   An event memorializing both Anne Frank and Diana Aron is
                held at Villa Grimaldi by the Centro Progresista Judío.

December 6   A funeral is held for Bernardo Lejderman, who was murdered
                with his wife, María del Rosario Avalos, by the Chilean army
                on December 8, 1973, in the presence of their two-year old
                son, in an abandoned mine while they were trying to flee
                Chile on foot. The remains of Avalos have yet to be found.

December 10   Augusto Pinochet dies.

                                   2011
October 28   A funeral is held for psychiatrist Jorge Klein, a forcibly
                disappeared detainee as of September 11, 1973. Klein, who

had been a close advisor to President Allende, was arrested the day of the coup and taken along with twenty other presidential staff to the Arteaga military base in northern Santiago, where all of them were summarily executed. Fragments of the victims' remains were discovered in 2001 and 2009.

2012

September 4   A funeral is held for Ernesto Traubmann, a forcibly disappeared detainee as of September 13, 1974, who had been a journalist and radio operator.

2013

September 11   Chile marks thirty years since the military coup.

December 8   A memorial for seventeen Jewish victims is erected in a Jewish cemetery in Santiago.

December 19   A plaque honoring twenty Jewish victims is installed at Villa Grimaldi Peace Park by the Jewish Progressive Center.

2014

April 13   A funeral is held for journalist Carlos Berger, a forcibly disappeared detainee who had been sentenced to sixty days in jail but was summarily executed with twenty-six other political prisoners on October 19, 1973, on a road outside Calama.

2015

May 29   A funeral is held for Jacobo Stoulman and Matilde Pessa at Santiago's Sephardic Cemetery. Stoulman and Pessa were forcibly disappeared detainees, abducted in Buenos Aires in May 1977. Fragments of their skeletal remains were discovered in a former mining area in Chile, confirming that they were brought back to Chile and then murdered.

ABBREVIATIONS

ACU	Agrupación Cultural Universitaria (University Cultural Association)
AFDD	Agrupación de Familiares de Detenidos Desaparecidos (Association of Families of Disappeared Detainees)
AJI	Asociación de Jóvenes Israelitas (Association of Young Israelites)
AMIA	Asociación Mutual Israelita Argentina (Argentine Israelite Mutual Association)
ANEF	Agrupación Nacional de Empleados/as Fiscales (National Public Employees Association)
CIS	Centro Integral de Salud (Comprehensive Health Center)
CNI	Central Nacional de Informaciones (National Information Center)
CODELCO	Corporación Nacional del Cobre de Chile (National Copper Corporation of Chile)
CODEPU	Comité de Defensa de los Derechos del Pueblo (Committee for Defense of People's Rights)
CORFO	Corporación de Fomento de la Producción de Chile (Economic Development Agency)

CPJ	Centro Progresista Judío (Jewish Progressive Center)
CREJ	Comité Representativo de Entidades Judías de Chile (Jewish Representative Committee)
CUT	Central Unitaria de Trabajadores (Chilean Federation of Workers)
DICOMCAR	Dirección de Comunicaciones de Carabineros (Directorate of Police Communications)
DINA	Dirección de Inteligencia Nacional (National Intelligence Directorate)
ERP	Ejército Revolucionario del Pueblo (People's Revolutionary Army) (Argentina)
FASIC	Fundación de Ayuda Social de las Iglesias Cristianas (Christian Churches Social Assistance Foundation)
FECH	Federación de Estudiantes de la Universidad de Chile (Federation of University of Chile Students)
FEDEFAM	Federación Latinoamericana de Asociaciones de Familiares de Detenidos-Desaparecidos (Latin American Federation of Associations for Relatives of the Detained-Disappeared)
FIS	Frente de Izquierda Sionista (Zionist Left Front)
FLASCO	Facultad Latinoamericana de Ciencias Sociales (Latin American Faculty of the Social Sciences) (Santiago)
Fundación PIDEE	Fundación de Protección a la Infancia Dañada por los Estados de Emergencian (Program for Children Injured by States of Emergency)
HIJOS	Hijos por la Identidad y la Justicia contra el Olvido y el Silencio (Sons and Daughter for Identity and Justice against Forgetting and Silence)
IC	Partido Izquierda Cristiana (Christian Left Party)
INSA	Industria Nacional de Neumáticos (National Tire Industry)

MAPAM	Mifleget HaPoalim HaMeuhedet (United Workers Party)
MIR	Movimiento de Izquierda Revolucionaria (Revolutionary Left Movement)
PDC	Partido Demócrata Cristiano (Christian Democratic Party)
Propeace Committee	Comité de Cooperación para la Paz (Committee of Cooperation for Peace in Chile)
RAF	Royal Air Force
SA	Sturmabteilung
UDI	Unión Demócrata Independiente (Independent Democratic Union)
UNHCR	United Nations High Commissioner for Refugees
WIZO	Women's International Zionist Organization

Latent Memory

Introduction

I grew up in the Deep South in the late 1950s and 1960s, the daughter of a father from New York and a mother from Argentina. The essence of my Jewish identity could be synthesized as follows: "We are members of one of the most persecuted groups on earth and that compels us to take a stand against injustice today."

Later, I would add other elements to this foundation of my Jewish identity, but during the first eighteen years of my life, an acute awareness of a history of persecution as well as a sense of social responsibility arising from that history comprised its core. My parents and several in their circle of progressive, mostly Jewish, friends, all transplants to Baton Rouge, Louisiana, shared these beliefs, which spurred them to participate in the early civil rights movement. As Jews and civil rights activists, our family was a curiosity to our neighbors. That sense of being "different" was another thread in the fabric of my nebulous identity as a Jew.

Jews, including Reform and Orthodox rabbis, figured prominently in the civil rights movement, raising funds and participating directly in actions during the Freedom Summer of 1964. But it is important to recall that, by and large, these were northern Jews.[1] Most southern Jewish communities did not take a vocal stand against the white majority that outright rejected integration and full citizenship for Black people. In the South, racism and antisemitism went hand in hand, and shop windows had signs that read "No blacks, no Jews, no dogs," which might explain, though not justify, the hesitancy of southern Jews to publicly align themselves with the civil rights cause.

The commitment to social justice my parents upheld was not always the norm among Jews. For centuries, Jews had been "the other" in marginalized and isolated communities of Europe. A strategy these Jewish communities adopted to mitigate their precarious and insecure condition is summarized in the Yiddish expression *sha-shtil*, which loosely translates as "keep quiet and don't make waves." Fearful of negative repercussions that could befall the entire community, they preferred to keep a low profile, to avoid voicing an opinion outside their communities.[2]

In 1990 I moved to Santiago, Chile, where I still live, leading me to more deeply reflect on the significance of this othering and the impact of centuries of Jewish marginalization on the collective psyche of the Jewish people. My condition as newcomer and outsider during the time I was assimilating into both the human rights and Jewish communities afforded me a different perspective on how Jewish institutions had responded to human rights violations under the Chilean dictatorship, leading to the development of this book, *Latent Memory*.

The 1970 election of Salvador Allende as president, followed by a military coup in 1973, sharply polarized Chilean society and presented a moral crossroads for the Jewish community. Despite reassurances from Allende, the Jewish community was wary of his leftist Popular Unity government, and a third of the nation's Jewish population fled the country.

When the military abruptly upended democracy on September 11, 1973, shutting down Congress, suspending all civil and human rights, and introducing a radical neoliberal economic policy, most Jewish community leaders explicitly applauded the authoritarian regime. Despite the implementation of a systematic policy of state terrorism and repression, they preferred to ignore the persecution and suffering of fellow Chileans. Progressive Jews who suffered physical and psychological abuse in unjust, brutal detentions now became the "other," ostracized by Jewish communities.

The Jewish community's silence and complicity during the years of the military dictatorship still hurts those Jews who directly suffered from the repression. The American rabbi and political activist Michael Lerner offers a possible explanation for why the Jewish community remained largely silent. While not referring specifically to Chile, he has noted in his book *Jewish Renewal: A Path to Healing and Transformation* that "there are moments when the pain [passed from generation to generation] becomes so overwhelming, the fears so intense, that human beings seem to be acting only out of the collective memory of anger, frustration and humiliation. . . . It is precisely one of the continuing consequences of the pains of the past that we become blind to the pains of others, unable to hear their pain and their cries because we are so overwhelmed with our own."[3]

Lerner's words raise a couple of weighty questions. Is a human collective with a history of marginalization and persecution engraved in its cultural psyche bound by a higher ethical imperative? How can Chilean Jews make amends for ignoring the pain and suffering of their coreligionists during the years of dictatorship?

In the Jewish tradition, when a person causes an offense against another, the possibility for *teshuva*, restoration of confidence, always exists. Yet for such a renewal of faith to occur, the offender must first recognize the damage he or she caused, then make justice, and lastly repair the damage. In Chile, however, the road map for restoring trust, both within the Jewish community and society as a whole, cannot follow the traditional process of *teshuva*. Within the Chilean Jewish community, the point of departure for this process must be acknowledgment of a shared history and respect for different ways of assuming Jewish identity.

From that standpoint, Chile and the Chilean Jewish community can provide a lesson for all nations and peoples who have endured systematic persecution and discrimination. A latent dimension of historical memory can be activated to the extent that collective consciousness incorporates an ethical mandate that does not tolerate cruel treatment of other human beings, regardless of where they come from. If I fail to raise the human rights banner everywhere, I deny my own history.

Pinochet's Chile spans beyond the official conclusion of his dictatorship, at the inauguration in March 1990 of the first democratically elected president in twenty years. The failure to dismantle the economic, social, and political framework installed during the dictatorship contributes to a persistent human rights problem that needles Chile's very soul, manifested today in negationism, lenient court sentences for perpetrators of human rights crimes, and harsh police repression in response to pressing social issues. The tension between human rights and Jewish identity simply mirrors the nagging, unresolved legacy of dictatorship in Chile as a whole. Only by harnessing the latent memory of both Jewish and Chilean history can the wounds of the past be healed and give rise to a society founded on respect for the inherent dignity of every human being.

PART I

SHARED HISTORIES AND A DIVERGENCE

I

Exodus

Monumental structures—splendid palaces and temples, obelisks and colossal statues—conceived by Ramses II were built throughout the Nile delta region during ancient times. Such enormous and extensive public works required a constant production of bricks, mortar, other construction material, and especially abundant manpower.

A settlement of foreigners whose prolific reproduction appeared to pose a threat to the hegemonic stability of the nineteenth dynasty was worrisome for the pharaoh. The god-king wisely decided to conscript them into his state slave labor program. Here was the labor force needed to implement the kingdom's ambitious construction projects. And the hard work would weaken that haughty nation.

With this double objective, the foremen were instructed not to spare their whips. The slave who let a brick fall from his hands, who slipped in the mud while digging ditches and dikes to contain the annual river floods, felt the lash on his back. One time, the monarch decreed that all male babies born in that slave colony be killed, but the midwives refused to be accomplices to genocide and would not carry out the order.

From that degraded generation there emerged a charismatic leader, one of the babies saved from the infanticide decree, who convinced his people that they need not suffer; lives of freedom, he proclaimed, were within reach. This group of slaves may have been one of the first in the history of humanity to rebel against their taskmasters. They also established the first link of a chain that would extend infinitely into the future, wandering Jews obligated to undertake an exodus to seek gentler lands in which to raise a new generation in freedom. They had been strangers in a strange land, and, except for brief spans here and there, their descendants would be too.

The oppression of the Hebrew people and their subsequent liberation from Egypt are at the crux of the formation of Jewish identity. Religious Jews remember this foundational event every week upon blessing the Shabbat wine. In addition, for eight days of every year through the celebration of Passover, they relive the story of how an enslaved people took its first step toward becoming a free nation. Even for nonreligious Jews who participate in the Passover ritual, the yearly repetition becomes incorporated in their psyche as a social ethic. The story is particular to Judaism; it is also universal. Its prophetic message of the possibility of societal transformation resonates beyond the Jewish setting, inspiring African American aspirations for freedom and providing the foundation of Latin American liberation theology.

Every so often, a biblical historian announces that he or she has calculated the precise date of the Exodus, and biblical archaeologists have also claimed to have discovered hieroglyphics that register the presence of Hebrew slaves. For many Jews, however, the historicity of the Exodus is of little importance. Mitzrayim, the Hebrew word for Egypt, has a metaphorical meaning of "a narrow, constricted place": in other words, any place where a population lives in narrow straits. Every generation has its Egypt. And any place we live may be or become "Egypt." But, in contrast with Moses, who was able to demand that the monarch let his people go, in centuries to come Jews would rarely be in a position to demand anything. Time and time again, they would be expelled or would rapidly flee without having time to plan.

CROSSING FORBIDDEN BORDERS

As a story goes, a long time ago, a bear escaped from a circus. Police ordered that the bear be shot on sight. Upon hearing about the order, a Jew announced to his neighbor: "I'm leaving town. As soon as the bear surfaces, it will be shot."

"But you are not a bear," the neighbor replied.

"That's what you say. Soon they'll shoot a Jew and only after he's dead they'll discover he wasn't a bear."[1]

The precarious nature and danger of everyday life for the four million Jews expelled by the czars from their villages in the early years of the nineteenth century and forced to live in a territory that extended more than six hundred thousand square kilometers from the shores of the Black Sea to the Baltic fed anecdotes that evoked the nervous laughter of recognition.[2] "If there was too much sun, it was our fault, and if it rained too much, that was also our fault," a grandmother used to tell her Chilean grandson to illustrate the suffocating atmosphere of her native village near the Russian-Ukraine border.[3]

In that expanse of land, known as the Pale of Settlement, the most extensive community of Jews up to that point in history lived in numerous villages and towns.[4] The rationale for designating a zone for Jewish habitation originated from complaints by Moscow shop owners that they could not compete with Byelorussian Jews. In 1804 a series of laws specified the provinces from which Jews were banned, as well as major cities within the zone such as Kiev, Niko-layev, and Sebastopol. Kiev officials periodically raided every house, conduct-ing *oblavy* (hunts) to track down Jews illegally residing in the city and then chain and return them to the Pale.

The classic work *Life Is with People* describes the insecurity of Jewish life in these villages, where long spans of tranquility were subject to an unpredictable burst of violence.

> Most Jews knew, by experience or by eyewitness account, of pogroms. They had direct evidence of the strange fashion in which their neighbors might sud-denly become pillagers and murderers. They knew equally well the reverse tran-sition, when, the pogrom over, these same killers once again became neighbors, customers, salesmen, and relations settled back into the old routine "as if noth-ing had happened." Nothing had happened,—except that one's friend, one's uncle, one's sister, one's father was now dead.[5]

Some Christians protected Jews during a pogrom, and others demanded a bribe to keep the hordes at bay. There were also villages where Jews always had good relations with their Christian neighbors.

The lack of contact with contemporary currents of society and culture (according to an 1897 census, 96.7 percent of Jews residing in the Pale spoke Yiddish and only 1.3 percent spoke Russian as their mother tongue) fostered the creation of an autonomous Jewish life, nurtured exclusively by Jewish sources.[6]

March 1, 1881, the day Russian czar Alexander II was assassinated, has been described as "a turning point in the history of the Jewish people as decisive as that of 70 A.D. when Titus's legions burned the temple at Jerusalem, or 1492, when Ferdinand and Isabella decreed the expulsion from Spain."[7] The death of Alexander II brought the end of a peaceful era for the Jewish com-munity; Jews were subsequently subject to mass executions, expulsions, racial and religious persecution, and pogroms led either by groups of bandits while police looked the other way or, at times, by the police itself.

These circumstances spurred the first major wave of Jews to leave for the *goldene medina*, the golden lands of opportunity and freedom, New York City in North America, and Buenos Aires in the southern hemisphere. The much-dreaded military service that forced Jewish males—boys as young as ten—to serve ten, fifteen, or even twenty-five years in the czar's army also drove families to send their sons far away.

In the town of Zlovota, about one hundred kilometers from Kiev, a city Jews were prohibited from living in, Marcos Svigilsky was born. The house he grew up in was built, brick by brick, by his mother, or so she claimed to her granddaughter Perla Aron. When Marcos received the order to present himself for the army medical checkup, his mother devised a scheme whereby he could avoid military service.

"For three days she kept him from falling asleep, while she sat on a chair and he on a low bench. Whenever he started nodding off, she would wake him up. The idea was to weaken him so he would fail the military conscription medical exam," said Perla. The strategy worked. He was weakened to such an extent that the army did not accept him. A short time later, Marcos Svigilsky and his cousin Benjamin Slachevsky became the first members of their family to embark for the southern hemisphere, arriving at the shores of the River Plate in 1908.[8] The recollections of the people left behind, the houses where they were born, and a way of life remained frozen in time.

Between 1880 and 1914, two million Jews immigrated to the United States from Russia, the Pale of Settlement, and regions of Poland under Russian dominion.[9] In the same years, another million Russian Jews immigrated to Argentina.[10]

With the advent of the October 1917 revolution, the czars' power collapsed, but the Bolsheviks only assumed power in a very small part of Russia, limited to the zone between Saint Petersburg and Moscow. Meanwhile, in the villages where the Lawner family lived, near the Polish border, the White Bands were established. Taking advantage of the subsequent political chaos, these bandits assaulted villages, robbing everything they could find, including the animals. Miguel Lawner explains that his

old folks were modest farmers. They had to learn how to coexist in this situation. They had a guard lookout system. When dust was seen rising in the distance along the road, they knew the bandits were on their way. And they would scramble into underground shelters they had built under the houses for that purpose. They lay low in those basements, even anesthetizing the animals to keep them from making noise. They could hear the bandits above them destroying everything.[11]

Increasingly, it was impossible to live a normal life. After several years of great hardship, in 1921, they decided to leave forever. Eight of the Lawner brothers, several with their wives and families, as well as their father and mother, left for the American continent. Two brothers stayed behind, later reuniting with the family in Argentina some years later.

Crossing the broad Dniester River that formed the border between Russia and Poland was the first step of an exodus that thousands participated in. Frequently in the history of that corner of the world, the 524 feet between the two riverbanks was the distance between life and death. So it had been in the past and so it would again when the Lawners were far away, safe in Chile. Six years earlier, on June 25, 1915, the Dniester's rapid course did not intimidate Prussian troops, who waded with their cannons in the dark, through chest-high water, to destroy the Russians. And on July 25, 1941, near the town of Coslav, Romanian troops herded a convoy of twenty-five thousand Romanian Jews, delivering them to the German forces occupying Ukraine.[12]

But on the night the Lawners crossed, they were guided by the spirit of the great eighteenth-century mystic known as Baal Shem Tov (Master of the Good Name), renowned for his legendary generosity. It has been said that as a youth, Israel ben Eliezer, who would later come to be known as Baal Shem Tov, made use of his knowledge of Kabala to cross the Dniester. Hurling his *gartel* (cloth belt) over the water, he pronounced the secret name of God and was able to cross to the other bank of the river. For the rest of his life, he regretted having invoked the sacred name of God for his personal gain. In the cold darkness of 1921, it was as if Baal Shem Tov's *gartel* had transformed into the ferry that enabled the Lawners to reach the Polish side and leave the shtetl behind forever. The family then boarded a ship that left from Poland and anchored in the port of Buenos Aires. In February 1922, the family moved to Rosario, where they found the humid semitropical summer weather unbearable. "My mother would always tell us how they would lie on the tile floor, practically undressed, to sleep," says Miguel.[13]

The youngest of the Lawner brothers, Miguel's uncle Samuel, who was still single, got a tip about the country on the other side of the Andes range. He crossed the mountains to take a look and returned to report his findings: "Chile is better. You can breathe there and you can make *kishef*, business." A few months later, the family set out for the third and final leg of their odyssey. They lifted their suitcases once more, closed the doors of another house behind them, and crossed the Andes into Chile.

A Luminary Ventures into the World

Vilna, today the capital of Lithuania, was once known as the Jerusalem of Eastern Europe. During the eighteenth century, it was not only a major Jewish industrial center, dominating the apparel and glove market through exports to Russia and Germany, but the focal point of Eastern European cultural activity, Torah study, and the Jewish enlightenment known as Haskalah. Adherents of Haskalah believed Western education would make full equality between Jews and Christians possible. The enlightened ones, or *maskilim*, maintained that only by exposure to non-Jewish thought, to the effervescent political and intellectual movements of eighteenth- and nineteenth-century Russia, could ghetto isolation be overcome.

In 1720, the mystic sage Elias Ben Solomon was born in Vilna. Legend has it that at three he knew the Holy Scriptures by heart and that at six he gave his first public speech. During his adolescence, he roamed communities of Europe on foot, dressed as a beggar, sharing his wisdom. Several years later, upon returning to Vilna, by which time he was known as Gaon Hasid, the saintly and wise man of Vilna, he argued that the only way to fully grasp Talmud was through the study of secular matters such as astronomy, mathematics, and botany.

More than a century later, on December 29, 1898, Jacobo Pilowsky was born in Vilna, which had by then been annexed to the Russian Empire. We do not know whether his genealogy can be traced back to Elias Ben Solomon, but his family did include acclaimed rabbis, and he himself, like Ben Solomon, was an avid scholar as well as leader in the Jewish community. Jacobo was born and grew up in an era of persistent attacks on the Jews of Vilna. His son Jorín recalls what his father told him.

> My grandfather and great grandfather were rabbis. My father was born into a very religious household but broke with that to become a Yiddishist, a passionate practitioner of Yiddish culture and writer in that language, which was spoken by the Jewish masses. The socialist revolution of October greatly affected that region. Many shared the expectation that the Soviet Union would not only solve prevailing social problems and end man's exploitation by other men but would also end all forms of discrimination against minority peoples.[14]

But Jews who had grasped onto the revolutionary hope that antisemitism would be extinguished would be disillusioned. The roots of hatred were so deep that revolution did not erase them.

In that context of insecurity and fear, messianic dreams were born. By the early twentieth century, Vilna had become the center of Russia's Zionist movement as well as the headquarters of the Zionist Worker Party. But in 1941, Nazi military forces would snuff out Vilna's light forever. By then Jacobo would be safe and thriving in Latin America. Around 1923, he, his wife, and their first son, two years old, had joined the stream of immigrants who crossed the Atlantic. As with the Lawner family and the Svigilsky cousins, they first arrived in Argentina. There Jacobo worked as a teacher of Yiddish before continuing on to Chile.

The Righteous of Ulm and Contulmo

Thousands lay dying in the medieval cities of Europe. Their bodies remained where they had breathed their last breath until they could be buried in mass graves. Rats, probably transported aboard a merchant ship from Messina, Italy, introduced the bubonic plague in Europe in the fourth decade of the fourteenth century.[15]

Survivors of the black plague were convinced that Jews had caused the calamity by poisoning wells, even though Jews died at the same rates as everyone else. The belief ignited collective hysteria as widespread as the disease itself, leading to massacres and mass burning of Jewish communities, despite Pope Clement VI's condemnation of the violence against Jews. In various zones of Germany, where pogroms of notorious fervor and ferocity were carried out, by late 1390 few Jews remained.[16]

But by the mid-fifteenth century, after the last major outbreak of the plague, large landowners in Germany permitted Jews to settle on their territory, offering them a degree of protection in exchange for the payment of a special tax. A man known only by the name of Loew, meaning "lion," a surname derived from Levi, arrived at a large landholding on the outskirts of the city of Ulm. Loew learned to work leather, one of few trades permitted to Jews. The next ten generations of Loews worked in tanneries in the village of Fraunloch and later in Ulm itself.

The lords allowed many Jews to purchase names to camouflage their true identity, a strategy designed to minimize repression. Other Jews were given names in return for favors rendered. In this way, the descendants of the Loews became Lebrechts, which derives from "lebe recht," or "live right," referring to a person who lives a righteous life.

In Ulm, where the Danube meets the Blau and the Iller, Walter Libricht Koln was born in 1912 to a family of prosperous industrialists of the leather trades.[17] His ancestors had lived in that city since the Middle Ages. Walter Libricht Koln's father was a German republican, proud of having fought for Germany in World War I. His father was also a musician, a member of a string quartet, and his mother was a patron of the arts of Ulm, known for its artistic traditions. Walter went to the Heidelberg University, ninety-three miles to the north, to study law. However, his higher education ended prematurely, frustrating his intellectual aspirations. A portent of what was to come was the controversy that arose at the university over the appointment of Emil Gumbel, a socialist and pacifist Jew, whose academic credentials were impeccable, as extraordinary associate professor of mathematics.[18] Over a period of two years, Nazi professors and students created a tense setting by holding fiery rallies.

Their incitement culminated in Gumbel's dismissal in 1932 on the grounds that he was a traitor to the German people owing to his Jewish origins. A year later, in April 1933, with Hitler in power, a law was passed to "cleanse" universities of non-Aryan faculty, defined as having at least one Jewish grandparent. One fourth of Heidelberg University professors were fired. The following month another law came into effect banning Jewish students from attending universities.

Unable to continue studying, Walter went to a *hajshara*, one of many agricultural organizations that proliferated in Eastern Europe in the years between the two world wars, that trained Jewish youth to be pioneers in Israel. They learned to plant, irrigate, raise animals, and gather eggs, skills intended to prepare them for life as part of a kibbutz, an agrarian collective. However, in Walter's case, these skills prepared him for Chile.

The business run by Walter's father was Aryanized; in other words, he was forced to sell to a non-Jew at a ridiculously low price. Different countries extended visas to the Lebrecht family. The parents and eldest son, Kurt, went to southern Brazil; brother Hans went to Israel; Walter and the youngest brother, Weiner, went to Chile.

Utopian enthusiasm for working the land lifted Walter's spirits as he crossed the Atlantic at twenty-five years of age. During his journey, he imagined the land promised him by a German settler, whom his father had helped in Ulm. In 1937 he arrived in the town of Contulmo, founded in 1884 in the Nahuelbuta forest by Baptist craftsmen and farmers from Berlin, located in southern Chile's Arauco Province.[19]

FROM RUDOLPH TO RODOLFO

Embraced by soft verdant hills on the south; forests of birch, beech, and larch trees on the north; and by the Leine and Ruhme rivers on the west is the town of Northeim, formerly belonging to the kingdom of Hanover in Germany. Medieval walls still surround narrow cobblestoned streets in the vicinity of the town's central oval plaza. In its days of glory, during the fifteenth century, the town was practically independent and its walls impervious to invaders. When the town converted to the Lutheran religion in 1625, it resisted a blockade by Catholic forces for two years.

Among the dangers its walls were meant to keep out were Jews. The Duchy of Brunswick-Lüneberg had expelled Jews, yet city historic records show it made a few exceptions. In 1576 a Jewish family composed of a man named Moses; his wife, Ana; and their children was admitted for a period of six years in exchange for annual payments of fifteen gulden to ensure their protection. In 1589 they were obliged to pay another twelve gulden and fifteen marks more in taxes to guarantee their children's lifetime right of residence. However, in 1639, the Diet, the assembly of Hanover nobles and ecclesiastical officials, banned Jews from living in Northeim. The dozen Jewish families still residing there, including descendants of the Moses family, were expelled. Not until 1809 did town records again note the presence of Jewish residents—two families— who had settled in Northeim.

In 1922, a Jewish couple, Adolph and Lotte Müller, living in Northeim had their second child, Rudolph. By the time Rudolph was born, Northeim's twenty thousand inhabitants counted among them one hundred Jewish families. The small Jewish community had a synagogue, a school, and its own cemetery. Adolph had enlisted at the outset of World War I, as had thousands of other German Jews. Their hope was that by volunteering for military service, doubts concerning their loyalty to Germany would be laid to rest and they would cease to be second-class citizens.

Many years later Adolph would tell his four sons how he led horse-drawn carts carrying ammunition to the front lines, a highly dangerous job that earned him an Iron Cross.[20] He served during the entire war, from 1914 to 1918, and was present at the bloody battle that took place in the hills outside Verdun-sur-Meuse. Of the more than one hundred thousand Jews who enlisted in the German army, an estimated twelve thousand died fighting for Germany.[21] But instead of winning acceptance as full-fledged German citizens, with all the rights this entailed, Jews were blamed for Germany's humiliating defeat and economic ruin. Ominous clouds were still distant on the horizon when Rudolph was born, though, and during his first ten years, life was good for him. Rudy, as he was known to his friends, discovered a passion for music and at seven began playing violin, accompanying his father, who played piano. He had two close friends—one Jewish and the other Lutheran—at the primary school. The Lutheran buddy, Bernard Baum, "was a very, very good friend of mine," he recalls, now an elderly grandfather on a continent far from his native town. In the summertime they would go together to the swimming pool, and Bernard invited him to the movie theater his father opened on the second floor of his house to see the first talking pictures.

The Great Depression upset Northeim's tranquil ambience and Rudy's placid days as a student. The ancient walls could not contain the new danger because it was brewing from within. In the national elections of 1928, the National Socialist Party received just 2 percent of the vote in Northeim, and in 1929 it was still a peripheral party of only five members in the town. But in the elections of 1933, Nazi propaganda yielded 63 percent of the vote for the National Socialist Party.[22] Capitalizing on this electoral triumph, Nazis expanded their indoctrination and recruitment work: rallies, marches of uniformed men, and

violent actions by the brown-shirted Sturmabteilung (SA) paramilitary organization were increasingly common in Northeim. The woodsy trails south of
town were no longer safe for Sunday strolls, as these had become one of the
favorite places for confrontations between Social Democrats and the SA.

Until then, anti-Jewish sentiments had been expressed only by the most visible Nazi leaders. The campaign against the Jews got under way in earnest on
March 29, 1933, according to historian William Sheridan Allen. On that date,
the Nazi Party launched a publicity campaign to decry "international Jewry"
for spreading negative reports about Germany. Germans were called upon to
stop patronizing Jewish businesses. In Northeim the order affected thirty Jewish businesses, including the A. H. Müller Bank.

Nazi Party members stood outside Jewish stores, writing down the names
of non-Jewish people who entered. After deploying this intimidation tactic
one time, the SA no longer needed to actively enforce the new policy. Posters
appeared throughout the business district that announced that a given shop
was a "Christian-owned business" or a "business without foreign capital."

At school, classmates tried to provoke the three Jewish boys: Rudy, his older
brother Ernest, and his friend Simon. "All that's happening to our country
is your fault," classmates chided them.[23] Simon was a very studious boy who
didn't participate in sports and went to synagogue with Rudy. On more than
one occasion, bullies tormented Simon, and Rudy rescued him. "They respected me a little more because I defended myself. One time they sat my
friend Simon on a closed garbage can and set it on fire underneath. I got him
out of there, and the both of us took off," Rudy recalls.

The situation deteriorated to such an extent that Rudy's father took him
and his brother out of the public school and sent them to a Jewish boarding
school in the city of Coburg, in southern Germany. In that large two-storied
house, where Jewish families from all over Europe were sending their children,
Rudy gained a greater appreciation for the Jewish tradition and celebrated his
bar mitzvah.[24] He also learned to play both the accordion and the violin, and
in 1934 he formed a band.

One time Rudy went with a boarding school friend to the movie theater. "We
had settled down in the middle of the theater, when the manager signaled to
us to get out. The manager realized we were from the Jewish boarding school.
He kicked us out and told us never to come back there again." Rudy could no
longer go to the movies in Northeim either. The father of his friend Bernard
was ordered to put a stop to his son's association with Jews and send the boy
to the Hitler Youth. If he did not obey, officials would close his movie theater.

The breaking point for the Müller family was the death in 1935 of grandfather Hermann Rodolph. The extended Müller family—an uncle's family as

well as Hermann—lived in the same house, above the bank the patriarch had founded. Hermann had been a conservative as well as a respected member of the glee club, the traditional *schutzenverein* marksman club, and other circles of Northeim high society. On holidays, he customarily raised the imperial flag above his bank. Some seventy businessmen chose to ignore the warnings and accompanied the funeral carriage to the Jewish cemetery. The next day, the Stuttgart daily newspaper ran a photograph taken by an SA leader of all who attended the funeral with the caption "Judenknechte aus Northeim!" (Servants of Northeim Jews!).

Sheltered from the outside world at the boarding school, Rudy and his brother Francisco, as well as Ernest at a *hajshara* near Berlin, received phone calls from their parents instructing them to pack their belongings at once. "Events were advancing so fast that we had no time to react," recalls Rudy.

At fourteen years of age, Rudy and his eleven-year-old brother Francisco, each carrying a single suitcase, left the boarding school. They boarded a train for Paris to meet their parents. Two days later, with the cold December wind in their faces, the family boarded a ship that left from the port of La Rochelle for a country called Chile. They reached Valparaíso, in the middle of the southern hemisphere summer. It was January 12, 1937, Rudy's birthday. On that day, he became Rodolfo.

ISLES OF FREEDOM AND CONFINEMENT

An Irish legend recounts the story of the light-haired giant Fionn mac Cumhaill, who dug up a chunk of Irish soil and hurled it at a Scottish rival. He missed the mark, and where the piece of land fell into the ocean, between Ireland and England arose the Isle of Man, a place of astounding beauty and mythology as singular as the great Chilean island of Chiloé. The thick fog that sometimes envelops its 193 square miles, 40 percent of which is uninhabited, is said to be the cape of the god of the sea Manannán mac Lir, a legendary king who gave his name to the island and protects it from invaders.

Today's tourist brochures tell us that the island's beaches welcome thousands of visitors every year, who arrive by plane or by boat for "unforgettable vacations." However, no word is found in those guides about the mandatory stay of thousands of people in the small towns of Knockaloe and Douglas, where England established detention camps during World War II.

German military prowess sowed panic but also mistrust in Germans as a whole, leading the British government to implement harsh measures against refugees. Germans, Italians, and Austrians in the country were deemed "enemy aliens" and as of September 1939 were placed in detention camps in various parts of England.

Erwin Grunpeter was a Jewish refugee. Born in Germany, Erwin met Martha Windolz in the Czech village of Ceski-Tesin, near the Czechoslovakian-Polish border, and they married. In late 1939, after the German invasion of Poland and the bombing of Warsaw on September 25, 1939, the couple fled with their young daughter, Hanni, to England. After the bombing of London, the family moved to the city of Bedford. They had just arrived in Bedford when Erwin, thirty-seven years old at the time, was arrested and sent to the Isle of Man. A year would pass before his wife and child saw him again.

Small wooden houses, some of which had previously served as hostels for vacationers, were requisitioned to house detainees. Over the course of the war, more than ten thousand persons were held in the six camps established on the Isle of Man. A demographic survey of a single camp on the Isle of Man in the village of Onchan, where barbed wire was extended along Royal Avenue, revealed that 1,230 people, or 8 percent of detainees, were Jews.[25]

During that seemingly interminable year, Erwin was permitted to write two letters per week that were inspected by the Liverpool Censor Office before being delivered. His wife, Martha; his daughter, Hanni; and his recently arrived father, Zumlein, settled down in a house in Bedford provided by a Jewish family, owners of a garment factory in London. Martha was a skillful seamstress who sewed girdles, bras, and dresses for the business. The family in London put its two children in Martha's care to protect them from the bombing. Once a week the family traveled to Bedford to see the children, bringing fruit and other food considered luxury items in those days of scarcity.

Beginning at four in the afternoon of September 7, 1940, and continuing until dawn the next day, 348 Luftwaffe planes unloaded incendiary bombs over London. The blitzkrieg continued over British cities until May 1941, resulting in heavy damage to many parts of London. The shrieking sirens warning of another aerial attack, the black curtains in the windows, and hunger remained etched in the memory of Erwin's daughter years later in Chile.

Upon his liberation from the Isle of Man, Erwin reunited with his family in a London flat that they shared with other Jewish refugees. In 1948, Erwin's sister wrote from a South American land called Chile, which she described as "flowing with milk and honey," insisting that they join her as soon as possible. Hanni had no idea on what continent Chile was located; she had not even heard about the country in her geography class. Soon she would come to know that distant country very well.

∼

During the Jewish ceremony of Passover, the following words are read from the Haggadah: "In every generation, each of us should feel as though we ourselves had gone forth from Egypt."[26] Few generations that read these words have had to make an effort to imagine bondage in Egypt. Each generation actually *lived* its own Egypt or soon would.

The Lebrecht family of Ulm, the Lawners and Svigilskys of Ukraine, the Müllers of Northeim, the Pilowskys of Lithuania, and the Grunpeter family of Czechoslovakia would experience the very real sensation of having passed through there. They had made their way to Chile one way or another and hoped to find a genuinely new and better world there. Thirty-five years later, the benevolent South American country would turn against them. Either they themselves or their offspring—children, grandchildren, nephews, and nieces—would be forced to undertake the journey back to the old continent. For them, Chile would become an Egypt.

2

Strangers in a Strange Land

On January 24, 1939, while the earth shook Concepción, Federico and Ana Seelmann and their two children left Germany. "We had no idea we would end up in Chile," says Gunter Seelmann, who was eight at the time. They had visas for the United States but while they waited in the Netherlands for their grandmother's visa that never arrived, their own visas to the United States expired. The last visas left were for Chile. "I can assure you that my parents did not know where Chile was, if it was in Africa, Asia, or Oceania," he adds.[1]

As he climbed aboard a ship in Antwerp, Jorge Hirsch, alone, and without even a suitcase, had not the slightest idea where that country was either. When an official explained that his visa was for Chile, "he thought they said China," says his son Tomás. "Never before had he heard of Chile."[2]

What Hans Stein, at twelve years of age, knew about the country that waited for him was equally minimal. After the Nazi invasion of Czechoslovakia, his family left for England. During their stay there, he developed a passion for soccer, and it occurred to him that he could introduce soccer to Chile. "A week after arriving in Chile, I went to the National Stadium to see the Colo Colo team play and I realized my project was utterly useless."[3]

On a globe, Rodolfo Müller saw the long thin line called Chile near the southern tip of the world. "We had no idea about it at all. On our voyage we learned that our destination was a port city, Valparaíso, and from there we would continue two or three hours more to Santiago, the capital. On the ship we had grammar books to learn Spanish; we learned easily."[4] For the Müller family, for most of the Jewish refugees who arrived at the port of Valparaíso in the late 1930s, Chile was a destination of last resort.

Jorge Hirsch had escaped from a forced labor camp that manufactured ammunition near the border between Germany and the Netherlands, not far from Burgsteinfurt, the town where he was born; almost the entire population was sent to the gas chambers. Of their family, he and a sister who also immigrated were the sole survivors.

Federico Seelmann and his brother had spent a month in the Buchenwald concentration camp. Despite the boycott on Jewish businesses, new laws severely restricting the ability to earn a living, and his own harrowing detention, it was hard for Federico to let go and leave the place. He still believed those bad times would soon pass. His wife persuaded him to leave for the family's sake. His son recalled the emotional intensity of the moment when he observed his father's boss, a gentleman who was not Jewish, weeping upon bidding the family farewell at the train station.

For them and so many others, it didn't matter where Chile was, as long as it got them away from Europe and the threat the continent posed to their survival. Some came to Chile because relatives had already settled there. Others chose Chile because it permitted immigrants to bring a greater number of belongings. Although this benefit was completely irrelevant for Jorge Hirsch, who had fled with nothing but the clothes on his back, it paid off for the Müllers. Rodolfo points to a small round table in his living room and other things that his family brought with them to Chile, tangible vestiges connecting the life they left behind in Northeim with the one they made for themselves in Santiago. Most Jews of Northeim did not have the coffee table's good fortune; understandably, Rodolfo is attached to it. "Not everyone had the possibility to immigrate," he acknowledges. "Few were able to leave."

Selective Immigrants

Chile's oldest Jewish communities had been founded by Sephardic Jews—descendants of Jews expelled from Spain in 1492 and Portugal in 1496, who settled along the Mediterranean—long before Ashkenazi Jews from Russia and Eastern Europe sought refuge in Chile from oppression. In 1916, Sephardic Jews established the Macedonian Israelite Center of Temuco and the Max Nordau Instruction and Beneficence Society of Valparaíso, and in the early 1920s, after the collapse of the Ottoman Empire, the Paz family immigrated from Cairo, Egypt; the Sharim family from Aleppo, Syria; the Caro family from Smyrna, Turkey; and the Benados family from Bulgaria, seeking better business horizons. According to official records, in 1914, there were five hundred Jews in all of Chile. In those times, when few Jews were coming to Chile, no major obstacles existed to impede their immigration.

In 1930, when the population of Chile totaled four million, its Jewish population numbered 3,697. In 1933 this figure leaped to ten thousand. Between 1932 and 1941, thirteen thousand Jews arrived from Europe, making Chile third among destinations for refugees in Latin America, surpassed only by Argentina and Brazil.[5] By 1959, when the Chilean population was more than seven million, thirty thousand Jews lived in the country.

Chile never developed a policy of mass immigration, except with respect to German as well as Austrian and Swiss colonists whom the Chilean government encouraged to settle in the southern regions in the mid-1800s. The arrival of these immigrants was promoted under the Selective Immigration Act of 1845, which initially specified they be Catholic (later amended to "Christian," to include Lutheran Germans). Much of the lands promised them south of the city of Valdivia were not in fact uninhabited but were traditional territory of the Huilliche indigenous communities, whom the government sought to displace.[6] With these intentions in mind, government officials were not interested in promoting large-scale immigration to the country.

Statistics for a single year speak for themselves. In 1895, 665 immigrants arrived in Chile, while on the other side of the Andes, Argentina received 44,169.[7] More than half of recent arrivals to Argentina were Italians, a third were Spaniards, and the rest were Poles and Russians, the vast majority of whom were Jews fleeing the pogroms of 1881.[8]

When the dribble of Jewish refugees trying to leave Europe became a steady stream in the mid to late 1930s, Chile followed the example of most of the world's nations. It either made it hard for such persecuted persons from Europe to emigrate or outright blocked them from entering the country. Nationalist and fascist elements in Chile also exercised pressure to restrict the entry of refugees.

On October 11, 1933, President Arturo Alessandri enacted Discretionary Law 4072, which required immigrants to prove they would not be a burden to the state and left selection and admission to the discretion of Chilean consuls. The following year that law was amended to clarify that Chilean firms could only hire foreigners if no qualified Chileans could be found to fill those jobs.

Ignoring the League of Nations' appeal to facilitate the entry of German Jews, in 1937, the Alessandri government introduced a regulation to limit the entry of immigrants in general and Jews in particular to people who had families in Chile. A quota of sixty Jewish families per year was eventually set; these families were selected by the Comité de Protección a los Inmigrantes Israelitas (Israelite Immigrant Protection Committee) in conjunction with the Foreign Relations Ministry.[9]

The deep division within Chilean society was indicated by the results of the 1937 congressional election. Chileans voted in five lower house representatives and one senator from the National Socialist Movement.[10] In the same elections, Natalio Berman of the Socialist Party, Marcos Chamudes of the Communist

Party, and Angel Faivovich of the Radical Party were elected the first Jewish congresspeople in Chilean history.[11]

The election of Natalio Berman, in particular, was a triumph over tremendous odds. Berman was a physician, public health advocate, and active member of the Jewish community, who left Russia at an early age with his family, arriving in Chile in 1915. His fervent opposition to policies promoted by conservative president Alessandri landed him in prison twice: first, in 1935, for opposing a regressive sales tax; and in 1936, when he was banished to the rocky, inhospitable Melinka Island. In 1937, President Alessandri invoked an obscure law that allowed the expulsion of "undesirable foreigners" to strip Berman of his Chilean citizenship. The outcry against the unjust and discriminatory measure obliged the president to retract the order. Berman, then twenty-nine years old, ran for office that same year and subsequently was reelected twice. Once, in a heated congressional session, a representative remarked, "How can you talk about Chile when you are a nationalized Jew!" To this Berman retorted, "I think I am a better Chilean than many of you here who have given away this country to foreign capitalists."[12]

The year the first three Jewish legislators took their seats in Congress, Walter Lebrecht left Ulm. After arriving at the port of Valparaíso, he still had another four hundred miles to travel to claim his promised plot of land in Contulmo in southern Chile. Soon after, Lebrecht set about working to bring his younger brother Heiner to Chile.[13] Under the recently ratified immigration regulation, his brother should have been permitted to emigrate because he was a direct family member. It did not turn out that way, however. When Heiner arrived at the Chilean port, exhausted from the ocean voyage and traumatized by Nazi persecution, Chilean immigration bureaucrats only accorded him a tourist vista. Like people today who enter Chile on a tourist visa but who want to stay longer and so have to travel to Mendoza, Argentina, to extend their visas another three months, Heiner had to leave Chile several times and then reenter the country. The denial of permanent residence status that would have allowed him to work wreaked havoc on Heiner. Believing himself to be a burden to his brother, Heiner, at twenty-two years of age, took his own life. Walter concealed from his family the truth about Heiner. Not until they were adults did his children learn that their uncle Heiner had not died from a heart attack.

But Heiner's tragic circumstances and that of thousands of Jews trapped in Europe were of no concern to President Alessandri, who governed the country a second time (1932–38), implementing emergency de facto laws and a state of siege. Alessandri had developed a plan to settle German, Swiss, and French immigrants in southern Chile, but Mapuche peasants lived on the land the government had promised these European immigrants. When, in July 1934, the Mapuche community of Ranquil ignored the government eviction order, Alessandri commanded police to open fire against one hundred rural people. This president did not care about the plight of Jewish refugees.

At the time, Austrians Francisco Sohr and Elsa Biss, both nineteen years old, were newlyweds.[14] But the future did not look bright after March 12, 1938, when Germany annexed Austria, in what is known as the Anchluss. With alarm, they saw thousands of people—Jews, social democrats, and communists— arrested within days after the invasion, while other Austrians joyfully welcomed the invaders, with bouquets of flowers and German flags. They applied for visas to Chile, but when the couple went to pick them up after the Chilean Consulate notified them that the visas had been approved, their interview at the consulate took an unexpected turn. What happened that day was so startling that years later they often recounted it to their children, born in Chile. As their son Raul explains,

> The Chilean consul in Vienna handed my parents the visa and said, "Well, have a good trip." Then he added, "By chance, are you Jews?" Yes, they said. "Let's see, give me your passports," the consul replied. And he repealed the visas! They went to the Chilean consulate in Prague, paid a hefty sum of money, and then received the visas. They sold them the visas!

The young couple reached England and were on the verge of staying there when they became aware of the atmosphere of mistrust of German-speaking people. It was the same climate of suspicion that a year later led to the detention of Czech-German refugee Erwin Grunpeter on the Isle of Man, as described in the previous chapter. As soon as it was possible, Francisco and Elsa resumed their journey, arriving in Chile in December 1938.

After the November 9, 1938, massive attack on Jewish communities in Germany that bore all the characteristics of pogroms from earlier in the century, thousands of Jewish families, who previously had not wanted to believe that terror was fast approaching, clamored for visas at all the diplomatic missions, including that of Chile. Two months earlier, Pedro Aguirre Cerda had won the presidential election, and he announced his intention to open the doors to refugees and remove the antisemitic consuls. But Aguirre Cerda faced a Congress dominated by the right that opposed the aspirations of his Frente Amplio political coalition, which negatively impacted Chile's approach to the Jewish refugee issue.

In a confidential memorandum dated April 26, 1939, to Chilean consul to Prague Gonzalo Montt Rivas, Consular Department director Carlos Errázuriz

Ovalle bluntly stated that "in regards to Israelite requests to come to Chile, . . . you have been instructed that this Department is not interested in these, no matter how wealthy they may be, yet you continue to authorize them to come under any pretext."[15] The reprimand to the consul in Prague notwithstanding, Chilean governmental officials were willing to consider exceptions to the rule, persuaded by influential non-Jewish people who sent letters of recommendation or, better yet, a well-placed banknote to a public employee. The latter practice proved so effective that HICEM, the Jewish committee that facilitated entry of Jewish immigrants, had to hire "a special employee to help government employees with their job to accelerate visa authorizations."[16]

In 1939, this bribery scheme came under congressional investigation, and two years later, Abraham Ortega, the foreign relations minister, was forced to resign. The following year, the emigration of Jews to Chile was suspended, pending the passage of an immigration law that was never implemented.

In the first two months of 1939, four German ships—the *St. Martin*, the *Oceanisa*, the *Artigas*, and the *Cap Norte*—tried to drop 411 Jewish refugees off at various ports. The *St. Martin*, according to an article published by the Jewish Telegraph Agency on March 31, 1939, "after trying in vain to disembark its passengers at every port of Latin America, was heading back to Germany to return the refugees to concentration camps when Lisbon permitted it to anchor." The British government eventually allowed *Oceanisa* to disembark its passengers at Gibraltar.[17]

The *Artigas* and *Cap Norte* found safe harbor in Montevideo, thanks to the intervention of three Chileans. At the time, which was March 1939, the International Democracies Congress was in session in that Uruguayan city. Natalio Berman, who was one of the Chilean delegates, heard about the urgent situation affecting the *Cap Norte* passengers, gathered signatures from fellow delegates, and then sent a telegram to President Pedro Aguirre Cerda asking that he authorize twenty-seven Jewish refugees to enter Chile. President Aguirre Cerda's positive response was applauded by the entire International Congress. "I feel deep satisfaction and am very grateful to the government," Berman later said. "These highly skilled people who had been subjected to humiliations, privations . . . , barbarity and exploitation, see our country as a paradise."[18]

Two key actors in this dramatic episode have been forgotten by other authors. The first, a person who dedicated all his soul and strength to the refugee cause, was Jacobo Pilowsky. The Vilna native who had arrived fifteen years earlier was acutely aware of the hardships endured by forcibly displaced persons. In his capacity as secretary of an organization that actively advocated for displaced people, Pilowsky helped another generation of Jews find a place where they could fully develop as human beings. In his memoir, published in 1970 in

Yiddish, Pilowsky describes the actions he took behind the scenes to provide shelter for Jewish refugees aboard the *Cap Norte*.[19]

Pilowsky appealed to a second equally forgotten actor of this story: Socialist Party general secretary Salvador Allende Gossens. It was Allende who dispatched an urgent cable to the Chilean congressional delegation in Montevideo through Berman.[20] Arye Pilowsky, who is translating his father's memoirs into Spanish, notes that "in the cable, Allende requested that the delegation ask Aguirre Cerda to allow the Jewish refugees on board the ship anchored in Montevideo to settle in Chile. Thus, Allende undertook efforts that prevented the refugees from being returned to Germany."[21]

Allende's efforts to secure entry and advocacy of a solidarity-oriented immigration policy for refugees from Nazism led Pilowsky to laud him as a *hasid umot haolam*, which is a Hebrew expression that means "righteous among the nations," the highest recognition reserved for people who save Jewish lives. Allende certainly deserved that accolade, but so did Pilowsky, the tireless fighter for the refugee cause.

CLASSIFIED INFORMATION

"They completely vanished, and no one knows how or where they have gone." Thus remarked England's ambassador in Berne, Switzerland, in November 1941, regarding nearly one-and-a-half-million Polish Jews.[22] On August 8, 1942, he and other British diplomatic offices in Switzerland received a telegram about the inexplicable disappearance of the Jews from Gerhart Riegner, the representative in Geneva for the World Jewish Congress.

> I received an alarming report about a plan being discussed in the Fuhrer's headquarters to exterminate all Jews in the countries controlled by Germany, consisting of three and a half to four million after deportation and concentration in the East in order to resolve the Jewish question once and for all in a campaign planned for the fall with methods that include hydro cyanuric acid.[23]

At a moment in time when evacuation of the Warsaw ghetto had begun and Jews were being deported to unknown locations, Riegner's telegram constituted the first reliable source regarding the deportees' destiny. However, officials of the United States and England decided to restrict dissemination of the telegram's contents.[24]

Two years later, officials would receive an eyewitness report about a concentration camp. Rodolf Vrba and Alfred Wetzler, two young Slovakian Jews, escaped from Auschwitz with help from members of the resistance within that extermination camp, their specific mission being to inform the world about what they had seen. After walking kilometers and kilometers only at night, "without a compass, map or arms," they reached Bratislava, Czechoslovakia. There they drafted a detailed report about what was going on in Auschwitz, even including a map of the concentration camp premises. Vrba had been a Sonderkommando, and he had firsthand knowledge of the crematoria at Birkenau. A chain of hands passed the report along to the Vatican, the Allied forces, and finally Roosevelt. The report called for the bombing of Auschwitz. It was April 1942, but the Allies decided to keep the report under wraps.[25]

It is not known whether the Riegner telegram or the report were leaked in Chile and therefore shaped its diplomatic policy of neutrality. However, today we do know that Chile possessed classified information earlier than most other nations. The source was Gonzalo Montt Rivas, the same Chilean consul in Prague who in April 1939 was reprimanded by the consular general for granting visas to Jews. Two years later, the consul had made a 180-degree turn in his position.

In a letter dated September 6, 1941, Montt informed the Chilean foreign relations minister that "in Warsaw the Jews have been concentrated into a single neighborhood of the city," which, he added, was a model that could likewise be followed in Czechoslovakia: "The example of Warsaw shows that there is a solution to this aspect of the Jewish question. No obstacles exist to impede doing the same in the Protectorate."[26] The consul described the restrictions placed on Jewish life and praised a measure that would become mandatory as of the nineteenth of that month: "Thus visibly marked with the star of David, the Jews will be unable to infiltrate where they do not belong; transgressors will be severely punished."[27]

November 24, 1941, the day before the order was issued that stripped Jews of citizenship in other countries—the step prior to expropriating their property—Montt translated the decree and sent it to the Chilean government, remarking that "the Jewish problem is being solved in part, in the Protectorate already, as the decision has been made to remove all Jews and send them to Poland and to the city of Terezin, while a more isolated location is sought."[28] Montt went on to offer the following prediction: "The German triumph will leave Europe clean of Semites. Those who manage to stay alive will certainly be deported to Siberia, where they will have few opportunities to make use of their financial abilities."[29] This indicates that the Chilean consul had early access to information about the Reich's plan to deprive Jews of citizenship, deport them, and eventually exterminate them.

Two months before the Wannsee Conference, where the "final solution" was sealed, Montt, with clear sympathy for the Nazi policy, informed his higher-ups in Chile about the plan to carry out genocide, although he lacked details about the methods that would be employed to achieve that. He concluded his report to the Foreign Relations Ministry by noting that "the exodus of Jews from the Reich has not had the consequences prophesized by Germany's enemies, quite the contrary: Aryans have replaced them at clear advantage in every way, except for the area of usury and similar activities at which they are the consecrated masters."[30]

Montt's reports were intercepted and their contents leaked to intelligence agencies of the United States and England. In 2001, Richard Breitman, a US historian, discovered the English translations of Montt's reports among the documents declassified by the State Department. Montt's original letters with his seal as consul general in Hamburg can be found in the National Archives of Chile.[31]

Breitman suggests that Montt had close relations with German officers in Prague, speculating that he may have been a Nazi collaborator. In 1940, Germany forced the Chilean consulate in Prague to shutter its consulate, as it did other countries, but it authorized it to reopen in 1941. At a time when Prague was no longer a national capital, and most of the diplomatic corps either had left or had been expelled, Gonzalo Montt Rivas's friendship with Nazi officials permitted him to resume his consular duties.

With full knowledge of these facts, England and the United States chose not to do anything. With the same classified information in its possession, Chile emulated the inaction of the superpowers, choosing trade interests over humanitarian demands.

Raúl Sohr, son of the previously mentioned young Austrian couple who arrived in late 1938, cautions not to judge Chile's neutrality too severely:

> If you look at it in the cold light of day, there was no reason for Chile to take a side one way or the other, especially since the United States chose not to involve itself in the war until it was directly attacked by Japan. The United States, the most powerful country, that always proclaimed itself to be the moral beacon of the world, refused entry to many refugees. . . . Had I been a statesman in those times, I too would have called for neutrality. Why should I get involved in a war that has nothing to do with me? If they allow such atrocities to occur, why should I, like Quixote, fourteen thousand kilometers away, come out with my spear?[32]

Some twenty-five years later, indeed, in an entirely different political context, Chile would face international repudiation for its disregard for its citizens' fundamental rights, isolating the country from the league of civilized nations. The UN High Commissioner of Refugees (UNHCR) would launch its refugee protection program in Chile in 1973. The nations of the world that in 1938 refused to raise their immigrant entry quotas to save human lives opened their doors wide to harbor Chilean refugees.

The Medal

In the years when thousands clamored to leave Europe, one young Czech refugee, who had just arrived in Chile, chose to return to the eye of the hurricane. Ernesto Traubmann, born May 19, 1924, in Brno, Moravia, was the son of Sigmund Traubmann, a wealthy property owner. One building belonging to Sigmund later became the main offices of the Moravian public health services under the Communist Party government. When the Nazis took Czechoslovakia in March 1939 and forbid Jews from owning property, he sold the building for far below its real worth, because Jews were not only banned from owning property but also were not allowed to possess more than a certain amount of money.[33]

Sigmund used all the money he had left to obtain visas and tickets for himself, his wife, and his son in an effort to reach the United States. When they eventually arrived in Chile instead, he wrote to a sister who had succeeded in reaching the Northern Hemisphere that "Ernst and I studied English, and he received a certificate of achievement for his excellent English. Now we have to learn Spanish!"

Sigmund and his family did not come directly to Chile. Like other Jews, they looked for a country that would admit them. Like many other displaced people, they were turned away at each place they arrived. After passing through Colombia and Argentina, they finally arrived in Chile.

They arrived without a penny to their names. Sigmund took the only possession of value they had—his wife Lucia's fur coat—and sent it to his sister in the United States for her to sell and send the money from the sale to him. His sister never received the coat.[34] But Sigmund was resourceful and opened a small shop, which he named Casa Arta, on the corner of Monjitas Street near Plaza de Armas in Santiago. Along one side, he offered jackets, gloves, and all kinds of woolen garments; on the other side of the shop, he sold bathing suits.

As Sigmund began reestablishing himself financially and integrating himself into Chilean society, alarming news came from relatives in Czechoslovakia. Then letters from Brno stopped coming. Much later, they learned that in October 1939 trains carrying 1,292 Jewish men left Ostrava in the northern region of Moravia, where Sigmund and his father had been born.[35] In November 1939 the first train loaded with a thousand Jews left Brno, headed in the direction of the concentration camps. Practically all twelve thousand Jews of Brno were murdered during the years of Nazi occupation (1939–45). An estimated one thousand fortunate souls survived.

Sigmund and the rest of the Traubmann family were well aware how fortunate they were to be in Santiago, but they were naturally racked by anxiety over the fate of their relatives in Brno. The frightful information from Europe angered Ernesto, and when World War II broke out in September 1939, he was determined to return to fight. Under no circumstances would his parents allow him to carry out what they considered a senseless idea. But Ernesto had made up his mind to fight against Nazism and would lecture anyone who would listen about how critical it was. His friends from those years remember how "he concluded his harangue with the phrase: 'It's now or never!'"[36] As a minor of seventeen, he would not be able to obtain a passport or even leave the country without his parents' permission, so he procured a false identity card and passport, making his way first to Argentina and eventually to England. He joined the Czech Battalion of the British Royal Air Force, better known as the RAF, and was trained as a telecommunications specialist.

As a radio operator, he flew in missions over Ostrava, his grandfather's native town, where the Nazis now used slave labor to run the coal refinery plants. He also participated in reconnaissance flights that searched for German submarines. People who had enlisted in the RAF were free to leave upon completing a certain number of flying hours. Ernesto completed those hours and continued until the end of the war. The queen of England decorated him with a medal.[37]

Ernesto returned to Chile with a medal pinned to his uniform, but the indignation that had driven him to leave his home to join the RAF burned in this chest stronger than ever. It infuriated him that the Allied forces had not done everything in their power to save Jews en route to extermination camps. What he saw and learned during the war shaped his identity as a progressive as much as his certainty regarding the need to create the state of Israel, a double militancy arising from a deeply held belief in freedom.

Fast forward to the 1960s. A young boy flips through a photo album. From one picture a tall, thin, man, with gaunt cheeks and timid smile gazes out at him. Next to the man, dressed in an elegant blue uniform with small white wings embroidered over the left breast pocket, stands another uniformed man, his comrade and best friend. The two young comrades were Ernesto and Denni. Each promised the other that if one of them died, the other would name his son for him. The boy who scrutinized the photo learned this many years later, when he was an adult. At that time, he reached the conclusion that his father's comrade died, because the boy's name was Denni.[38]

The story behind the photo was one of many mysteries associated with his father that Denni Traubman has tried to decipher. For years he wondered about the medal on the uniform that he enjoyed taking out of the closet and putting on. His father never told him what it meant. Many years later, when he learned it was an award for valor, everything made sense. He finally under-stood why the unbending and deeply idealistic man who was his father did not attempt to flee before the foreseeable arrival of those who came to arrest him in the early hours of September 12, 1973. Just like his family members in Brno, Ernesto's nightmare began and ended with men in khaki green uni-forms. And just like his comrade Denni, fallen in battle against the Nazis, Ernesto would disappear in action.

3

Community Dilemmas

CROSSROADS

Every immigrant brings baggage to his or her adoptive country containing family, social, and political experiences from the country left behind. The Jews who arrived in Chile brought along a wide range of experiences. Some came from small villages and others from large, cosmopolitan urban centers; some followed traditional religious practices, while others had participated in vibrant union and socialist movements.[1]

Sometimes the sense of being uprooted and coping with the adjustments common to many immigrants is compounded by trauma. When an immigrant's departure is not the result of his or her decision to seek better economic or educational horizons but rather due to untenable conditions like war and oppression or the outright expulsion from one's native country, the insecurities intrinsic to refugees may make their process of adaptation and their relationship to the new country different from that of immigrants who choose to emigrate to a new country. Such was the case for many Jews in Chile in 1970. Less than twenty-five years after the unfathomable slaughter known as Shoah, the history of marginalization and persecution was deeply rooted and culturally entrenched.

Between September 1948 and June 1949, at a time when the ashes of the six million had barely ceased to smolder, several Jewish intellectuals were arrested in the Soviet Union. On August 12, 1952, thirteen of them were executed in Lubyanka prison, in what came to be known as the "night of the murdered poets." In 1951, thirty-seven Jewish doctors were arrested and were subsequently released following Stalin's death in March 1953.

That persecution against loyal Jewish Communist Party members in the Soviet Union prompted many members in other countries to abandon it, disillusioned by the party's failure to acknowledge and denounce antisemitism.

34

One person who left the Communist Party in Chile was Jacobo Pilowsky, the Yiddishist from Vilna. He had left the party years earlier when the Soviet Union signed the nonaggression pact with Germany in August 1939. He rejoined after observing the Soviet Union's decisive role in defeating the Nazis, only to leave the party definitively after the murders of the Jewish writers. "Many people from the party's progressive wing were also dismayed but lacked the courage to follow his example," affirms his son Jorín Pilowsky.[2]

The Círculo Israelita de Santiago (synagogue also known as CIS and Mercaz) held a commemorative event in August 1972 honoring the murdered Soviet writers, "who joined the centuries and centuries of Jewish martyrs."[3] Twenty years after the fact, the memory of these murders was still vivid for Jewish communities.

Among Jews in Chile who had been traumatized by the Shoah, there was a marked mistrust in anything resembling the left, except perhaps among active socialists or those with union backgrounds. Economic class interests also played a role in pushing Jews who had prospered away from the left. Prior to 1970, Chilean politics were centrist, and Chilean Jews likewise gravitated toward moderate political positions. Many were attracted to the Radical Party's nonreligious, anticlerical, and strong social doctrine.[4]

For the Jews of Chile, two years of the country's contemporary history—1970 and 1973—accentuated the differences they brought to the country and other differences subsequently constructed there, marking an ethical crossroads.

First Crossroad: 1970

As Salvador Allende's electoral campaign advanced and a presidential victory began to look like a real possibility, many Jews prepared to leave Chile. The rise of the socialist president revived old fears among segments of the Jewish community. They worried once again about becoming targets of persecution and having their property expropriated, as happened in 1935 in Nazi Germany. Estimations of the number of Jews who left Chile due to Allende's election fluctuate between three thousand and eight thousand, according to different sources.[5]

Chilean society as a whole was polarized, and the Jewish community reflected that polarization. But the condition of being Jewish added another element that other Chileans did not experience: the old latent fear of totalitarianism. International analyst Raúl Sohr observed the situation close up, as the son of Austrian Jewish refugees. He states that the reaction among certain Chilean Jews to Allende

> was more a psychological phenomenon rather than a fear of anything concrete. Jews have the little worm of anti-Communism inside them, but it's an

anti-Communism related to the past with no connection to Chilean Communism. It is characterized by vulnerability, experience, and history of a people who had arrived fleeing an atrocious process and had no desire to stumble into the same hole twice.[6]

Perla Aron, the granddaughter of Marcos Svigilsky, the immigrant from Ukraine who avoided military service by going three days without sleep, describes the panic aroused by the possibility that Allende might be elected president of Chile:

> My husband was afraid of the communists. He was terrified! Everyone said that if Allende were to win, a delegation would come to our big, elegant house and ask us "how many people live here?" And you had to answer "three people or five." "How many bedrooms does the house have? How many bathrooms do you have?" And they would send two or three families to live with you. It was a lie. But he believed it.[7]

A few months after Allende's electoral victory, the Arons left for Israel, while their daughters, Anamaría and Diana, stayed in Chile to continue their university studies.

The year Allende was inaugurated as the first socialist president elected in a democratic nation, a socialist was also elected president of the Federación Sionista de Chile (Zionist Federation of Chile), representing Mifleget HaPoalim HaMeuhedet (MAPAM, United Workers Party), the socialist worker party of Israel. The doctor and accomplished violinist Isaac "Ica" Icekson had arrived in Chile from Warsaw with his parents in 1935 when he was six years old. In his youth, Icekson had been an active member of the Hashomer Hatzair movement and, like many of his friends, he "had a very critical attitude toward community institutions" such as the Círculo Israelita, the Zionist Federation, the Comité Representativo de Entidades Judías de Chile (CREJ, Jewish Representative Committee), and the Women's International Zionist Organizaton (WIZO).[8] "For us," he explains, "they were all bourgeois." Now he was at the head of the Zionist Federation of Chile. "It was amazing and I never understood how we won that democratic election," he says, still marveling at his electoral achievement forty-three years earlier.

"Fear motivated many families to leave Chile. It was like a stampede," he says. "So much so that Jews would come to the Zionist organization I presided over offering to sell their property for very cheap. Some sold their cars at ridiculous prices because they were overcome by genuine panic." One event was burned into his memory and had stayed with him ever since. A Zionist

Federation leader named Miguel Maldavsky proposed organizing a mass exodus after Allende had been elected. He told them, "You have to get buses and transportation to take all the Jews out of here because Allende will take reprisals against the Jewish community" for not fully supporting him. "We of MAPAM disagreed with him. The only ones who supported that position were right-wing and religious Jews." Icekson believes the reaction was exaggerated: "There was a collective hysteria. Jews born here simply believed their property was in jeopardy; they thought everything they had would be taken away from them: their house, their car, their cat."

Icekson supported the candidacy of Salvador Allende and was one of the organizers of a meeting between the socialist candidate and young people of the Frente de Izquierda Sionista (FIS, Zionist Leftist Front), and Hashomer Hatzair held in early 1970. A dozen young people hosted the future president. Mauricio Guzmán, at the time youth coordinator (*madrij*) for Hashomer Hatzair, was present and remembers it as "a very pleasant, very sincere meeting."[9] They spoke about Israel and the kibbutz collective agricultural system; Allende, he says, "was very interested in everything we told him about Israel, and he was quite pleased to know there were leftist Jews who shared many of the principles he advocated."

At the same time, the young people expressed concern about Allende's doctoral thesis on race and the supposed hereditary Jewish tendency toward criminal behavior that Allende posited in 1933 to earn his MD. "Allende responded that he no longer believed it and that he had been mistaken. He told us that in those years he did not yet understand what Judaism was. He knew we would ask him that question," Guzmán recalls.[10]

Guzmán and his twin brother, Leo, were part of a group of sixty youths from Hashomer who for many years had been planning to immigrate to Israel. Their departure date approached, set for one month after the presidential election. "We explained to Allende that we were on the verge of going to Israel. We agreed with his ideas, but we envisioned our future in Israel, not Chile. Allende completely understood," he says.

Satisfied with Allende's response to their concerns, the young people pledged to support his campaign, Guzmán recalls. Hashomer Hatzair members along with Zionist Left Front college students attended campaign rallies, handed out election material on the street, painted murals, and participated in other volunteer campaign activities.

The Jewish establishment criticized Hashomer Hatzair and the Zionist Left Front for having met with Allende and for their involvement in his campaign. Haim Hayet, who arrived from Israel in 1971 as emissary and adult coordinator (commonly known as *sheliaj* in Hebrew) for Hashomer Hatzair, recollects how the support the Zionist Left Front and Hashomer showed "for Allende caused discontent in the Jewish community and the Israeli embassy."[11] Before Allende took office and prior to the assassination of René Schneider, the army commander in chief who died on October 22, 1970, Hayet learned that the Israeli ambassador had written to the foreign relations department of Israel to say that Zionist Left Front coordinator Pesaj Zaskin's support of Allende was problematic.

Six weeks after the elections and just four days before Congress confirmed him, president-elect Salvador Allende received a delegation of seven Jewish community leaders, led by Gil Sinay, president of the Jewish Representative Committee, an umbrella organization uniting forty Jewish institutions. As president of the Zionist Federation of Chile, Ickeson was present as well.

Sinay addressed Allende on behalf of the delegation, congratulating him for the electoral victory, and thanking him for his Rosh Hashanah message, published October 1, 1970, in the *La Palabra Israelita* weekly newspaper, which was also read aloud in the Círculo Israelita, Chile's largest synagogue. Sinay stated that "as a people who inherited the teachings of the Prophets inspired by principles of social justice, I am able to assure Dr. Allende that our community is not apprehensive regarding social and economic change, which, as the new President of Chile has repeatedly expressed, will be carried out with complete respect for the principles of freedom and democracy."[12]

Allende reassured the delegation that "the measures that will be adopted in the economic arena will be general in nature and under no circumstances shall

President Salvador Allende (*center*) meeting with Jewish community leaders, 1970 (La Palabra Israelita)

they be aimed at a particular group or community." In the Jewish community, he added, "I have deep friendships and I would never dream of even considering discriminatory measures." The president-elect went on to emphasize that it was important for him "to receive representatives of the Jewish community, whose members, like all Chileans, exercise their citizen rights," and noted that "as individuals you have every right to disagree and as a group you have nothing to fear."[13]

At least twenty people of Jewish origin were members of Allende's government; one of these, Jacques Chonchol, served as agriculture minister and was responsible for implementing agrarian reform. Others had positions in various government ministries and offices.

David Baytelman was named director of the Agrarian Reform Corporation and Jaime Faivovich became governor of Santiago. Miguel Lawner, the son of the family who started its journey to the New World along the banks of the Dniester River, was named executive director of a new department within the Housing Ministry whose mandate was to remodel old neighborhoods. Lawner explains that the agency sought "to end social segregation by building public housing complexes such as Villa Carlos Cortés on the former San Luis agricultural lands of Las Condes."

Architect Miguel Lawner (*right*) with President Allende (*left, with hat*) at a ground-breaking ceremony for a new housing development, July 1971 (Miguel Lawner)

Jorín Pilowsky, son of the Yiddishist who helped rescue Jewish refugees, served as lawyer for the Corporación Nacional del Cobre de Chile (CODELCO, National Copper Corporation of Chile) in 1971 and was later appointed executive of the state-owned El Teniente copper mine. Carlos Berger was public relations director for the Finance Ministry and was later appointed communications director for the Chuquicamata mine in Calama. David Silberman was mining undersecretary, and later general manager for CODELCO. Attorney Washington Domb worked in the Interior Ministry and in 1973 was appointed director of the Tax Crimes Department. Eliana Bronfman was a lawyer with the Foreign Relations Ministry. Benjamin Teplizky was director of National Television (1970–71) and then the National Cement Industry (1970–73). Oscar Waiss was director of the daily official newspaper *La Nación*. Elías Jana, a member of the Socialist Party and personal friend of President Salvador Allende, was elected mayor of the town of Cañete in 1971 in a landslide vote. Hanni Grunpeter, who arrived as a child from Czechoslovakia after a stopover in England, won a seat on the Talcahuano city council in southern Chile in these same municipal elections.

Never before had a Chilean government incorporated such a high percentage of members of Jewish origin. However, few publicly acknowledged their Jewish identity, nor was it a factor in the appointments of these officials. They belonged to parties that formed part of the Popular Unity alliance and were mainly known for their leftist politics rather than their Jewish origins. Moreover, according to Icekson, the Allende administration's Jewish officials "were stigmatized by the community." In any event, Allende's gestures of friendship did not reassure community leaders, and the effort he made in 1939 together with Jacobo Pilowsky and Natalio Berman to find safe harbor for the Jewish refugees on the Cap Norte ship was not a part of their collective memory.

In December 1970, President Allende announced the nationalization of banks through the acquisition of their stock by the state-owned Banco de Estado. The Banco Israelita de Chile was the first bank to be nationalized, with 94.8 percent of its shares purchased by the Banco de Estado. Enrique Testa Arueste, president of the Sephardic religious community, was appointed comptroller of the Banco Israelita. As a result of the agrarian reform, the lands of José Levi Guggenheim, Enrique Assael Levy, and David Luft were redistributed to destitute tenant farmers and significant acreage was returned to its original Mapuche indigenous owners.[14] Jewish businessmen, some recalling the Nazi Ayrianization of Jewish businesses, viewed state interventions like these with apprehension.

Although two of Rodolfo Müller's brothers left Chile, he remained, occasionally lending his old Citroneta car to his son Jorge, a cameraman who crisscrossed the country filming Popular Unity events.[15] Jorge was driving the Citroneta when he visited the encampment of the truck drivers who in October 1972 went on strike for a month against the Popular Unity government. He filmed many events after the election of Allende, including practically everything that took place in the National Stadium. Much of Jorge's work is recorded in the documentary *La batalla de Chile*, directed by filmmaker Patricio Guzmán.[16] He was the official Chilean cameraman for the state visit of Clodomiro Almeyda, foreign relations minister, to the Soviet bloc. "Many times we told him, 'Jorge, you are getting far too involved. You are placing yourself in danger.' He would answer, 'I'm not doing anything bad. I just film what I see.' Later, they [the military] did not understand it like that," his father says.[17]

Rodolfo Müller also argued with his son about the state's intervention in the factories.

> Allende's supporters took over factories, but they didn't know how to manage them. They weren't prepared for that. In those years I told Jorge several times: "You staked everything on this government but you lack training to run it. Not even public administration training." A friend of Jorge's was the government-appointed official who assumed control of the Yarur textile factory. This young man knew nothing about the textile industry. What could he possibly do there? Nothing. So the workers did whatever they wanted. I was worried when I saw this. I feared the government would not last long.

Invariably, every morning, Walter Rosenberg, manager of the Marmicoc kitchenware factory, would remark to his family as he was leaving for work that "every day I'm afraid of finding a flag [signaling an occupation] flying from the factory roof."[18] The factory, owned by Enrique Alcalay, a Sephardic community leader, had good relations with the union and was never taken over by its workers.

The Marmicoc factory was not expropriated; however, the small metallurgical factory owned by Walter Rosenfeld was. Rosenfeld, born in Vienna, witnessed the humiliating treatment of Jews and the confiscation of their businesses after the German invasion. He and his wife arrived in Chile in 1948. His shop manufactured metal parts for car seats, and his business was doing well. The union took over the shop administration but allowed him to continue going there every day. They treated him respectfully because he had been a good boss, says his niece Corina Rosenfeld.[19] Nonetheless, the expropriation of that car body shop instilled fear among other businessmen.

Like Icekson, attorney Isaac Frenkel, a man of left-leaning politics not affiliated with any party, who grew up in the Dror progressive Zionist movement, is another insider who was critical of organized politics: "I have always been independent left. Why didn't I belong to a political party? Because I was and continue to be a Zionist. Zionism didn't sit well with Marxist politics," he states. In the early 1970s, Frenkel began his career in the B'nai B'rith organization, serving as president of the district comprising all Latin America B'nai B'rith groups from 1975 to 1979 and later as vice president of B'nai B'rith International. "I really believed in Allende," says Frenkel, who knew him personally during the 1960s.

Frenkel says that "many Jewish businesses were taken over. But most Jews were already against the Allende government before the takeovers of nationalized businesses began." One such businessman, Emerico Letay Altman, a Hungarian Jew who arrived in Chile in 1950 and was a partner of the Santa Barbara mining company, he explains, was involved in trying to broker an agreement between Alessandri and Tomic whereby one or the other of them would drop out of the race so that there would be just two candidates for the 1970 elections instead of three. "That way, they would have blocked Allende."

Mauricio Guzmán, the youth coordinator for Hashomer Hatzair who met with Allende and volunteered on his campaign, immigrated to Israel in October 1970 with a large group of Chilean Jews. He observed Chileans arrive in Israel after the election.

> Something was happening, and we were worried. The people who began arriving in Israel were afraid Chile would become a communist country that persecuted Jews, although this did not end up happening. People who had lived through the Shoah and others who had escaped Stalinism in Hungary didn't want to repeat the experience. Jews are always afraid. Here people were very frightened. That's why a very large number left, although no more than thirty percent came to Israel.[20]

Second Crossroad: 1973

In August 1973, conservative Chilean media published a series of letters from unidentified readers "denouncing" the Jewish community's influence on the Allende government. Before the military coup, propaganda of the extreme rightist National Party and the paramilitary nationalist Patria y Libertad (Fatherland and Liberty) movement claimed that Allende was dominated by Jews. He was not to blame for what was happening in Chile, they contended; rather, it was the Jews around him who were to blame for his socialist public policy.[21]

During the second week of August in 1973, Representative Committee leaders Gil Sinay, Robert Levy, and Raul Perlovich met with Augusto Olivares, director of the TVN state television station, to express their concern over the

accusations. The Jewish leaders presented him with an open letter that was
read during TVN's news hour on August 11. The statement reiterated Jewish institutions' absolutely neutral position regarding contemporary Chilean
politics that was outlined in the organization's bylaws approved in 1940: "The
community has a completely apolitical position locally and shall maintain said
position, and for no reason whatsoever shall alter that position; therefore it
prohibits any individual, group, or organization from seeking to make undue
use of collective representation on matters related to Chilean national politics."[22]

The statement, published August 17, 1973, in *La Palabra Israelita*, concluded
with the following paragraph:

> This Representative Committee repudiates any endeavor that may aim to con-
> fuse public opinion by making the Israelite community appear to be in favor or
> against any specific government, given that each Jewish inhabitant, like those
> within any other group, ethnicity, or religion, individually assumes responsibili-
> ties to the national community.

Near the end of the same month, *El Siglo*, a newspaper published by the
Communist Party of Chile, added its own condemnation of antisemitism exhibited by the media. It noted, among other things, a letter by "an alleged
reader" of the daily *La Segunda* who recommended hanging "citizens of Jewish origin who belong to the Popular Unity government" from the lamp posts
of Alameda Boulevard.[23] The article also pointed out that another newspaper,
La Prensa, affiliated with the Partido Demócrata Cristiano (PDC, Christian
Democratic Party), published diatribes against the Allende government that
had antisemitic overtones. An example cited is an article on the *La Prensa* editorial page that warns that "a cell of Jewish and Communist extraction has
gained domination over Chile."[24] As happened during the Weimar Republic,
Jews who held key positions in the government caught the attention of the far
right in Chile.

Whenever a new president took office, the Jewish Representative Committee had the custom of extending Chile's chief executive a formal greeting
through its institutional newspaper *La Palabra Israelita*. In keeping with that
tradition, on October 1, 1970, the front page of *La Palabra Israelita* featured a
photograph of Salvador Allende as the newly elected president of the republic.
On October 15, 1971, in the same publication, leaders of the committee returned a Rosh Hashanah greeting from President Allende at the beginning of
the Jewish new year. This protocol was repeated two years later, on September
28, 1973, with the front-page photo of Augusto Pinochet and the "greetings to
the Honorable Government Junta" and "Mr. President." These formal greetings

to both chiefs of state speak to a neutrality policy that did not differentiate between one leader chosen by democratic vote and the other self-imposed through a military coup.

Various statements on the part of the Jewish Representative Committee over the course of the subsequent seventeen years cast doubt as to whether it maintained the neutrality that its leaders had affirmed less than a month before the military coup. The impression in those years was that the 1940 bylaws had been brushed aside and that the institutions that made up the Jewish Representative Committee had decidedly chosen to take sides.

A status report on the Chilean Jewish community, written in April 1974 by the United States Embassy in Santiago that it sent to the State Department in Washington, DC, notes in its first point that the "Chilean Jewish community" was satisfied with the "current military government."[25]

1. SUMMARY: CHILEAN JEWISH COMMUNITY PLEASED WITH CURRENT MILITARY GOVERNMENT AND ADAMANT IN ITS REFUTATION OF REPORTS CIRCULATING ABROAD OF GOC-FOMENTED ANTISEMITIC DISCRIMINATION.

The document goes on to describe the characteristics of Chile's Jewish community, a population of approximately between twenty-five and thirty thousand, noting that "an estimated 5,000 Jews left Chile during the Allende years." It adds that "there was no antisemitism fomented or condoned by Allende government. Jewish leaders energetically state that this policy continues under present government."

The final paragraph of the same report states:

7. LOCAL JEWISH COMMUNITY LEADERS HAVE BEEN EMPHATIC IN THEIR CONVERSATIONS WITH EMBASSY OFFICERS IN THEIR EFFORT TO DISPEL RUMORS CIRCULATING ABROAD OF ANTISEMITIC ATTITUDES OR ACTIONS ON PART OF MILITARY GOVERNMENT. THEY NOTE THAT RELATIONS WITH GOVERNMENT ARE EXCELLENT AND THAT "95 PER CENT OF JEWISH COMMUNITY" IS AVIDLY PRO-JUNTA. THEY ADD THAT THE GOVERNMENT HAS MADE SEVERAL SYMBOLIC GESTURES SUCH AS THE PRESENCE AT HIGH HOLY DAY SERVICES OF AIDES-DE-CAMP OF JUNTA MEMBERS TO PUBLICLY DEMONSTRATE ITS EXCELLENT RELATIONS WITH COMMUNITY. EMBASSY AGREES WITH JEWISH LEADERS' VIEWS. THERE IS AT THIS TIME NO POLICY OR INTIMATION OF ANTISEMITIC DISCRIMINATORY POLICY ON THE PART OF THE GOC.

This memorandum was confidential and only declassified in 1999, and yet its contents do not reveal any secret information. Rather, it corroborated what was public knowledge. Throughout the nearly two decades the military junta ruled the country, Jewish institutions showed their support, beginning with the invitation to the high command to attend synagogues during Yom Kippur to greet the community. That tradition, which began on October 5, 1973, with the attendance of military attachés at Yom Kippur services, continued throughout the de facto government rule and even in subsequent years.

In 1974, Rosh Hashanah coincided with September 18, Chilean independence day, when a national interfaith service is held. Since it was impossible for rabbis to attend, Rabbi Angel Kreiman proposed "inviting the governing junta to Yom Kippur of 1974 near our noontime prayer for the nation, so military officials could see firsthand that, like Protestants and Catholics, Jews also pray for the nation. Afterward, they kept up the tradition."[26]

In the September 21, 1973, issue of *La Palabra Israelita*, the Comisión Mixta Colectiva Ampliada (Community-Wide Mixed Commission) announced that it was "encouraging contributions of money and valuable objects from Jewish residents" to the Chile National Reconstruction Fund, a campaign concocted by civilian supporters of the military junta. At an end-of-year gathering in 1973, the Women's International Zionist Organization welcomed Gabriela de Leigh and Alicia de Mendoza. They were the wives, respectively, of military junta members air force commander Gustavo Leigh and national police director César Mendoza, who honored the women's group with the Silver Clover award in gratitude for its contribution to this campaign.[27] The organization's donations contributed to a total of $11,188,573 escudos (US$54,285) that the Jewish community deposited over the following five months in a special account opened for that purpose with the Banco Israelita.[28]

Thus, on different and repeated occasions, the Jewish community and the Representative Committee, in particular, made known their support for the new regime from the early days following the military coup and throughout the duration of the dictatorship. "Externally, they wanted to appear neutral, colorless, but beneath the surface there was financial support, ideological support, and straightforward support in every sense," Ickson argues. He adds, "Not from the community's membership but from its most affluent segments. Up until the coup, I saw a fairly neutral community, with a slight inclination toward the right due to economic interests. Later, there was outright support for the military regime."[29]

Ickson was president of the Estadio Maccabi recreational complex in 1980 and again in 1984. On one occasion two businessmen came to a board meeting with a proposal. They asked that the Estadio Israelita offer a Rosh Hashanah dinner in honor of the military junta leadership. "I immediately and curtly opposed the idea," says Ickson, with evident indignation.

I said, "During my presidency this is not going to happen." They defended themselves like lions, saying it was an offense to the military junta that the Jewish community would not hold a dinner in its honor. I replied, "We are totally apolitical regarding what's going on in the government." I proposed that the board, dominated by a right-wing majority, vote on it. And they refused to allow that celebration. It was never held anywhere.

In another Jewish institution, the B'nai B'rith, Isaac Frenkel was also an iconoclast.[30] He had been a classmate of Orlando Letelier, Chilean ambassador to the United States, foreign relations minister, and defense minister in the Allende government, at the University of Chile Law School.[31] They had a deep friendship. In the days after the military coup, Frenkel "frequently intervened on behalf of Jews and non-Jews," meeting constantly with Israeli ambassador Moshe Tov to discuss ways they could protect people. A major part of B'nai B'rith brethren supported the Pinochet regime or was silenced by fear. "We wanted to issue public statements, but the discussions on wording would go on so long that in the end nothing was done. The statements ended up with no *schmortz*, without any punch. It was very frustrating for me," he says.[32]

During the last weeks of Salvador Allende's government, B'nai B'rith put its building, located on the second block of Vicuña Mackenna Avenue, up for sale in order to build new offices. The cost of the building had been in part covered by donations from German Jewish refugees who had received reparations compensation from the German government. None other than the military junta's Housing Ministry wanted to buy the property, and it agreed verbally to a price. Six months passed without the purchase being finalized. At that point into the dictatorship, inflation had reached 400 percent, and military officials refused to take the inflation into account in their payment. However, if B'nai B'rith would not sell, military officials warned they would take it by force and expropriate the property.[33]

Frenkel audaciously proposed that B'nai B'rith sue the military officials. Many B'nai B'rith members were Shoah survivors, and they were frightened. The board of directors believed it had no choice but to sell it to the military. Finally, Frenkel convinced them: "I staunchly opposed the idea of accepting the despicable money offered by the officials. At last the board approved the bold proposition of confronting the powerful military regime, a challenge few would dare to take." In December 1975 the military expropriated the building. "At that point, I personally began defending the lawsuit in court. Many thought it was madness, but I was convinced justice would prevail." Eleven months later, the first instance ruling proved him right. "And I won the case quite nicely," he says.

On August 12, 1974, another commemoration of the massacre of the Soviet Jewish poets was held at the Círculo Israelita synagogue. Jewish Representative Committee president Gil Sinay opened the ceremony by stating that "we must not continue to silence the martyrdom of these Jewish writers, victims of a judicial farce, whose only crime was having been born in the heart of our people."[34]

At that time, thousands had been arbitrarily imprisoned in Chile with no charges brought against them. More than fifteen hundred people, including several of Jewish origin, had been summarily executed. Less than a year earlier, a war council—a kangaroo court that often afforded defense attorneys no more than an hour's access to their clients—sentenced Carlos Berger to sixty days in jail. During the night of October 19, 1973, however, he was removed from the prison and shot along the road between Calama and Antofagasta. The Jewish community newspaper made no mention of the "judicial farce" that was occurring in Chile. *La Palabra Israelita* did not routinely cover political or court matters, but during such extraordinary times, its silence weighed heavily.

Fourteen years later, when the 1988 referendum provided an opportunity for Chilean citizens to embrace the resurgence of democratic aspirations, Jewish institutions of Chile preferred to reaffirm their loyalty to the military junta, even holding events in support of General Augusto Pinochet. The neutrality avowed by the 1940 bylaws had become dead letter.

Raúl Sohr, who had insisted that Chile's feigned neutrality during World War II should not be judged too harshly, made the same argument regarding the Jewish community's official position.[35] "Neutrality was a fantasy," he remarks. Perhaps "neutrality in the sense that one refrains from taking action" was possible, but, he argues, that is not truly "neutrality and never has been. No resident immigrant community is ever neutral—not the English, German or anyone else. They all have their interests." But before 1970 and especially before 1973, Chilean Jews did not have a prevailing or perceived political identity. "The coup radicalized Chilean society," he explains, "and Jews remained collectively identified with dictatorship, just like Israel, which reinforces that image."[36]

The Jewish Representative Committee realized it had to shift gears politically with the onset of democratic transition. In 1991, the organization that represented the community to non-Jewish Chileans appointed Isaac Frenkel its president. Nearly twenty-five years later, he said, "Do you think they chose me because they loved me? They appointed me because they realized they had to change the perception Chileans have of Jews. In my opinion, the Jewish people should have greater social and humanitarian sensitivity than other people who have suffered less. But Jews are only human. We too forget our history."

FROM THE DANUBE TO THE MAPOCHO

"When Allende was elected, what we felt was terror," says Marita Feldmann, born in Budapest in 1934. "We felt sheer terror that another government would harm Jews."[37] Sheer terror transformed Marita's childhood on the morning of March 19, 1944. It was a Sunday, and Marita's mother had sent her to buy bread. "I crossed a wide street and as I was returning with the bread, I heard a deafening sound. I was very frightened. German tanks were crossing the Santa Margarita Bridge into Buda. It was a horrific sound; I had never seen a tank before." The Germans had invaded Hungary.

Antisemitism had flourished in Hungary before World War II. Between 1938 and 1940, the Hungarian Parliament passed a number of racial laws that followed the Nuremberg model. In 1940, Hungary became an Axis member, and in 1941 it sent soldiers to buttress the German invasions of Yugoslavia and the Soviet Union. That same year—three years before German tanks entered Budapest—Hungarian authorities deported the first Jews from the provinces.

Until that moment, Marita's family had not been directly affected. Her mother was widowed when the girl was two years old and then married a second time. In an attempt to ward off stigmatization Jews commonly endured in the country, they pretended to be Christians. They lived in an elegant, safe district behind the Gothic building that housed the Hungarian Parliament. Now their lives would change abruptly.

A week after the occupation began, the Germans in collaboration with Hungarian officials decreed Jews had to be separated from Christians. Marita's family was forced to leave their apartment and move to a building marked with a yellow star on the exterior wall. In October they were alerted that quite soon the Jews of Budapest—the last remaining Jewish community in Hungary—would be deported. The family dispersed, with each member hiding in different parts of the city.

Marita's stepfather, a corpulent man, spent months hiding behind a false wall, sharing a narrow underground space with several people. Her mother scurried from one place to another, without a yellow star, to obtain food.

Marita was sheltered in a modest apartment and discovered that her maternal grandfather was hidden in the same building. When Marita greeted him, she was severely scolded and told not to come near him. On a cold dawn in January 1945, after the Soviets had surrounded the city, German soldiers raided the building. The building's residents, many in thin nightclothes, were forced to line up outside for inspection to confirm that no Jews were living in a place forbidden to them.

While the soldiers shouted at them, a Russian jet flying overhead dropped a bomb. Amid the thunderous explosion, the shattering of windows, and walls tumbling down, someone lifted the girl from the rubble. Inside the building, she was placed in the deepest corner of a cupboard and warned to keep absolutely quiet and not to move until the German soldiers left.

Budapestians endured two interminable days of fear and hunger, leading some to devour the cadaver of a horse that had fallen dead on the street, before Soviet forces were able to enter Budapest.[38] By March, survivors of the siege felt they could safely emerge from their hiding places.

Marita's family survived, with one exception. Fascist Hungarian militia were informed that her father's sister, Nicolette Nagel, a twenty-one-year-old, was a Jew. She and many other people were taken to the banks of the Danube River and ordered to take off their shoes. The Hungarian fascists fired, and the people fell into the water. "That was our great sorrow," says Marita.

The family encountered new difficulties when they went back to live in the sole inhabitable room of their former apartment in ruins. Some of the hardships they faced were to be expected in a city reemerging from the ashes. Others had social connotations corresponding to the political changes introduced by the Soviets who now controlled Hungary.

"My father began working in wheat and potato sacks that he imported. Importation was forbidden, and the business was nationalized. He had no means to earn a living," Marita recalls. "When the Russians came to Hungary, I was not accepted in the school because my family was bourgeois. My father's surname—Pietsch von Ritterschild—suggested noble origins. Before, I had not been allowed to go to school because I was Jewish. Now we could not find a school that would accept me either. In both 1944 and 1945 I was denied education," she adds.

In 1949, the family was able to travel to Chile with false passports. Her mother's brother Ladislao (Láci) Beck had immigrated in the 1930s, settling in the town of Angol. Marita did not join them until a year later because a bout of tuberculosis forced her to remain in a sanatorium in Hungary, under the care of her uncle Esteban (Pista) Pietsch.

By 1970, Marita was married to Pedro Feldmann, an Austrian Jewish refugee, and had two small sons. But her childhood suffering in Hungary under the Nazis and then under the Soviets never faded from her memory. "I feared what happened in Hungary was about to happen here in Chile. When the military pronouncement came, we were so happy. We hugged each other! We've been saved!"

In 1945, the Danube carried away the body of her young aunt and hundreds of other people. In Santiago of 1973, bodies of people shot by the military flowed down the Mapocho River. But "we did not wish to believe it," Marita now acknowledges. Her mother and husband were fervent supporters of Augusto Pinochet. The Feldmann family attended rallies in support of Pinochet and felt the ardor of the flaming torches in Chacarillas, where, on July 9, 1977, the dictatorship staged a dramatic pageant in which seventy-seven young civilians pledged loyalty to Pinochet. Most of their neighbors and immediate circle of friends also identified with the dictatorship.

Upon reaching adolescence, their sons Roberto and Andreas became more critical of what was happening around them in Chile. The country's political situation became a heated topic of family discussion. Andreas, Marita's youngest son, who was born in 1968, explains:

> It was a gradual process, but by time I was fourteen or fifteen, I had formed my own ideas. I went to school at the Instituto Hebreo, in those years located next to the "Pedagógico" [the education sciences college known for student activism].[39] During student protests there, we could hear the repression. Whoever did not wish to see it, did not. Then in 1986, I entered the University of Chile and met people whose views were different from my family's. It was an eye-opener.[40]

He adds, "Not only did we become aware of what was going on in the country; we believed it was ethically wrong. It was an intuitive thing to support democracy and the right to choose who governs us. A very deep cleavage was produced within the family, and many disputes began to take place at home."

Andreas is an associate professor of political science and Latin American studies at the University of Illinois at Chicago. Despite his academic training and his having authored numerous publications about international security, political violence, terrorism, and human rights, he still does not fully comprehend how the closest and dearest members of his nuclear family were capable of supporting what for him is "ethically reprehensible." However, he concedes that families like his "had experienced Nazi occupation and then lived a few years under Communist occupation. They lost everything. They were bourgeoisie who probably were mistreated and humiliated. The Communists probably had an antisemitic bias. Clearly, those people were tremendously frightened."[41]

This fear was heightened—both within the Jewish community as well as within his family—by a lack of political sophistication, observes Andreas. He believes many people had little understanding of political processes, and so they confused Allende's Socialist Party with Nazism and Stalinism. "Faced with the prospect of undergoing a similar experience again, their reaction was viscerally against it," he notes. "The community's more politically sophisticated members supported Allende because they rejected the prevailing societal model in Chile. It was an oligarchic, classist, elitist, and discriminatory model," he adds.

His analysis might explain the insecurity and fear that propelled a third of the Jewish community to flee the country. However, it still does not explain the resounding support for Augusto Pinochet, whose deployment of terror tactics to retain power was similar to Nazi totalitarian practices and certain aspects of Stalinism. "Some segments of the population simply felt comfortable with a regime that gave them security, that allowed them to do business and live without a care," Andreas notes. "Those right-wing people could care less if the regime killed Communists because they believed Communists to be bad people who wanted to take away everything they had," he concludes.

Another trait of the Jewish community that may have influenced its backing of the military dictatorship, he points out, was "a worrisome tendency" among Jews to always ask themselves how a government would affect them as Jews. "If the government has no antisemitic undertones, then it's good for Jews. But we are part of a society that is much larger than we Jews."

Searching for a logical explanation for what became a generational conflict in his family is a complicated process for Andreas, and it is also painful. "It was never clear to me why they were incapable of recognizing how bad the dictatorship was. Jews do not have a monopoly on persecution—many others have endured it—and precisely because we were victims we must not forget or be passive."

Roberto, the oldest Feldmann brother, earned a fine arts degree at Catholic University in Santiago and then went on to study at a rabbinical seminary in the United States, returning to Chile an ordained rabbi in 1994. Rabbi Feldmann has participated in interfaith dialogue, accompanied Christian base communities in their annual Holy Week pilgrimage to the former Villa Grimaldi torture center, and led tributes for victims of human rights violations in the religious communities he created in Santiago since 1997.[42] "History and reality gradually distanced me from the stubborn fantasy of those who wished to believe in the dictatorship and were incapable of seeing a world in which dictatorships of the left and military dictatorships of the rights existed," who were not able to accept that "we were living in the middle of torture, repression, disappearances, lies and the cynicism of de facto powers," he notes.[43] In 1996 and 1997, he lived in Cuba, serving as rabbi for the Cuban Jewish community. "Perhaps," he says, "I came full circle from the day the USSR conquered Hungary, the military coup in Chile, and the entire subtle curvature of a straight line."

Today his mother recognizes the reality that she did not see, or preferred not to see, at the time. The widely disseminated Rettig and Valech human rights commissions reports, the proliferation of special televised news pro-grams and documentaries in the last twenty years, and her own sons' opinions converged. As a result, a small window opened for Marita. "We shut our eyes; we didn't want to know anything. We did not want to believe that people were being tortured, that people were being taken away and killed. I can no longer ignore the fact that so many people were tortured and others were thrown into the sea," she says.

On September 10, 2013, CNN journalists interviewed Manuel Contreras, former director of the repressive Dirección de Inteligencia Nacional (DINA, National Intelligence Directorate), the Chilean secret police. From a comfort-able cabin that served in lieu of a cell on premises of the regime's former tele-communications and where a number of human rights violators served their sentences, Contreras, serene in a brown sweater and yellow shirt, denied hav-ing tortured people at Villa Grimaldi and Tejas Verdes or any involvement in other crimes for which he had been sentenced to nearly six hundred years in prison. He also stated that disappeared people had actually died in combat and the armed forces then threw some into the sea. His claims provoked indig-nation and led to a transfer for him and nine other former military officers to Punta Peuco prison, which was created for human rights crime violators. From her home, Marita Feldmann watched the television interview and had this to say: "I listened to that man, who had been chief of the DINA, answer the question about what happened to the people he arrested. Well, he said, we questioned them—that means they tortured those people—and then we shot them and threw them into the sea. He said it as calmly as you might say, 'Let's have empanadas for lunch.' I found it shocking. For me, all the barbarities they committed are intolerable." Marita adds, "My thinking has changed."

RABBI ANGEL KREIMAN

Shabbat services were drawing to a close that Saturday, September 15, 1973, at Bnei Jisroel synagogue when Rabbi Angel Kreiman received a telephone call. Traditional rabbis like Kreiman do not use the phone on Shabbat, and their acquaintances know not to call. Therefore, he deduced that the ringing phone indicated an urgent matter. The person calling him on that first Shabbat after the military coup was the Catholic archbishop of Santiago, Cardinal Raul Silva Henriquez.

Practically all other rabbis had joined the Jewish flight after the election of Salvador Allende, and so community leaders requested that Kreiman, an Argen-tine at the time serving in Barranquilla, Colombia, take charge as rabbi for Santiago's Jewish community. His mentor, the US-born rabbi Marshall Meyer who subsequently became a noted defender of human rights in Argentina, asked him to accept the post to help prevent Judaism from vanishing from Chile in the wake of the election of a socialist government.[44]

Kreiman arrived in Santiago in 1972, with the challenge of serving as spiritual guide for five religious communities ranging from orthodox to liberal. They had joined forces to hire him. He faced challenges unique to a country under economic siege. The scarcity of foreign currency had led the government to restrict imports, including meat from animals slaughtered in a manner that adhered to the requirements of Jewish kosher laws, for which the primary source was Argentina. Rabbi Kreiman appealed directly to Allende to permit the slaughter of seven to ten cattle each month; he requested that a ritual slaughterer be brought from Argentina and that the product be sold at a kosher meat shop at 10 de Julio Street. The proposal was accepted, but with the proviso that the shop curtain had to be down and the shop itself "under police guard to ensure that the meat was sold only upon presentation of a certificate signed by me that the person was from a family that customarily ate kosher."[45]

Several weeks before the military coup, Rabbi Kreiman had participated in an interfaith effort to create a bridge for dialogue between the president and Congress. This "peacemaking group," which also included Cardinal Silva, Lutheran bishop Helmut Frenz, and Methodist Tomas Stevens, went back and forth six times between the president and Congress. But, Kreiman notes, "Eduardo Frei Montalva, then Senate president, insisted that the crisis would only be resolved at 'gunpoint.'"[46] On Sunday, September 9, 1973, the group convened thousands at Constitution Plaza, which faced La Moneda presidential palace, to pray for peace.

Now, just four days after the bombing of La Moneda, the defeat of the Popular Unity government, and the death of president Salvador Allende, thousands were held in prison under no charge and increasingly troubling reports were emerging of generalized violence and arbitrary abuse throughout the country. The times demanded not only the voice of conscience from the nation's spiritual leaders but also decisive action to protect so many persecuted people.

Cardinal Silva made his urgent call to Kreiman on Shabbat to ask him to join a group called the Comité de Cooperación para la Paz (Committee of Cooperation for Peace in Chile). With consent of Jewish community leaders, who debated the proposal at length, the rabbi joined the new organization, soon to be known as the Propeace Committee.

Every morning from 8:00 a.m. to 10:00 a.m., members of the interfaith team had breakfast together to discuss how to address pressing cases that were referred to them. "Cases increased to such an extent that it was no longer possible for five clergymen alone to handle them. This led to the organization's expansion to new areas of support that incorporated lawyers, psychologists and sociologists. Some people needed protection, the unemployed needed work, and the wives of disappeared prisoners needed vocational training workshops."[47]

Rabbi Kreiman explained how he proceeded when a person was jailed:

> Family members turned to me, and immediately I would go to Diego Portales building and meet with Pinochet in every case. I would take the prisoners from the place of detention to the embassies, sometimes even in the trunk of my car, and at other times, directly to the airport. I obtained contacts and airplane tickets to various European countries, and I had special cooperation from the grand rabbi of France Jacob Kaplan as well as the grand rabbi of Israel Shlomo Goren.[48]

Kreiman points out that in his humanitarian work, he did not question a person's Jewish credentials: "In every case in which I helped, either on my own or referred to me by the Propeace Committee, there were Jews with active religious practice, others more active in lay organizations, some with family ties to Círculo leaders, as well as others who were quite indifferent to Judaism."[49]

Benjamin Teplizky, Luis Vega, Julio Laks, Jorín Pilowsky and Sara Sharim are among the many who attributed their freedom to Angel Kreiman's interventions. In a letter dated December 1, 1974, Teplizky thanked Kreiman for obtaining his release after fourteen months in prison: "My father told me about your sleepless nights and sacrifices in obtaining my freedom . . . ; for that reason, Mr. Rabbi, before leaving my native land, the undersigned wishes to express his deepest gratitude for your courageous intervention."[50]

When Sara Sharim was arrested in her home one night in August 1975, her husband and her younger brother Nissim, the actor and theater director, spoke to Kreiman. They had learned that Sara was being held at Cuatro Alamos along with another Jewish woman, Elena Dobry, mother of the writer Carla Guelfenbein. The rabbi spoke to the US ambassador. Kreiman told him, "Mr. Ambassador, two ladies from my community have been imprisoned. You must intervene." But the ambassador told Kreiman he could do nothing without orders from his government. "Look, if you do not intervene, I will speak with the grand rabbi of Paris and he will contact the Jewish community of New York. And they will talk with rabbis in the United States capital, and you will indeed receive orders!" And that's how it happened. He received instructions from Washington, DC, and went to Pinochet to request their release. That night, after eight days in the detention camp, both were released.[51]

Julio Laks, who first moved to Jerusalem and then Paris, where he still lives today, also thanked Kreiman for his efforts to gain his release after he had spent four months held in various DINA detention and torture centers. In a letter addressed to Rabbi Kreiman dated January 25, 1975, Laks writes: "The destiny of the Jewish people could not be better fulfilled and represented than in this fight for the most essential human rights that at this moment in Chile are being trampled on by a boot similar to Hitler's, whether or not this is understood by some segments of our community who have blinders on."[52] Laks also requested that the rabbi intercede for his friend María Cristina López Stewart, arrested at the same time as he and his wife. Whether or not Kreiman tried to do something for her is unknown, but she remains disappeared to this day.

Kreiman states that he was "most involved" in the David Silberman case. Silberman, director of CODELCO, was arrested on September 12, 1973, in the northern city of Calama and transferred to the Santiago penitentiary: "I went to see him Yom Kippur eve when he was arrested; I brought him clothing and a prayer book, and two days later he disappeared during a transfer."[53] Despite Kreiman's efforts to arrange for Silberman to leave the country, on October 4, 1974, he was kidnapped by the DINA. Many surviving prisoners later testified that they had seen him at the José Domingo Cañas and Cuatro Alamos torture centers before he disappeared forever.

At one critical juncture, Kreiman moved the conscience of a Jewish military judge who had in his power the lives or deaths of four people. Sergeant Belarmino Constanzo, Captain Raul Vergara, Commander Ernesto Galaz, and the vice president of the Banco de Estado Carlos Lazo had been accused of fictitious crimes for which the dictatorship's first war council had sentenced them to die, in a case called *Aviación contra Bachelet y Otros (Aviation vs. Bachelet and Others)*. All were air force officials who had been tortured for upholding the Constitution and opposing the military coup. Air force brigadier general Alberto Bachelet, father of future president Michelle Bachelet (2006–10 and 2014–18), died March 12, 1974, as a result of torture. The war council sentence stated that "all of them must face the firing squad."[54] The entire world was engrossed by the news reports about the aberrant air force court proceedings, which at one point the Argentine ambassador and other officials were allowed to attend. Outside the country, groups held rallies and issued statements in solidarity with the illegally convicted prisoners.

General José Berdichewsky Scher, an air force judge, had the last word. Berdichewsky asked the rabbi to meet with him. When the general arrived, Kreiman was waiting, completely clear regarding the ethics of life at play and having built up strong arguments against the death penalty the night before with his colleagues of the Propeace Committee. On August 5, 1974, Berdichewsky announced his sentence: in consideration of their past irreproachable conduct, the death penalty was disproportionate punishment. The rabbi had appealed to *pekuaj nefesh*, the highest Jewish principle that holds that saving a life must reign above any other consideration.

Rabbi Kreiman also participated in efforts to halt the military regime's re-pressive policies. In a letter addressed to the military junta, dated August 23, 1974, and published in Chile's newspapers, the interfaith group echoed Pope Paul VI's appeal in the context of the Catholic Church's jubilee year calling for the "cessation of the state war," pardons for all imprisoned people, and the transfer of legal proceedings to ordinary civilian courts.

On August 30, 1974, *La Segunda*'s editorial page carried an unusual letter titled "Something Else about Rabbi Angel Kreiman" ("Algo más sobre el rabino Angel Kreiman"). It stated:

> With great indignation we have read in *La Segunda* that Rabbi Angel Kreiman has had the audacity to request pardons for the Marxists who have been justly punished by the Honorable Government Junta. . . . The rabbi, like his great friend Salvador Allende, has had power to divide the Jewish community, as the vast majority does not tolerate him and this signed letter provides the opportune moment to suggest that he leave this country soon.[55]

The letter's authors identified themselves as "several Chileans of the Jewish faith who fight for the reconstruction of Chile," signing only with their ini-tials: J. S. D., A. W. S., O. R. L., J. D. K., O. K. B., M. F. S., and J. B. S.[56]

Jewish community leaders had authorized Kreiman to take part in the Pro-peace Committee because they viewed it as a strategy for cultivating better relations with the Catholic Church. But when that participation publicly com-promised the Jewish institutional position of maintaining good relations with the military junta, they tried to rein him in, which resulted in verbal confron-tations such as exemplified by the anonymous letter printed in *La Segunda*. Kreiman came to be questioned not only by Jewish institutions but also by people who expressed frustration with what they thought were less than ener-getic efforts to protect and save their loved ones.

Shortly after arriving in Chile, the rabbi traveled to Concepción to meet the Jewish community in that southern city. The community had no rabbi, but Gunter Seelmann served as its president. Hanni Grunpeter, his wife, was a Socialist Party city councilwoman in the neighboring town of Talcahuano. Kreiman asked her for support in securing a long-term loan for a tract of land near Hualpen to establish a summer camp for Jewish youth. Finding the rabbi friendly and "definitely a Popular Unity supporter," she pulled strings to enable him to acquire the land.

On September 11, Gunter, also a Socialist Party member, was arrested and taken with many others to Quiriquina Island. In the course of her efforts to free her husband, Hanni learned that the rabbi was part of the new interfaith entity that sought to protect people persecuted by the dictatorship. Hanni traveled to Santiago with her sister, arriving a Saturday afternoon. She rang the condominium doorbell and through the intercom described Gunter's situation to the rabbi. The rabbi responded through the intercom that he could not help her that afternoon because it was Shabbat. Determined not to have traveled in vain, from there the two sisters proceeded to the home of Lutheran bishop Helmut Frenz, who was also a member of the Propeace Committee. Frenz was in bed with the flu but met with them just the same and proposed that they make a visit to the German ambassador the next day. Bishop Frenz's support was key in getting Gunter out of prison and enabling him to obtain refugee status in Germany. Neither Hanni nor Gunter had any further contact with Rabbi Kreiman.

When her daughter Diana was apprehended and abducted on November 18, 1974, Perla Aron turned to the rabbi. "We went to talk to Angel Kreiman. 'Buy a plane ticket and pack a suitcase to have it ready for her to travel. In fifteen days you will have her in Israel.' That's what he told us. A week later, we received a letter from him. It read: 'The community forbids me from getting involved in this matter. I'm very sorry. Angel Kreiman.'"[57]

Not two weeks transpired and cameraman Jorge Müller was also arrested. His father, Rodolfo, met with the rabbi. "We described the situation, and he told us he would talk to Jewish leaders. A couple of weeks later we spoke to him again. Kreiman said he had spoken with his higher-ups who recommended not getting involved in this type of thing."[58]

Rabbi Kreiman's apparent easy access to the high-ranking military officials that other Propeace Committee members did not share also generated alarm and suspicion that he might be collaborating with the military junta. On one occasion he stated, "I must acknowledge that if I was able to help get Jews with problems out of the country in thirty-six cases, independent of my participation in the Propeace Committee or my subsequent nominal involvement with the Vicariate of Solidarity, it was thanks to the opening that the president of the republic [Pinochet] and in particular the interior minister, General Bonilla, extended to me."[59]

Law philosophy professor Miguel Orellano Benado, who knew Kreiman well, believes the rabbi formed close relations with the military as a way to gain the support he sought to help people in need. "How can people criticize Angel Kreiman for his contacts with the military? Of course he had them. How could he have interceded without those contacts? It's very primitive. He was the flame that represented this community that approved support but wanted to keep it low profile, while he was actively and publicly involved." Nevertheless, historian Valeria Navarro insists that "Rabbi Kreiman's position exhibits certain dichotomy," pointing out his close ties to the highest military junta officials on the one hand and his aid to prisoners on the other.

The rabbi himself offered another explanation for the military's good will toward him: "The military government gave me special attention to avoid being perceived as antisemitic." A desire to maintain good relations with Israel may have also encouraged the military to sustain cordial relations with the rabbi and to be careful not to make gestures toward him that could be interpreted as antisemitic.

Kreiman cultivated those good relations, inviting military junta members to greet the Jewish community on Rosh Hashanah and Yom Kippur. In October 1973, when the tradition began of having the junta visit Círculo Israelita synagogue on Yom Kippur, the delegation included air force general José Berdichewsky. Ten months later, the same official would turn to the rabbi to help him decide whether or not to save four human lives.

In his Yizkor memorial service sermon on Yom Kippur in October 1974, the rabbi offered an explanation about his involvement to his congregation as well as the military junta representatives present at Temple Bnei Jisroel.

> Much has been said about the interfaith work underway to aid all those in need. Even my own actions have been criticized. However, I must clarify that as a Jew I do not adopt political positions; what moves me is a profoundly religious and Jewish human vision that should inspire us all to help and love our neighbor because every man is made in the image of the Creator.

In the sphere of Jewish liturgical practice, Kreiman had an indelible impact, infusing new vitality in Judaism in Chile. He introduced egalitarian religious services, bilingual prayer books in Spanish and Hebrew, and encouraged a generation of young people to explore their Judaic heritage through organizations such as Camp Rama in Hualpén. It was also Kreiman who incorporated more progressive practices associated with the Rabbinical Seminary of Buenos Aires. When his wife, Susy, was killed in the bombing on Asociación Mutual Israelita Argentina (AMIA, Argentine Israelite Mutual Association), on July 19, 1994, that left eighty-five dead, he lost the center of his existence and the anchor of his life. He returned to Chile a few years later. When Pinochet was arrested in London in 1998, he criticized the move, which perplexed many people inside Chile.

People well acquainted with Angel Kreiman contend that his seeming vacillation reflected not a political view but rather his complex personality. Endowed with a fairly well-developed ego, he felt compelled to insert himself as a protagonist in different scenes that at times did not comport with one another,

according to Isaac Icekson, Zionist Federation president during the Popular
Unity era. The rabbi was a member of the federation during Icekson's presidency, and Icekson affirms that they greatly respected each other: "With us,
he adopted a progressive view similar to the leftist Zionist position. But he
displayed true schizophrenia in the situation we experienced under the dictatorship. On the one hand, he had to support the military, but on the other he
aided people in need."

People who attended synagogues presided over by Rabbi Kreiman recall a
recurrent theme in his sermons related to the Jewish concepts of yetzer hatov
and yetzer hara. Yetzer hatov is the impulse for good that corresponds to a
moral conscience and altruistic inclinations, while yetzer hara is the source
of all human suffering and what drives us to be competitive, ambitious, and
violent. In underscoring this duality, perhaps the rabbi implicitly sought to
explain to others as well as to himself his own apparent contradictions.

Unpredictable to the end, Rabbi Kreiman died suddenly on January 5, 2014.
His funeral brought together people who had always supported him uncondi-
tionally with others who had been among his harshest critics.

ARE THEY REALLY JEWS?

In the weeks that followed the military coup, Chilean agents at the border
with Argentina arrested a group of university students belonging to the Frente
de Izquierda Sionista (FIS, Zionist Left Front) as they attempted to leave the
country. Community leaders met to map out a strategy to compel the military
government to commit to protecting the group of students.

"All of us spoke, and we were all concerned about securing assurances that
the student would be well treated and that they would be allowed to leave
the country," recalls Icekson. But he also remembers something that occurred
in that urgent meeting that continues to disturb him to this day: "Observing
how passionately we defended the safety of those young people, Gil Sinay
uttered a phrase that has stayed in my head, despite all the respect I had for
him as community leader. His question, posed almost in an innocent tone,
was 'But are those young people really Jewish?' That is the sentence he used."[60]

Israel's education minister was also present. He had been on an official visit
to the government of Salvador Allende when the coup occurred and had been
stranded in Chile ever since, unable to leave. "That official's reaction was ex-
plosive," says Icekson. "He rose from his chair, livid, and addressed Gil Sinay:
'How dare you say such a thing in this situation?'"

Some thirty-five years after these events, historian Valeria Navarro interviewed Sinay, who had been president of the Jewish Representative Committee from 1956 to 1982 and director of the newspaper *La Palabra Israelita* from

1985 until his death in 2013. When Navarro asked him about his thoughts regarding people of Jewish origin arrested during the military dictatorship, Sinay answered with a question: "What relation did they have to the community?' Answering his own question, he said, "None," adding that "they had Jewish last names but they had no relation to the community; they were assimilated and never had ties to the community. No one knew them."[61]

According to this eminent community leader, Jewish identity is defined in terms of affiliation or participation in an institutional community framework. Casting doubt as to whether these people of leftist politics were indeed Jews implied that that they were not sufficiently Jewish to be concerned about. This narrow definition of Jewish identity that ties it to community affiliation ignores the diverse ways it is elaborated and the fact that these do not always center on participation in a synagogue or other community institutions. As Navarro puts it, "People who feel represented by these Jewish community organizations are not necessarily the only ones who consider themselves Jews."[62]

How do people of progressive and left-leaning politics relate to their Jewish origins? Is it a significant component of their personal identity?

Denni Traubmann remembers the exact moment he became aware that he was a Jew. "When I was five or six years old, I don't know why, I blurted out, 'The Jews killed Christ!' My father looked at me, my mother looked at me, and they said, 'But you are Jewish!' They must have said it with particular emphasis because those four words became etched forever in my mind: 'But you are Jewish!'"[63]

His father was Ernesto Traubmann, who arrived in Chile with his parents as refugees and went back to Europe to fight against the Nazis. After the defeat of Germany, he had returned to Chile but not to the Jewish youth movements; instead, he became a member of the Communist Party. The fact that he was a Communist as well as freedom fighter did not diminish his sense of Jewish identity, nor did it mean he would fail to instill a sense of Jewish identity in his son.

Carlos Berger grew up in a family that was both Communist and Jewish. His father, Julius Zoltan Berger, born in a town in Transylvanian Hungary, arrived in Chile at the age of seventeen after he and his family had fled the approaching Nazi threat in the mid-1930s. All his Hungarian uncles and aunts perished in the Shoah. The family of his mother, Dora Guralnik, originally from Ukraine, came to Chile in the late 1920s speaking only Yiddish. A great number of the Berger-Guralnik couple's circle of friends were, like them, Jews who belonged to the Communist Party. During the administration of President Gabriel González Videla, who outlawed the Communist Party in 1948 and persecuted its members, the well-known leader Volodia Teitelboim spent long stretches of time hidden in the Bergers' home.

Carmen Hertz, widow of Carlos Berger, who was murdered on October 19, 1973, in Calama by the so-called Caravan of Death, describes what she thinks being Jewish meant to her husband:

> Carlos Berger's DNA certainly is marked as a member of a people persecuted simply for who they were. His awareness helped make him a better person and choose the political options he did. He inherited his great personal generosity from his parents, especially his mother. I cannot separate these elements—they were interconnected. They merged together into a single trait. Carlos was highly sensitive to injustice in Chile with its extremely high illiteracy rate and feudal, essentially enslaved, peasants. It was a generation forged in a collective desire to change Chilean society and create a more just world. And they were willing to give their lives for that.[64]

Rolly Baltiansky is the daughter of Isaac Baltiansky, who was born in the Ukrainian town of Jarkov, where Rolly's grandfather was an orchestra director. In 1912, when Isaac Baltiansky was twelve, he arrived in Valparaíso with his older brother, a socialist who had been jailed for conspiring against the czar. The whole Baltiansky family, according to Rolly, were socialists and all believed in the need for a Jewish state.[65]

> The creation of the state of Israel was very important for us as a family. We believed it to be a historic achievement of Jews who had been persecuted for thousands of years. Our father made sure to teach us and have us read about Israel. All of us are conscious of the importance of Israel's existence as a refuge for all those persecuted souls.[66]

Her brother was accorded refugee status by Israel after the military coup. Her husband, Ricardo García, a Communist Party member and general manager of the Cobresal mine, was killed by the Caravan of Death in Copiapó on October 18, 1973.

Miguel Lawner practically grew up in and around Santiago's vast central produce market called La Vega, where smells of dust, wicker, and spices permeated the air, playing with the stray cats. Facing Vega Central in a narrow, enclosed corridor still known as El Baratillo, his father, Luis Lawner, opened a small store that sold used flour sacks, a very modest business that years later his sister Ester expanded considerably. From an early age, Miguel witnessed not only impoverished people around La Vega but also the diligence and dignity with which they lifted themselves out of their poverty. In his home neighborhood near the corner of Matta and Portugal streets, Miguel played in the spacious gardens of Bikur Jolim, one of Santiago's oldest synagogues. It was founded as a beneficent society to assist newly arrived Jewish immigrants to Chile.

On Sundays, the Lawner home was the center of family gatherings that frequently included new arrivals who they welcomed to Chile. Miguel recalls how, during all the years his family worked in La Vega,

> my dad had a man who came nearly every Saturday to sell him two mullets, the best quality river fish. My mother would get up at five in the morning on Sundays to bake the two fish because you never knew how many people would show up for lunch. A lovely table was set on Sundays. After lunch we would play cards with the cousins or listen to records, frequently recordings of Jewish songs.
>
> I feel I—and my sister Ester too—inherited from my parents a feeling for relationships with other people, especially solidarity. My mother was an exemplary person, a very warm and supportive person. That's why her house was the place where everybody gathered. I feel that my sister and I inherited that. And we both transmitted this to our own children.[67]

In 1940, when Miguel was twelve years old, his connection to the Jewish community was through an organization called the Asociación de Jóvenes Israelitas (AJI, Association of Young Israelites), which met in the basement of the Círculo Israelita synagogue on Serrano Street, at the corner of Tarapacá Street. Perla and Elías Aron, parents of Diana Aron, met in these gatherings. Youngsters of AJI closely followed the course of events in Europe during World War II and were excited about the creation of the state of Israel.

Another Jewish youth movement, the Hashomer Hatzair, was decisive in forming the Jewish identity and worldview in general of Gunter Seelmann and Hanni Grunpeter, in the southern city of Concepción. Gunter explains that with Hashomer Hatzair he had his "first contact with a community-oriented experience that encouraged friendship and solidarity and with a group that had a socialist outlook. Everything focused on a single long-term objective, which was to immigrate to Israel and live in a kibbutz, which in those years was my primary goal."[68]

The birth of the state of Israel led to a greater Jewish consciousness for Hanni, one that was no longer associated with the intense religiosity of her childhood but instead with Israel. In 1950, after a journey by ship with a stop in prerevolutionary Cuba and a long stay in England, she arrived at a kibbutz in Israel. She thoroughly enjoyed the experience of a pure collective system: "It was considered bourgeois to have belongings, so we shared everything. It was also bourgeois to have a bathroom. There was no toilet—just a hole in the ground. Showers were shared. I thought it was the most beautiful thing in the world."[69] She would have stayed, but she heeded her parents' plea to return to Concepción to finish high school.

Israel—which they support but not unquestioningly—continues to be a fundamental element of Gunter's and Hanni's Jewish identity. Both were Socialist Party leaders who grew up in Concepción in an era when it was an industrial city of intense social and political activity. Gunter in his capacity as president of the Concepción Jewish community was not a Jew who "just had a Jewish last name."

Sara Caro, her two sisters, and the daughter of another family were the only Jewish girls of their grade in La Serena, northern Chile. "When I was seven, eight, and later twelve, I would go out to the schoolyard at recess and my classmates would sing and play, 'Burnt bread. Who burned it? The Jewish dog. Set it on fire, because there I go.' They often sang me that song and played that game. They would also tell me, 'You killed Jesus.'"[70] Her mother said to her, "You have to be the best student of the school. You have to be outstanding. Jews have been known for outstanding intelligence, wisdom, and knowledge. And she would name great Jewish thinkers such as Einstein and Freud. You have to be open. Walk straight and be proud that you are a Jew."

Sara explains, "When we were bullied, we would begin naming the great Jews of the world. But I suffered on account of it. It marked me." Just like for Sara, for many other Jews, a primary component of Jewish identity is the awareness of being "different" and always subject to discrimination and antisemitism.

Tomás Hirsch is representative of a common type of cultural Jewish identification not associated with any specific element yet characterized by a strong sense of belonging.

> For us and for me in particular, Judaism is more a family tradition than a religion. It is difficult to define. I've spent the greater part of my life asking myself what it means to be a Jew, even though it is not a priority issue for me. I have no religious belief, but I feel very strong ties to Judaism. If you ask me why, I would have to say I don't know. But I experience it, I feel it.[71]

Diana Aron and her siblings were raised by a family that embraced the concept of Jewish identity described by former community leader Gil Sinay. Her maternal great-grandfather Samuel Rotter may well have been Santiago's first rabbi, when the Jewish community consisted of less than a thousand people who met in a building on San Diego Street.[72] Her maternal grandfather was one of the founders of the Círculo Israelita synagogue, and her father, Elías Aron, had been director of the same synagogue as well as president of the Culture and Education Commission, known as the Vadajinu, of the Instituto Hebreo Jewish school. Her mother, Perla Aron, was the WIZO president and an active lobbyist in the cause of persuading Chile to vote in favor of the creation of the state of Israel.

Despite her parents' active institutional participation, Diana did not think the values she considered intrinsic to Judaism were stressed enough by them. This is exemplified in her mother's account of the family's Passover celebration.

> For me Passover was a dinner of traditional foods, gefilte fish, and knaidel. But Diana insisted on reading the entire Haggadah, the whole Passover story. As you know, reading the entire Haggadah, the seder may well run on to midnight. Diana was about thirteen years old when she said to me during a Passover seder, "What kind of celebration is this? Are we only going to eat?" And I said, "Oh, Diana, stop your foolish talk." She got up from the table, went to the second floor, and slammed her bedroom door shut. And she did not come back to join us. Diana was an extremist.[73]

The Haggadah that Diana wanted to read in its entirety included the allegorical and pedagogical narrative about four types of children—the wise, the wicked, the simple, and the one who knows not what to ask. These represent four ways of transmitting Jewish tradition or approaching Jewish identity. The second child is called the *rashá*, or rebellious child. However, a contemporary interpretation suggests that this boy or girl only challenges their elders to infuse the ritual with meaning, thereby uniting it to a true commitment to social justice. Diana's indignation over the social inequities of Chilean society and her willingness to pay the highest price for that cause exemplified this linking of Jewish values and practice.

If you had asked Diana if she considered herself Jewish, she would have replied, "Yes!" says her sister, the psychologist Anamaría Aron. The same as Ernesto Traubmann would have, according to his son Denni. This is how they and other progressive Jews feel about their identity.

Implicit in Gil Sinay's suggestion that leftist Jews are not true Jews is the idea that Jewish community leaders must focus their attention on certain Jews and not others. For Chilean Jewish institutions during dictatorship years, certain people who shared Jewish origins became "others." In the context of a threat to life, this translated as a reluctance to intercede for persons persecuted for their political beliefs because they were regarded as assimilated Jews. Miguel Orellana Benado, a philosopher and professor at the University of Chile Law School, maintains that this view is reasonable.

> It's very common for assimilated leftist Jews to call themselves Jews only when they need the Jewish institutions. And later they are surprised that these same Jewish institutions they had always scorned fail to take action in their cases, that they don't want to endanger their own people in order to save those who are Jews but only just now realized they are. . . . You could say the Jewish community did very little to protect persecuted Jews. But were these Jews integrated in Jewish life? Were they stakeholders who had grounds to plea for help from Jews in particular?[74]

In the early twentieth century, the rabbi Chaim Soloveitchik (1853–1918) faced a similar dilemma in Bresk, a city in Byelorussia located on the border with Poland. Commonly known as Chaim of Brisk, the rabbi was a sage who left his mark on an extensive dynasty of orthodox rabbis who founded seminaries and schools in Eastern Europe and other parts of the world. In those years, the General Union of Jewish Workers, better known as the Bund, was established in Lithuania, Poland, and Russia. It was an amalgam of Jewish intellectuals and socialist workers that totaled thirty-four thousand members.

A certain young Bundist of Bresk habitually exhibited his contempt for Jewish religious tradition and whenever he passed the rabbi on the street on Shabbat, he would deliberately light a cigarette.[75] One day he shot a poster featuring a portrait of Czar Nicolas. Just before Rosh Hashanah he was arrested, charged with sedition, and sentenced to death. However, the czar's government announced that if Jews paid a ransom of five thousand rubles, charges would be dropped and the sentence would be repealed.

Rabbi Chaim ordered the community to collect the sum to save the young man's life. His followers were perplexed. Pointing to Deuteronomy 17:7, which says "to eliminate the evil from your midst" (New American Standard version), an exemplary student asked what could better fulfill that precept than killing the Bundist. "Your interpretation of that verse is erroneous," replied Rabbi Chaim, forcefully but patiently. "To consider the words 'eliminate evil' carte blanche for eliminating any unpleasant individual from the city is not a correct application of Torah," he emphasized. To seal his argument, Chaim asked his students to read the immediately preceding verse, which requires there be three witnesses if a capital sentence is to be carried out. "This poor man has been condemned by the words of one single witness," he pointed out. And the rabbi again insisted on collecting the rubles because saving a Jewish life is the highest precept of the Holy Law.

In the twenty-first century, another rabbi listened attentively to the narrative about the wise Chaim of Bresk. "It's a beautiful story," says Rabbi Joel Oseran, director of the World Union for Progressive Judaism, an organization dedicated to strengthening and revitalizing small Jewish communities throughout the world. Rabbi Oseran, who had just visited the Museum of Memory and Human Rights of Santiago, adds, "But I would raise the standard from Jew to human being. It makes no difference whether or not the person facing danger is Jewish. And whether or not one is a member of the community is absolutely irrelevant. One is a human being. That reason alone should suffice to concern ourselves."[76]

DISSIDENT VOICES: LESSONS IN DEMOCRACY

For more than forty years, Rosita Schaulsohn Brodsky has been known for her vocation as a Jewish educator. She has taught in synagogues, in Hashomer Hatzair, and in several schools, but she doesn't just impart facts about Judaism and Jewish history. Her classes also address the universal values of freedom and critical thinking that she considers fundamental to Jewish culture and identity.

Her father, Jacobo Schaulsohn Numhauser, was elected deputy to Chile's lower legislative house in 1949 for the Radical Party and was reelected four times, becoming president of the Chamber of Deputies in 1961. In 1971 Allende appointed him to the Constitutional Tribunal, "one more piece of evidence for Chile that his would not be an authoritarian Communist government," comments Rosita.

During the Popular Unity years, when, as she observes, many Jews "were so frightened [of the government] that everyone went over to the right," she was given a great opportunity.[77] After the Popular Unity government was installed, Rabbi Kreiman approached the Education Ministry with a proposal: introduce Jewish religion classes in the schools. Both public schools and private schools today as well as in those years were required to teach religion classes. When his proposal was approved, he called two experienced teachers, Tamara Baron and Rosita Schaulsohn. Rosita recalls, "Never will I forget what he told us: 'You will be representatives of Judaism and Israel. You have to study hard to explain what Judaism and Shoah are,'" immediately adding that "this was during the government of Salvador Allende."

Rosita was assigned to teach at the Grange School, where wealthy Jews send their children. She explains that she "did not give them Jewish religious classes but rather Jewish classes." She would lower the blinds, and everyone had the right to ask questions. "We addressed each other with the informal 'tu,' and there were no grades. There were no tests." It was an exercise in democracy for young Jews.

She was working at that school when the military coup took place. Her young brother, Jorge Schaulsohn, after spending several weeks in the Israeli Embassy, left Chile. Her twin sister, Nora, a Socialist Party member who was an active member of the Popular Unity government and married to a Communist Party member, also went into exile.

When classes resumed several days after the coup, she discovered that "you walked through the school gate and it was as if nothing had happened. Most of the parents were delighted about the coup. Ninety percent of the parents had opposed Allende. They would have taken their children out of my classroom had they known I was a leftist," she says. Rosita introduced her teenage students to the thought of politically progressive Jews in Chilean history, such as Alejandro Lipschutz, Natalio Berman, Angel Faivovich, Jacobo Schaulsohn, and Moises Brodsky. At one point, she invited her mother-in-law and two other older women, the three of them former refugees from Nazism, to her classroom to share their experiences with students, using their experiences to draw certain parallels with what was happening in their own country.

At interfaith events at the Grange School, she was frequently asked to speak, "because they knew I was more open." Once "I gave an overview of Judaism and I ended up saying that Israel should not be a nation of saints but a nation of prophets. 'But are you crazy?' several parents asked me afterward. They nearly insulted me. I told them, 'To be a prophet means you question everything around you.' Many conflicts shaped my own Jewish identity."

In the early 1980s, Rosita was teaching Jewish "religion" classes at Santiago College high school. She talked to them about Nazi fascism.

> The school's directors called to clarify that I couldn't talk about political subjects— not even about fascism or antisemitism. I thought I would die from the shock! They were all seated there: the school principal, the twelfth-grade principal, and a rabbi who was about to leave for the United States. The three of them told me "no politics." Politics meant fascism, Zionism, and Nazism.

Her response was "How can I teach Jewish history without talking about these things?" Later, she says, "I talked it over with the students. 'There are two options,' I told them. 'Either we keep talking about these things in secret or I resign. I cannot evade certain content.' They wanted to learn. I have never been able to understand Judaism outside its historical context."

Hashomer Hatzair

The Hashomer Hatzair youth movement was founded 1913 in Poland, on the eve of World War I. In Germany thousands of Jews enlisted voluntarily, hoping to expel any doubts as to their loyalty to the country and put an end to their status as second-class citizens. In Eastern Europe as well, modernity entered Jewish communities, and the bright glow of assimilation enticed many. In this context, and with the resurgence of antisemitism on the horizon, Hashomer Hatzair was conceived as a scout movement through which young Jewish boys and girls would be instilled with greater self-reliance and autonomy, qualities that years later would make them outstanding fighters in the rebellions against the Nazis in the concentration camps and ghettos.

Recent immigrant arrivals from Germany founded the first Chilean Hashomer Hatzair group in 1939, and it became affiliated with the international organization in 1943.[78] In the 1960s and early 1970s, the organization sowed values of justice, compassion, and solidarity in many young people who subsequently went on to participate in the contemporary social and political movements emerging in Chile during those years.

Salvador Allende gave more than one talk at the Hashomer Hatzair house, known as the *ken*, during his presidential campaign, according to Mauricio Guzmán. The group's participation in Allende's electoral campaign, even as a sizeable number of them were finalizing details to immigrate to Israel, created a complicated duality, he notes.

> Often people of the left said we were betraying the cause. We could not be leftists and also be Zionists. But we were clear on that score. Yes, we agreed with Allende's ideas, but we saw our future as being in Israel. The country was still young and needed a great many people. Our conscience was clear about the need for us to go to Israel.[79]

Darío Teitelbaum, Latin America director for Hashomer Hatzair, notes that throughout the Latin American continent, "dual membership" was common, meaning that young people who participated in Hashomer were also "engaged in the local political and social situation." In Chile both Hashomer and the Zionist Left Front supported Salvador Allende's platform, to the irritation of Jewish community institutions and the Israeli Embassy. Teitelbaum observed leftist support among Chilean Zionists when he was an adult coordinator for Hashomer in 1986 and 1987: "I witnessed the last years before the referendum in Chile. I observed some young people go far beyond their Jewish identity and progressive Zionism. They saw that democracy was on the rise, and they wanted to be part of that process."[80]

Haim Hayet, born in Cuba to a Lithuanian-born cobbler, immigrated to Israel in 1960 at a young age to live on a kibbutz. He remembers the fervor with which he looked forward to his stay in Popular Unity Chile when he was sent to serve as a *sheliaj* emissary in the Santiago office of Hashomer: "The revolutionary sun of Chile was strong. I expected to combine the revolutionary and youthful fire of those people with the fact that I had gone to work for revolution in Israel."[81]

He describes his impressions of the first Chile he knew. "Chile was a democratic country. We were impressed that the Chilean national police were as cultured as they were. They spoke to people with respect. Traffic police did not simply give you a ticket but would explain what you had done wrong. We were very impressed." After the coup, he witnessed a second Chile emerge, "as if overnight." He observed, incredulous, how those refined policemen "turned into thugs," adding that "it was shocking" and that it helped him "understand how refined German people became murderers."

Hayet and other Hashomer Hatzair leaders brought cots the organization used in its summer camps to the Israeli Embassy, as it was as overcrowded with asylum seekers as most of the other embassies. Ambassador Moshe Tov smuggled people into the embassy in his car. According to Hayet, this "annoyed some segments of the community. 'How is it possible that the embassy harbors and hides Communists?' they charged. Moshe Tov replied, 'I'm not going to turn my back on the same people I went asking to support the government in Israel a week ago.' Many people were saved thanks to Moshe Tov," Hayet insists.[82]

He also remembered that once while dining in the ambassador's house, a staff person from the embassy, located on Santo Domingo Street facing Forestal Park, called to say that soldiers wanted to search the premises for subversives and that they were threatening to knock down the door if the embassy didn't let them in. The embassy had given refuge to a great many people on the building's second floor. The ambassador told the caller to let the military enter. Fortunately, they didn't discover the entrance to the second floor.

Hayet protected himself with a diplomatic corps ID card provided by the Israeli Embassy and his press credentials issued as journalist for the newspaper *Al Hamishmar*, the organ of MAPAM, the Israeli socialist party. A few weeks after the coup, someone told the police he was a Cuban revolutionary, and his house was raided. The curfew had started when a military patrol armed with bazookas entered his house. "As they turned my house upside down, I told the commanding officer, 'Sir, you are making a mistake,' and I showed him the diplomat credentials the embassy had provided me. The officer answered, "You are the one who's mistaken.' That card carried absolutely no weight," says Hayet. The raid was the second on his house, and it persuaded him to leave the country with his wife and three children as fast as possible. In a caravan of diplomatic vehicles owned by the Israeli Embassy, they went to the airport to board a flight bound for Buenos Aires. He later learned that he could not have more precisely timed his fleeing. Barely two hours after Hayet's family abandoned their home, security agents returned, this time intending to arrest him, only to find the house empty.

Soldiers also raided Isaac Icekson's house on Eliecer Parada Street near Tobalaba Avenue looking for Hashomer members. It was the night of October 6, 1973, during curfew, and Icekson was watching television when eighty armed soldiers invaded his home. Announcing that they had information that subversives held meetings there, the soldiers proceeded to search the house, while Icekson calmly continued to watch television. "I told them, 'I haven't the slightest idea about that. Please do inspect these premises. There are no weapons here.' They finished, and they left. In fact, two days before, some kids from Hashomer, my son's friends, had been there playing guitar, singing, and talking. That was the subversive meeting."[83]

During the dictatorship, especially in the early years, the Hashomer Hatzair house on Los Capitanes Street in well-to-do Providencia was raided repeatedly. The dangerous climate led the organization to suspend its activities for children and adolescents for a time. All the *sheliaj* sent from Israel after activities were resumed were opponents of the dictatorship—Dov Fishblein, David Maldavsky, and Dario Teitelbaum, to name a few. In those years—late 1973, 1974, 1977, 1980, and 1982—five groups of young Chilean Jews, many of whom were former Hashomer members, immigrated to Israel to live in a kibbutz.

Kathy Castro, who actively participated in Hashomer in those years, recalls that "in those times the position was clear: either you went to a kibbutz in Israel or you stayed in Chile as a leftist to actively oppose the dictatorship. Thousands of things were happening in Chile."[84] Kathy was among those who remained in Chile and continued to participate in Hashomer until her loyalties to Chile and her loyalty to Israel collided. "Hashomer was very important for me in those years," she emphasizes.

> Living in dictatorship was frightening. But Hashomer was a place of freedom, a place where I felt safe; it was a space for all of us who, one way or another, were suffering the consequences of our parents' involvement with the Allende government. We were frightened about living in dictatorship. It was a beautiful place where we grew up intellectually and emotionally. The *ken* was like a protective uterus within all that terrible violence outside. It gave us a space where we could talk, listen to each other, sing, where our activities had a very clear ideological meaning, where one built community with a pioneer spirit. My first notions about collective living, that it was possible and could be sustained, originated there. A good part of my ethical structure originated there: solidarity and respect for others.

In 1976, when she was sixteen years old, Kathy joined the Movimiento de Izquierda Revolucionaria (MIR, Revolutionary Left Movement), but she continued going to Hashomer. She began "to use Hashomer for political objectives," entering the building at night when no one was there to print leaflets for the MIR on Hashomer's mimeograph machine. One night in 1979, she carelessly left the first page of the movement's newspaper *El Rebelde* stuck to the machine. The adult coordinator and her teenage peers held a trial and ended up expelling her from the organization. Today she recognizes that her political utilization of Hashomer was irresponsible and that she had not fathomed the risk to which she was exposing the group.

In August 1984, Kathy's husband, Mario Lagos, was murdered in Concepción, and she ended up in prison. She was set free and expelled from the country thanks to representation by attorney Washington Domb from the Vicariate of Solidarity. In his youth, Domb had been a Hashomer member and had recently returned to Chile after he left for exile following his own arrest. Two people who spent their adolescence in Hashomer were killed by the dictatorship: Ernesto Traubmann, arrested and forcibly disappeared on September 13, 1973; and Abraham Muskablit Edelstein, summarily executed on September 9, 1986.

Dario Teitelbaum searches for precise words to convey Hashomer's role in forming citizens of conscience who the organization hopes will, in contrast to the majority of the Jewish community, be concerned with the social good.

> The shomrim always viewed themselves as protagonists and agents of change.[85] It is an ongoing debate that has resurfaced at different times throughout our history, and quite strongly in Chile. . . . Once I asked my *sheliaj* in Buenos Aires why Hashomer Hatzair was so important for us. He replied, "Hashomer Hatzair was the place where you could free yourselves from the repression that reigned in society at large." I've never forgotten that sentence; it has guided me my whole life long. Because Hashomer Hatzair must free people, not just nations. Not just support Israel, but fundamentally free people from their own oppressions.[86]

Jews for Peace

In early September 1988, a group of Jewish leaders announced an event in honor of Augusto Pinochet in *El Mercurio*. This event would seal their support for his intention to remain in power another nine years, which was to be voted on in a national referendum scheduled for October 5.

Juan Flores was indignant reading the news about Jewish support for Pinochet.[87] Sandra Oksenberg was likewise outraged that "Jews would endorse such a criminal stance, especially since Jewish people had lived through Shoah and discrimination."[88] Both were members of Jews for Peace, an organization founded in 1985 that assessed what was happening in the county and abroad, in Israel, from an ethical Jewish perspective.

The organization, which was made up of approximately thirty-five people, mainly Jewish university students, was based in an office on Bilbao Avenue, near the corner of Manuel Montt Street. The house of the Hashomer Hatzair movement was nearby, and the two organizations worked closely together.

Several Jews for Peace members also were actively involved in university organizations and political parties, most notably the Partido Izquierda Cristiana (IC, Christian Left Party). The organization's leaders included José Bitran, secretary of the Federación de Estudiantes de la Universidad de Chile (FECH, Federation of University of Chile Students), Rubén Dueñas, a Partido Demócrata Cristiano (PDC) member, Daniel Farcas, an IC party member and also a member of the federation, and Sandra Oksenberg and Juan Flores, both IC members and psychology students at Catholic University. Flores was elected student body president for the School of Psychology, in 1979, when the school disobeyed the prohibition against holding democratic elections.

The article they read in *El Mercurio* led them to organize a parallel event, called the "Forum for a Democratic Option," on September 22, 1988—thirteen days before the referendum—at the Hotel Galerías in downtown Santiago. The eighty endorsers of the "Jews for No" gathering included Irene Bronfman, who would one day be Chile's ambassador to Israel; actor Gregory Cohen;

Hashomer Hatzair dancers at Jews for No rally, September 1988 (Juan Flores)

Jews for No event participants greeting actor Nissim Sharim, September 1988
(Juan Flores)

Humanist Party leader Tomás Hirsch; artist Patricia Israel; architect Miguel
Lawner; playwright Nissim Sharim and his wife psychologist, Juana Kovalskys;
professor of voice Hans Stein; psychiatrist Luis Weinstein, and many others.

The invitation convening the event stated:

> The Jewish community, like any other human group, is made up of people
> who hold different political positions, opinions, and preferences. We therefore
> reject any suggestion that all of us identify with the regime and its candidate.
> We do not intend to speak on behalf of anyone else, beyond our personal views,
> our own views about life, and our identity. However, freedom and the constant
> striving for freedom have always been part of the Jewish tradition as well as the
> hope to live in a more just and fraternal society.

Flores, a psychologist and one of the organization's founders and a coordinator of the "No" campaign event, explains that the origins of Jews for Peace
is a deep sense of Jewish ethics: "We felt that we could not remain indifferent
to what was happening here, right next to us. And it seemed to us that Jewish
ethics imposes an immense obligation: to take a stand, play a role, to have a
voice, and to act in regard to what was happening" in the country. To take
a public stand was an act of courage not only due to the inherent danger of

opposing the military dictatorship but also because it meant facing ostracism from the Jewish community. Jews for Peace was "absolutely criticized and regarded as dangerous by the Jewish institutional base," says Flores.

The critical view of Jews for Peace in regard to Israel was possibly more incendiary than its opposition to the military dictatorship owing to the good relations between Israel and Chile and the fact that Israel was one of Chile's few avenues for obtaining military supplies. Non-Jewish leftists were perplexed by the organization's defense of the state of Israel, on the one hand, and its criticism of Israel's military policy, on the other. During Jews for Peace's five-year existence, the organization always maintained a double focus: it both opposed the military regime that was oppressing Chile and advocated peace in the Middle East, pioneering Jewish-Palestinian dialogue in Chile.

In 1988 the newspaper *Fortín Mapocho* interviewed Jews for Peace leaders and published the interview under the title "Jewish Youth Escape from the Caricature." In a way, the organization was driven by "the notion of breaking the equation that to be a Jew meant to be a right-winger," says Flores. Oksenberg expresses a similar sentiment. "It was not easy to defend something, but not in its totality," she notes. "There was much ignorance. Culturally, Chile is different from Argentina, where everyone is familiar with Jews. Here many students had never met a Jewish person before, and there was much prejudice. The Jewish institutional position that identified with the far right also contributed to that. We had to open new roads." She stresses that even though they "were a small group," they "tried to show that we were Jews and that we too were fighting against the dictatorship."

PART 2

CHRONICLES OF
PRISONERS AND PROTECTORS

These We Shall Remember

A young woman with light-brown hair got off a public bus and asked a pedestrian, "Where is Ricardo Lyon Street?"[1] The person she was addressing happened to be going to the same street and guessed they might be going to the same place. That afternoon of October 26, 2011, the Centro Progresista Judío (CPJ, Jewish Progressive Center) was showing the documentary film *Mi vida con Carlos* (*My Life with Carlos*) at the B'nai B'rith center on Ricardo Lyon Street. The young woman, a third-year journalism student, was interning at the *La Palabra Israelita* community newspaper and planned to cover the event. However, she didn't know what the documentary was about.

When the pedestrian explained that the movie by Germán Berger tells the story of the filmmaker's father, Carlos Berger, whose family was Jewish, and that he was summarily executed by the Caravan of Death in 1973, she replied in surprise, "I had no idea there were Jewish victims of Pinochet!"

Two years later, that young woman, Yael Mandler, now a journalism school graduate, thought about why she was so surprised to learn there were Jewish victims. "Never before had I heard about disappeared prisoners from the Jewish community. Never before had I made a connection between dictatorship and the Jewish community. Those subjects were entirely separate in my mind," Yael says.[2]

Yael's parents are progressive Jews. She studied at the Instituto Hebreo high school; as a child she spent weekends at the Jewish recreational complex Estadio Maccabi, and she attended Mercaz synagogue. Many events and activities in her life took place in a Jewish setting, yet until that moment, she did not realize that the roster of Chile's executed, disappeared, and tortured people included Jews. "Everything related to the dictatorship deeply moves me even though I didn't experience those years. Yet, I never asked myself, 'Might there be disappeared Jews?' The idea never crossed my mind until I saw that film."

Berger's documentary spurred her on to find out more. She discovered stories such as the one about Diana Aron, who, like her, studied journalism at Catholic University.

> It opened my eyes to a more critical view of my community. I thought we Jews were very united and that everyone always helped each other because a small community should support one another. But that's not how it was. We complain about German citizens' complicity in their silence, but who from our community did something about the dictatorship here?

Yael pauses and then says, "I try to understand why I had never asked myself that question. Memory is the foundation of Jewish tradition. The community always remembers its dead. If Jews had died in dictatorship, they would have been remembered, or so I thought. But that was not the case."

In the decade before the civil-military coup of 1973, people of Jewish origin had a significant presence in social and political movements as well as the political parties that comprised the Popular Unity coalition. They also had considerable involvement in the Revolutionary Left Movement (MIR). Therefore, it makes sense that persons persecuted by the military dictatorship would include Jews.

In fact, the list of 3,195 forcibly disappeared and summarily executed people confirmed by the National Reparation and Reconciliation Corporation as well as the earlier National Truth and Reconciliation Commission includes at least nineteen people of Jewish origin (one other case, that of Boris Weisfeiler, is not included in that list). Furthermore, two independent reviews of the list of 28,459 people confirmed in the first report of the National Commission on Political Imprisonment and Torture of 2005 conclude that at least 145, and possibly as many as 200, individuals are of Jewish origin.

Thinking of Yael's generation who grew up unaware and others from previous generations who preferred not to know, the following narratives chronicle Jewish lives affected by the military dictatorship's repressive policies.

In the National Stadium

A single bowl of soup each day. Shivering from cold at night in the locker room and burning during the daytime from the hours sitting in the bleachers under the sun. Sleeping crowded together, the head of one against the feet of another. Arbitrary blows and kicks. Senseless interrogations accompanied by beatings and electric current. Covered by a blanket when taken from the locker room cell.

Washington Domb never told anyone what he went through in the months imprisoned as one of twenty thousand people held in the National Stadium, converted into the largest prison of Chile.[3] He did mention that he was held in locker room 5, shared with other Popular Unity government employees. When this tall, robust man left the stadium, he was all skin and bones, and his skin was as black as coffee from the sun.

But he would not talk about what happened during his ordeal. It seemed to have been erased from his memory, people close to him say. However, considering that he was held in the stadium practically from the first day it opened to the last day it was used as a detention camp, one can speculate that he endured all manner of suffering in the place that other former prisoners have called a nightmare and an inferno.

Washington Isaac Domb Scott, or Icho, as friends and family called him, was the son of Polish Jews who, in the years between the two wars, arrived in Uruguay, where he was born in 1931. When Icho was a newborn, his parents moved to Chile and settled in Ovalle. His parents subsequently separated, and his mother brought her children to live on Condor Street in Santiago, near the old Bikur Jolim synagogue. His mother, Rosa Scott, who grew up in a modest agricultural family, made pickles, and her son recalls that her hands were leathery from their exposure to so much salt. Until the last days of her life, he says, she kept kashrut dietary laws, despite the challenge of obtaining kosher meat in Santiago. She would take live chickens to the rabbi, who would kill them in the proper ritual manner.

Icho went to Valentín Letelier secondary school, as did many young Jews in those days, and participated in Hashomer Hatzair. His boyhood friends were Jews with a social conscience who gravitated toward leftist politics. He entered the University of Chile Law School and became a lawyer. During the administration of President Eduardo Frei Montalva, he worked for the National Health Service drafting legislative proposals. As a Socialist Party member, he participated actively in Salvador Allende's presidential campaign.

During the Popular Unity government, he was a close associate of José Tohá, the interior minister. Their office was located in La Moneda, and Icho's daughter remembers the awe she felt as a young girl accompanying her father to his office at the Interior Ministry and meeting José Tohá. Her father traveled constantly to southern Chile to manage land expropriations in the context of agrarian reform. His job was to contain the violence that some land occupations had given rise to. He entered fields unarmed in an attempt to prevent further violence. In 1973, he was named director of the Tax Crimes

Department, a job that required him to confront powerful businessmen tax evaders. With his staff of five people, he would go to companies and inspect their accounting records to ensure they had paid their taxes. It was in his capacity as director of tax enforcement that Icho gained his main enemies.

On the morning of September 11, 1973, he, along with his wife, the psychologist Dina Krauskopf, listened to Allende's final speech transmitted on Radio Magallanes. "We realized it was not advisable to go out," says Krauskopf, but three days after the coup, an employee called asking to borrow his office keys.[4] The man was a coworker who was also a friend. Icho trusted him. No sooner had Icho walked into the office than he was arrested; he had fallen into a trap. They took him away lying face down on the floor of a bus.

Several days later, an anonymous telephone call from someone who had been released from the National Stadium informed his wife that Washington was there. As of that moment, Dina Krauskopf directed all her energy into the task of gaining her husband's release.

> I contacted a priest associated with the military . . . who explained the official reason for his arrest. The accusation against him was that the five pistols belonging to the Tax Crimes Department had vanished. Each member of Washington's staff had a personal pistol for protection. Obviously, after the coup no one was about to turn in their pistols. I contacted his colleagues, who, in an extraordinarily courageous gesture, entered the building, carrying the hidden pistols, and left them in the office. They did it to save Washington. It was an impressive display of loyalty. Later some of them were also arrested. If that were the reason for Washington's arrest, the charge had to be dropped.

But Washington was not released. One of Dina's colleagues, who lived in a military neighborhood, was very supportive. She discovered that a neighbor was the guard in the locker room where Washington was being held. Through him, she sent and received news. One day her colleague informed Dina that she had the keys to Washington's car and the parking garage ticket. "With a friend, we recovered Washington's car. We were so nervous," Dina recalls. "We were told that all the cars in the ministry parking garage were being requisitioned because their owners were in prison."

Dina visited the Defense Ministry offices several times to seek information and help. There she met the military officer who ultimately helped secure Washington's release. The man was a military psychologist, and they chatted amicably about psychology and art. Trust was built between them, to the point that one day he told her that the stadium was about to be closed and that all the prisoners would be sent to Chacabuco prison camp in northern

Chile. At that moment, without changing the relaxed tone of their conversation, she said, "But how can that be? You know perfectly well that you can get him released instead of sending him to Chacabuco." "We'll see; we'll see," was all the official replied.

Washington was not sent to Chacabuco. Dina was informed that he would be freed the same day the stadium closed. All day long, people kept filing out, released from the stadium prison, but not Washington. Upon inquiring with the military officials, she was told that the court record had not arrived. Dina Krauskopf remembers how from somewhere deep inside she found a commanding voice and called her friend who had served as a courier of letters and food between her and Washington to request that she call the office of the army major whose staff she was on. "I told her: 'Tell him to deliver those court records, now!' Incredibly, they were indeed delivered." Two other people regained their freedom without ever knowing that it was thanks to her action.

But Washington was not released through the main gate, where Dina waited all day for him. Instead, he was sent out through a side door to the stadium. Dina feared he would be shot and that the fugitive law would be invoked as justification. But that did not occur. He left alone and walked to a friend's house. The friend called Dina's sister and told her to go to the stadium, where Dina was waiting for Washington to tell her there was no need to wait any longer at the gate where the prisoners were being officially released.

"We went home. He was very afraid for his life. Immediately we began working on obtaining political asylum," Dina said. She obtained asylum at the Panamanian Embassy unofficially through a secretary because the ambassador was not allowing anyone else to enter. By that time, in early November, the embassies were filled with political asylum seekers.

With help from David Baytelman, the former vice president of the government agency that had implemented agrarian reform during the Allende administration and who was already refuged inside the Panamanian embassy, a plan was devised. "Washington went walking along, and suddenly he entered the yard of the house next door to the embassy. He climbed the wall into the embassy as if he were an athlete or a spider. We saw pairs of hands appear from the other side of the wall. And wham! He was safe inside embassy grounds."

Washington left Chile on December 26, 1973. After a sad stay in Panama where he slept on the floor of an empty apartment, he was able to move to Costa Rica. Moshe Tov, Israeli ambassador to Chile, facilitated his move to Costa Rica. Washington spent twelve years in Costa Rica and returned to Chile on the first flight after the letter *l* (which indicated the passport holder was on a "lista nacional" and could not return to the country) was erased from his passport. Once back in Santiago, he joined the Vicariate of Solidarity's legal assistance staff.

In Transit

On September 13, 1973, Lily Traubmann learned she was pregnant. At the time, she was unaware that at dawn that day, her father, Ernesto Traubmann, had been arrested and that she would never see him again. Ernesto Traubmann was the same Czech immigrant who came to Chile with his parents, only to voluntarily return to Europe to fight against the German Nazis.

Those days, the future was uncertain, and all the more so for a seventeen-year-old future mother. Practically the only certainty was the imminent danger. For this young member of the MIR and daughter of a Communist, the threat to life was real. But Lily clung to the optimism she felt from the baby growing inside her. As anxiety and horror increasingly dominated everyday life, her pregnancy gave her "great happiness" that helped her "keep smiling," she affirms.

In the following nine months of pregnancy and during the first six months of her daughter Tamara's life, Lily went from one place to another, in an effort to hide from the security forces. Her mother, also in Chile, had no idea where she was; her brother Denni in Israel knew even less. Although worried about what might happen to herself and her daughter if she were apprehended, Lily says she was not overcome with anxiety thanks to her faith in the future that her daughter embodied.

Among the first to offer her support was a leader of Betar, a right-wing Jewish organization, who promised to take care of her daughter and send her to live with her uncle Denni in Israel if the worst-case scenario were to occur. "It sounds terrible now," admits Lily, "but at the time it was reassuring."

Over the next few months, "a wonderful priest" from a church in a middle-class district of Las Condes harbored her through a network formed by his parishioners, who hid Lily and Tamara in their homes. The priest—she doesn't remember if he was from Belgium or the Netherlands—had helped Jews during World War II. A member of that church network helped her obtain asylum in the Colombian Embassy along with another twenty people.

Finally, the Israeli embassy arranged for Lily and Tamara to leave on the Brazilian airline Varig, on a Santiago–Río de Janeiro flight with a stopover in Buenos Aires. Brazil was also under a dictatorship, and Varig was known to collaborate with Chilean security forces. To ensure an added measure of security, the plan called for them to get off in Buenos Aires, where the embassy would provide airline tickets to Israel.

They arrived in Buenos Aires on November 22, 1974, a day before Lily's nineteenth birthday. Less than two months earlier, Chile's former army commander-in-chief general Carlos Prats and his wife, Sofia Cuthbert, had been murdered in Buenos Aires. Their murder exposed the existence of a network of collaboration between Chilean and Argentine intelligence a year and a half before the military coup in Argentina. Lily was warned to conceal the fact that she was a political refugee to avoid arousing suspicion.

At the Buenos Aires airport, immigration agents attempted to prevent her from traveling with Tamara, demanding that she exhibit the father's authorization. After this barrier was overcome, given that she was not married to Tamara's father, the officials continued looking for one reason after another to prevent them from continuing in transit. During the four hours she was interrogated, the Israeli Embassy officer and the UN Peace Commission representative, waiting at the airport, were informed that Lily and her daughter had not been on the flight from Santiago. Subsequently, these officials told Lily that the bureaucratic delay clearly had been undertaken to try to devise a reason to return her to Chile to be arrested.

Despite Lily's apprehension about exposing her refugee status, ultimately the UN laissez-passer issued to her as a political refugee ended the impasse, permitting her to enter Argentina for twenty-four hours. An embassy guard was stationed outside her hotel room all night long. The next day, she and Tamara were escorted to the jet that would take them to Israel.

In 1939, after the Germans invaded Czechoslovakia, Sigmund and Lucia Traubmann, with their teenaged son Ernst—Lily's grandparents and father— arrived in Chile. Lily and Tamara were the second generation of the Traubmann family forced to leave their native country. Lily and Tamara have now lived more than forty years in Kibbutz Meguido, Israel.

Ever since Tamara was a child, her disappeared grandfather has been an ever-present, larger-than-life figure. Her grandfather Ernesto's story provided her mother with a vehicle for transmitting to Tamara the value of human rights. From the grandfather who disappeared the same day she began to exist, Tamara inherited a deep commitment to fight for justice, which she carries out today as a journalist and social activist.

In a Small Southern Town

In the heart of ancient Mapuche indigenous territory, in the town of Cañete, 135 kilometers south of Concepción, two Jewish brothers—a mayor and a regional governor—coordinated local implementation of the Popular Unity's policies.

Land occupations by homeless families demanding dignified housing began under the presidency of Eduardo Frei Montalva. During the Popular Unity government, the movement of downtrodden groups who occupied empty land to demand homes became a strong force throughout the country. Cañete, a town that in the 1950s was twelve blocks long by four blocks wide, was built on a hilltop. The new neighborhoods arising from land occupations extended below the hilltop town center. The Cañete municipal government provided electricity and water and paved the streets of the new neighborhoods.

Until the mid-1960s, Cañete's economy and society revolved around the institution known as the *latifundio*. An estimated ten to twelve individuals, most possessing French surnames, owned all the land in this province. Most of the population consisted of employees or sharecroppers who were perpetually indebted to these large landowners. Poverty was rampant, and conditions were even more miserable on the small properties where the indigenous Mapuche communities were now forced to live.

After the new government of Salvador Allende took office, land was distributed to groups of peasants who had previously labored for the wealthy *latifundistas*.[5] This was not accompanied by adequate technical assistance, however, and the lack of means to purchase tools and fertilizer caused many problems. Beneficiaries were frustrated, and former property owners were resentful, even though the land had been purchased, not expropriated.

Elías Jana, the mayor, and Daniel Jana, the regional governor, were in charge of implementation and support for these and other Popular Unity policies locally. The Jana brothers, both born in Cañete, were the sons of Daniel Jana Levy, who arrived in Chile with their two uncles in the early years of the twentieth century, from Smyrna, Turkey. Daniel Jana Levy and his brothers journeyed across the Atlantic and to South America at the insistence of their mother, who feared the Turks would force her sons to serve as soldiers in their battles.

After some years in Santiago, Daniel Jana Levy, with a basket of merchandise on his shoulder, arrived in the small southern town where he ended up settling. One block from the town's plaza, he opened El Martillo, a large dry goods store that sold a bit of everything, from food and fabrics to agricultural tools. The family lived in a large but simple wooden house behind the store.

Around the dining room table with its fifteen chairs, Daniel Jana Levy transmitted a sense of connection to Jewish roots to his children and later to his grandchildren. The grandchildren observed him pray from his Siddur prayer book on Shabbat, although he did not close the store. The grandfather was the main teacher of the Jewish tradition for his children and grandchildren.

They were Cañete's only Jews. "From a very young age we knew we were Jewish because people would call us 'judíos de mierda,'" says Daniel Jana Calderón, the governor's son and the mayor's nephew. Each year the Lions Club and the Rotary Club came to his grandfather asking for donations, but they never allowed him to become a member. Four of the six largest stores in Cañete eventually belonged to the Jana family, yet none of its members were invited to join these organizations. "We were always 'Jewish businessmen,'" Daniel Jana Calderón states.[6]

The Janas stood out in Cañete not only because they were the only Jewish family but also because they advocated for social justice. Class and poverty differences were evident in this provincial town. In the years when Daniel Jana Calderón was growing up, most of his classmates came from rural areas. "They would come carrying their shoes over their shoulder to the town limits where horse troughs were located. There they washed their feet, put on their shoes, and arrived at school with their shoes on," he recalls.

Beyond observing these class differences in daily life, they also acquired "a sense of justice" at home, he says. His grandfather "always told us we had to act in solidarity and help other people," he said. His granddad showed generosity even toward animals. "After eating watermelon, he would cut the rind into small pieces. Once I asked him why he cut the rind that way. His response: 'Because this will go to the garbage dump and hungry animals go there to eat. It's easier for them to eat the small pieces.' In every way he was a person of conscience," his grandson said. "I still get choked up whenever I remember that," he added.

Such lessons led three of his children to become politically active, both locally and nationally. Elías first met Salvador Allende when he visited Cañete in 1952, during his first presidential campaign. Both brothers participated in Allende's three presidential campaigns. For the 1958 campaign, "we traveled together by car in the entire province of Arauco with my uncle Elías and my father. At each stop, they would give speeches in support of Allende," recalls Daniel Jana Calderón. They did the same during Allende's 1970 election campaign.

Elías's son, also named Daniel in honor of Daniel Jana Levy, remembers that Allende once slept in their house. Daniel Jana Torres, the mayor's son, recalls that "Allende and my father called each other *compadres*. The President had deep affection for my mother (Laura Rosa Torres Lopez) because, as he liked to point out, 'she has the same name as my mother.'"[7]

In 1971, Elías was elected mayor of Cañete, and later the same year, Socialist Party regional president. In those years his brother Daniel, a Communist Party member who previously had been a Cañete city councilman, was appointed governor of Arauco province.

After the military coup, Elías was arrested and imprisoned on Quiriquina Island, remaining twenty-two days in that inhospitable place. In 1974, he was arrested again, this time together with his brother and sister, and held in the

Concepción regional stadium. When they were allowed to return to Cañete, the siblings became targets of unrelenting harassment. The Regional Business Board, created under the presidency of Pedro Aguirre Cerda (1938–41) to ensure fair business practices, constantly sent inspectors to the family's store, repeatedly closing it down.

When, in February 1975, his store was once again obliged to close, Elías requested a meeting with Gastón Elgueta Bahamondes, the military regional governor. Elías was well aware that it amounted to political persecution. The meeting was scheduled for February 14, and he traveled to the city of Lebu, capital city of Arauco province and the seat of the regional governor, accompanied by his wife and four children. When, from afar, they saw him leave the building escorted by two men, his wife thought they were taking him to another location to speak to the governor.

Three days later, the national police appeared at the family home in Cañete and announced that Laura should pick up her husband at Talcahuano Naval Base. She received a sealed coffin and was warned not to open it. That night, breaking from the Jewish tradition of not viewing a body in a coffin and defying the police order, the brothers opened the coffin. They confirmed that the coffin contained the body of Elías, which showed evident signs of torture.

Before their eyes, they had proof of the lies in the navy report that alleged Elías had committed suicide inside a truck. Several months later, the Jewish community of Concepción requested a court investigation, which the military manipulated, misrepresenting the facts. However, thirty-eight years later, in 2013, Judge Carlos Aldana indicted three former members of the navy for the first-degree murder of Elías Jana. In January 2015, the Concepción Court of Appeals reopened the investigation.

Orlando Correa, a major in the national police force who was appointed mayor of Cañete after the military coup, had ordered the demolition of the family mausoleum built by Elías in Cañete Cemetery on the grounds that "no Communist can be near the cemetery entrance."[8] Elías's body remained in a burial crypt until 2009, when the family recovered the cemetery plot and transferred his remains.

No one else from Cañete was forcibly disappeared or executed for political motives. Other leftist political leaders were arrested and held in the regional stadium but did not subsequently face the kind of harassment the Jana brothers did. In small towns such as Cañete, observes Elías's son Daniel, envy and resentment simmer for years. As in the rest of the country, the military coup provided resentful individuals the chance to take revenge against the most visible representatives of the Allende government, and in this case, the only Jewish family of Cañete.

El Cuyano

El Cuyano, El Rey de las Medias (Cuyano, King of Socks) was a store known by everyone in La Serena. The shop, which Moreno Caro opened in late 1930 and later comanaged with his younger brother Samuel, offered the latest fashion in women's stockings. Moreno subsequently left Chile and bequeathed the shop to Samuel. Women would frequently stop by just to take a look at the new owner with his blue eyes and wavy blondish hair. "Is Samuel in?" they would ask. If Samuel was there, they would come in and browse; if not, they would wander on.

Just as El Cuyano—named for the central western Argentine region where the Caro brothers were born—had a reputation for its excellent products, so too its owner was widely known in different spheres of La Serena social and community life. His parents, Elías Caro and Katempka Baron, arrived in Chile from Smyrna, Turkey, in the first decade of the twentieth century, and went on to Mendoza, Argentina, where their children were born. Moreno traveled to La Serena to assess the possibility of living there and then convinced his brother Samuel that life was better in that Chilean coastal city. Both soon returned together, and the rest of the family followed later.

In those years, La Serena's Jewish community consisted of twenty families who, like the Caros, were mostly of Sephardic origin. By the time the four children of Samuel and his wife, the writer and painter Fresia Benquis, were born, the Jewish population of La Serena had increased to approximately two hundred. They celebrated the traditional holidays, usually without a rabbi, in a community center called the Círculo Israelita. The men were in the habit of meeting there during their lunch hour and then returning to reopen their respective businesses at 4:00 p.m. In La Serena there was also a sizeable Arab community that enjoyed good relations with the Jewish community. When a Jewish boy and an Arab boy were born, a rabbi would come from Santiago to perform the bris circumcision rite for both.

Samuel was a man with a deep sense of justice. The common denominator between his leadership in the Lions Club and his support for Communist Party congressman Cipriano Pontigo (1969–72) was his unbending belief in human dignity. He could not remain indifferent to another person's suffering, and he enthusiastically served as business advisor to the regional government, backing social initiatives for the common good.

In the garage of his house, his children would help him fill bags with food for the Lions to distribute to needy people. At the same time, he participated in Salvador Allende's presidential campaigns. When Allende was elected and protests ensued against the Popular Unity government, El Cuyano was one of the few businesses that remained open. Samuel refused to participate in the boycotts, even though the shop became the object of violent attacks by government opponents.

After the military coup, La Serena's police stations and jail filled with hundreds of detainees. Samuel listened to news of friends arrested but refused to flee. The memory of his tense face, expecting something would happen at any moment, remains fresh in his children's memory. It was six in the morning when they came for him. The family was asleep when a slamming door awoke them. "They banged on my bedroom door," recalls his daughter Sara.[9] "I opened the door to find five soldiers pointing automatic rifles at us. They made us put our hands up on the wall for hours while they ransacked the place, pulling out furniture drawers, looking for something without offering any explanation."

The soldiers' last action was to forcibly remove Samuel from the house, kicking him as he went. They ordered him to lie on the floor of a truck and stepped on him, while his wife, children, and grandchildren looked on powerless and in horror. At the La Serena prison, Samuel was placed in a crowded cell with fifteen other men, who had to take turns lying on the floor to sleep. One of his cellmates was his friend Jorge Peña Hen, the noted musician and orchestra director. Samuel's daughter Sara came every day to leave lunch in a bag with his name, but he was only allowed to receive visitors once a week. On Sundays the whole family shared lunch in the prison yard. Smiling, he told them how he had helped organize the cell by setting a schedule for the prisoners.

On October 16, 1973, a Puma helicopter cast a dark shadow over La Serena. A contingent of soldiers from that helicopter arrived at the prison and demanded that fourteen prisoners be turned over to them. A fifteenth person was removed from the cells at the Arica military base. General Sergio Arellano Stark, commander of the military unit assigned to carry out the special mission by Augusto Pinochet, had circled their names in red that morning. As the group of prisoners was removed from the prison, several thought they were about to be released. When the helicopter took flight again, fifteen men, including Samuel's friend Jorge Peña Hen, were dead. The extrajudicial killings in La Serena were the first stop in the northern part of the country of the death squad that would come to be known as the Caravan of Death, which was headed by General Sergio Arellano Stark and resulted in ninety-seven detainees being summarily executed, and their bodies concealed, in southern and northern Chile. During the squad's stop in Calama three days later, one of the twenty-six people savagely murdered with a hooked knife and machine gun was Carlos Berger, also Jewish.

In La Serena, Ariosto Lapostol Orrego, the commander of the military base, argued with Arellano and is said to have tried to stop him from carrying out the plan. Lapostol did save at least one human life: that of El Cuyano's owner. Lapostol knew Samuel well because both belonged to the same Masonic Lodge. When Samuel was brought to the military base for interrogation, Lapostol saw him enter and shouted harshly, "Samuel Caro! I need you in my office!" Caro entered the commander's office, and the military commander said to him, "Samuelito, please forgive me" and offered him cigarettes.

Samuel left prison two months later, but he never completely shook off the anguish from those terrible days. It resurfaced in March 2002 when Juan Emilio Cheyre, the military officer who was so aggressive when he arrested Samuel in his home, was promoted to army commander-in-chief. Samuel died the following year, disillusioned and deeply sorrowful. In July 2016, Cheyre was indicted in the Caravan of Death case, prompting Caro's son-in-law to write: "Today, in some corner of another dimension, my father-in-law Samuel is at peace. . . . Dear Nonito, at last some people will understand your sorrow, and their complicity in acts of barbarism will weigh on their conscience."

Reappearance

Since 2012, Villa Grimaldi Peace Park has been building a list of survivors who spent hours, days, or even months imprisoned in the clandestine detention center located there from 1974 to 1978. Commonly known as Villa Grimaldi, it was the detention and torture center that operated the longest and was run by the military dictatorship's secret police known as DINA.

Catholic priest Mariano Puga, brought to Villa Grimaldi in July 1974, heads the roster of surviving prisoners. The fourth person on the list is Ivonne Szasz Pianta, a Socialist Party lawyer and supporter of the MIR, who was arrested in La Serena. Before she was taken to Santiago, Ivonne was permitted to get out at her house to let her family know not to expect her that night. Ivonne's husband ran out to the military vehicle and shouted, "Where are you taking her?" As the vehicle took off with Ivonne in the back, the captain shouted back, "Ask for her at the Second Military Prosecutor's Office!" His response saved Ivonne's life. The next day, her parents and brother were at the prosecutor office in Santiago to inquire about her.[10]

That Ivonne was one of the first survivors owes to the fact that she was arrested on October 2, 1974, when Villa Grimaldi, which in its capacity as a torture center came to be known as Cuartel Terranova, was not yet fully operational. In those days, the DINA's main detention center was at 1367 José Domingo Cañas Street, at the corner of Republic of Israel Street, a private house in the Santiago neighborhood of Ñuñoa that the military expropriated for that purpose. But that place was so crowded with Miristas (members of the Revolutionary Left Movement) who had been arrested at the time of the imminent capture of leader Miguel Enriquez that Ivonne ended up spending her first night in detention at the Defense Ministry. At dawn the next day, she was handed over to DINA agents, who brought her to a place evidently under construction.

Although it was night and she lay on the floor of a pickup truck, blind-folded and with a hood over her head, Ivonne could tell the vehicle was headed east along Matta Avenue. From the distance and duration traveled—during curfew without encountering other vehicles—she guessed it was not yet day-light, and that they were near the mountains. "Because I grew up in La Reina Alta, I recognized the crisp mountain air and the rustling of the poplar trees as the gate opened onto this place that was either under construction or in the process of remodeling. I was interrogated the entire day, always blindfolded," says Ivonne. Later, the sound of small planes from Tobalaba Airport enabled her to pinpoint the geographic location. From under the blindfold, Ivonne could see the edge of walls and other details that many years later, when the premises had been recovered and transformed into Peace Park, helped recon-struct her memory of the place where she was held.

"On October 4 they had to turn me over to prosecutor Rolando Melo of the Second Military Court. The night before—it was the night Lumi Videla Moya was murdered at José Domingo Cañas—I was taken to the women's correctional facility, where I slept. From there I was taken to the prosecutor's office, and the night of October 4, I was returned to solitary confinement at the women's correctional facility," she recalls.[11] "On October 5, 1974, through little holes in the cell wall, I could see a newspaper had been left outside my cell door. From that I learned not only the date but also that Miguel Enriquez had been captured and killed. From then on, the DINA guys only came to talk to me in a little room the nuns lent them, guarded by prison personnel."

That explains why Ivonne Szasz Pianta's name is one of the first on the Villa Grimaldi survivors' list. The main DINA facility on José Domingo Cañas Street, where most people were held, was full and so, fortunately, had no room for one more prisoner. For that reason, too, she did not spend a single night under the DINA's custody, only a single day, and "as of the night of the third day my name appeared on the official prison entry log" as a formally recognized detainee. "In other words, my 'disappearance' only lasted from 4:00 p.m. October 2 until the night of October 3, 1974. I am certainly the most fortunate of survivors," affirmed Ivonne.

Her interrogator at Villa Grimaldi was Basclay Zapata Reyes (aka "El Troglo"). During a short time at noon, the much-feared Miguel Krassnoff Martchenko participated in her interrogation, severely threatening her. "How did I know who they were? I recognized El Troglo from the countless times he later visited me in the two months I was in solitary at the correctional facility. As for Krassnoff, I recognized him by his metallic voice, his height (I was seated and his voice came from much higher than Troglo's voice), the tone, the attitude, the way he would restlessly pace from one side of the room to the other and scold Troglo." From glimpses caught from under the edge of the blindfold, Ivonne also observed that the man had light hair and stains or freckles on the back of his neck.

Ivonne was expelled from Chile and exiled to Mexico, where she continues to reside to this day. She was born in Bolivia, where her parents were admitted as refugees in 1939. After moving to Chile, her parents separated when she was five years old. When she was a teenager, Ivonne's mother told her that her father and paternal grandfather were Hungarian Jews. Her father had chosen to conceal his family history from his children, out of fear. Many of his relatives were deported to Auschwitz-Birkenau. The revelation about her father's origins moved Ivonne tremendously. It spurred her to continue researching her paternal family's history, and she began to build a Jewish identity for herself. Her father was stricken with cancer in 1980 and traveled to Mexico to say good-bye to his daughter, who was still banned from entering Chile. When she told him how pleased she was to learn that he descended from *cohanim*, "he virtually overflowed with immense happiness for what he considered to be the essence of the Jewish identity."[12]

"I am not Jewish by virtue of community membership or religious feelings but simply because I have a Jewish past on my father and grandmother's side," says Ivonne. "What returned me to Judaism was the shock and pain of learning about the Holocaust. Perhaps also the 'connecting thread' of the quest to become a just human being."[13]

Two Brothers

No sooner had the votes been counted that confirmed the electoral triumph of Salvador Allende than relatives and many acquaintances of Julio Budnik's left Chile. He calmly and with a certain curiosity contemplated what he called a "collective hysteria" that took hold of much of Chile's Jewish community.[14]

The Budniks were businessmen with socialist leanings. Their mother, Elsa Schwartzman, was a leader of Poalei Zion, a Jewish socialist workers' movement that began in the last years of the nineteenth century in Russia. The socialist freedom movement attracted many Jews who endured pogroms in czarist Russia, including the Budniks' grandfather and father.

Julio voted for Salvador Allende in 1970. Before that election, he had voted for Radical Party candidates and for his father's friend Jorge Alessandri, Chilean president (1958–64) from the conservative National Party. His brother Eduardo was a Communist Party member. Beginning in the early 1960s, both brothers were managers in their father Adolfo Budnik's tile factory.

In 1971, workers occupied the Industria Nacional de Neumáticos (INSA, National Tire Industry), a corporation with majority stock held by businessmen from the United States, demanding that the Maipu plant be transferred to the governmental Corporación de Fomento de la Producción de Chile (CORFO, Economic Development Agency). In July 1971, the agency purchased the factory for several million escudos and appointed Julio Budnik general manager of what was the largest tire factory of Chile. His brother Eduardo had previously been appointed the same position with the immense Celulosa Arauco wood pulp company.

"It was very, very difficult," admits Julio. The tire factory had five thousand employees who were affiliated with five different unions, three of which were directed by members of the Communist Party. It was nationalized under Allende, but as general manager, Budnik retained the structure it had before nationalization. "I was criticized for not firing all the managers and replacing them with socialists. But I ran it from a business perspective. That was why I had been placed there. It was very difficult, but we increased production and it was going fairly well for us," he recalled. However, tension mounted to such a degree that Budnik wanted to resign. In July 1973, he was transferred to CODELCO to serve as procurement manager.

On the morning of September 11, Julio went to his office at CODELCO, which faced La Moneda. At the building entrance, police warned him, "Don't go in because we can't guarantee you will leave alive." Despite the warning, he entered the building. From his office window, he saw the planes bomb La Moneda. In his office, for the last time, he tore up his party membership card and left. "I walked the eight blocks from La Moneda to the Mapocho River with my arms up, taking care not to run. A week later all CODELCO staff were fired."

"None of us could believe the coup was happening in Chile," comments his wife, Raquel Lipovetzky.[15] She was in Buenos Aires at the time and read Argentine newspaper reports about how Chile's National Stadium had been converted into a prison. "Afterward, I returned to my hotel and vomited. I could not believe the things that were happening in Chile. I couldn't fathom it," she said.

They were afraid. It was not safe to return to their house, but it was not easy to find someone willing to take the family in. Three years earlier, when Allende was elected, no one wanted to rent them a house because Julio was working for the Popular Unity government. Now people wouldn't receive them either. "It was unseemly to be friends with us; 'best not be too close to them.' We experienced that. It completely changed my view of people's values. I thought that to be a Jew meant that you had a set of values," Raquel says.

Julio's brother-in-law harbored them the first night. No one would dream of bothering them there, across the street from the home of Augusto Pinochet. They returned to their own house only to gather personal documents and items of value and to burn their books. It pained Raquel to see the poems of Vladimir Mayakofsky and other Russian writers whose writings she loved reduced to ashes.

They overcame the initial fear and surged forward again with their lives. Julio worked on "certain advisory activities and cooperation with the Communist Party." His wife recalls, "Our life was relatively peaceful. Twice we traveled to Europe without encountering any problems. Since we had been allowed to leave and return twice, we thought all was well. We were no longer afraid."

The illusion of a peaceful existence lasted until mid-1976. Between May 4 and 12, seven high-ranking leaders of the Communist Party were captured in an operation carried out by the DINA that began at 1587 Conferencia Street in the traditional Santiago district of Estación Central. From there, the secret police carried out raids in the municipalities of Quinta Normal, Conchalí, and Las Condes. In 2012, seventy-nine former DINA agents would be indicted for the abduction of the leaders who were taken to Villa Grimaldi on José Arrieta Avenue in Peñalolen and later brutally murdered at a house on Simón Bolivar Street that had been expropriated and converted into extermination center.

The arrests of numerous people can be traced to the operation at Conferencia Street. Julio and Eduardo Budnik were among the few survivors of that series of arrests. "They nabbed me in the parking garage," says Julio. He added, "Today I realize that had I kept my wits about me, I could have shouted because there were other people around. But they totally caught me by surprise." They brought him to Villa Grimaldi, and later that afternoon Eduardo was brought to the same place.

The day was Thursday, July 22, 1976. "Someone [arrested at Conferencia Street] must have said something about us. But you can't feel resentment or animosity if someone betrays you. It is very hard to withstand torture," says Julio, now eighty-seven years old. He describes what they endured:

> We were tortured. That day I began to become acquainted with electricity. I was questioned about many things that I knew nothing about. They also asked me for names of people from the Communist Party. After each question, and before you had the chance to answer, they hit you with the electric current. Obviously,

I said anything that came to my head. But in cross-examination the guy realized I was lying. What a kick I got then! At times the electric current was the mildest treatment they gave us. When you are blindfolded, you have no idea from what direction the blows will come. During the entire episode, physicians were observing everything and would tell them to keep at it or to stop. Or, out of the blue, a broad would speak to me so sweetly. . . . It was all calculated to alternate between being hard and being soft.

At one point they showed Julio a photograph of a distant relative, also Jewish, who he pretended not to recognize. The man was a Communist Party member, but he was never arrested and he managed to find refuge in Israel. He was also asked about two other people with Jewish-sounding names who he did not know.

In July 1976, a great many people were prisoners at Villa Grimaldi. At all times blindfolded and always together, the brothers were held in what appeared to be a large storage shed that had been divided in compartments. "We could hear people moaning, cries of pain, shouts, and insults. They brought one guy in who had just been beaten and was more dead than alive. Once in a while we were taken outside to sit in a terrace with several other people. Then came the hour for more kicking. It was all a routine," Julio recalls. Up to that point, Julio and Eduardo had been subjected to the same routine as other prisoners at Villa Grimaldi.

Two days after the Budnik brothers were abducted, the telephone rang, and Elsa Schwartzman experienced the overwhelming joy of hearing the voice of her son Eduardo. An anonymous caller had let her know earlier to expect a call from Eduardo and indicated the specific time to expect the call. "Don't worry; we are fine," Eduardo told her over the phone, while also insisting that she look for a small black address book.

Eduardo called at least twice more, always asking about the address book. "I knew the little address book he was talking about, but I told her to say it didn't exist," said Raquel.

When they inquired about the brothers' detention, the official response was that the family was lying because detainees were not allowed to make phone calls. Raquel was present when Rabbi Kreiman spoke directly to Pinochet over the telephone. "He said, 'Mr. President, they have to be here.' 'No, they are in Mendoza,' Pinochet replied."

The next time the family was told to expect another call from Eduardo, they were ready to tape the phone call. They then contacted the Mendoza telephone company and were told that Eduardo had not called from Argentina. Once again, the rabbi called Pinochet in the presence of Raquel. "In front of me, he said, 'General, Julio Budnik's wife recorded her brother-in-law's last call. And they have never been in Mendoza.' Pinochet responded: 'Angel, how fortunate they aren't there. You know, there they throw people into a canal straightaway.'"

Eduardo and Julio remained in Villa Grimaldi. Their abduction and detention were the subject of a series of intelligence memos, today declassified, between the US Embassy and the US Department of State. One memorandum, dated July 1976, identifies its subject as "The disappearance of the Budnik Brothers" and concludes with the following remarks about the practice of forced disappearances: "The modus operandi is nothing short of sadistic. It is not clear to us why officials who arrest them do not simply admit that they are questioning the individuals in the context of state of siege."

Julio continues to recall the ordeal. "At any time at all, they might take you out and beat you up. Sometimes they took my brother, at other times me, and sometimes we were taken out together. You got out from being tortured to recover a bit. Sometimes we could see a little from behind the blindfold. They told us, 'If we find out you can see us, we will liquidate you.'"

One day, still blindfolded, they were placed in a car. After traveling approximately thirty minutes, they arrived at a place that they have never been able to identify where they were the only prisoners. They heard someone tell the officer in charge of the premises: "Treat them well. You have to treat them well." According to Julio, the person "said it something like three times." The efforts to free the brothers were beginning to produce results. Two circumstances helped save them the fate of most disappeared persons: their friendship with Rabbi Kreiman and pressure brought to bear by the United States.

During 1974, the year when their son studied for his bar mitzvah, Julio and Raquel began attending Friday night services at the Círculo Israelita synagogue presided over by Rabbi Kreiman. The brothers were detained on a Thursday, and the next day, during Friday night religious services, the rabbi announced from the pulpit that the Budnik brothers, distinguished members of the synagogue, had been arrested. Kreiman turned to his close contacts in the military junta, while Raquel sought other Jewish contacts.

At around the same time, a letter made it into the hands of a member of B'nai B'rith who was traveling to New York. He hand-delivered the letter to Rabbi Morton Rosenthal, a well-known human rights advocate, who in turn contacted two influential senators, Jacob Javits of New York and Henry Jackson from Washington State. Later that week at a Foreign Relations Ministry reception Kreiman attended, a ministry staff person asked him, "Who are these Budnik brothers who are in detention? Javits and Jackson are driving us crazy, demanding an explanation."

That the detainees happened to be Jewish did not assure sympathy from other members of the Jewish community. Julio's wife met with air force general José Berdichewsky. "It was like talking to a wall. He was a cold, hardened guy who was completely indifferent to their plight," she recalls. And the deal the Jewish Representative Committee president told her he could arrange was outrageous. "Two or three days later, Gil Sinay called to ask me to meet him and his lawyer in his offices at the Israeli Bank. Gil told me, 'I can work something out so that Julio gets out, but Eduardo stays in.' How was Julio going to get out and leave his brother inside? It was a death sentence. I told him no."

Several times in the early 2000s, Santiago Appeals Court judge Alejandro Solis, assigned to investigate human rights violations committed at Villa Grimaldi, asked Julio Budnik to testify. Eduardo wasn't called because the imprisonment had left him traumatized and in fragile health. The judge showed him photos in an attempt to identify the place where they were held during the last five days in detention. Solis asked him whether he heard church bells, which would indicate he had been at the detention center at 38 Londres Street, near San Francisco Church in downtown Santiago. Civil police detectives also questioned him. As two of the few survivors from that period, testimony from the Budniks could help clarify several cases. "But I simply don't remember a thing," Julio states. "I seem to have lost selective memory; it's not that I don't want to remember."

Another State Department declassified report, dated August 1976, titled "Mysterious disappearance of the Budnik brothers," asserts in its first numbered point that "we may be on the verge of a fairly sensational discovery." A source, whose identity was expunged prior to the declassification of the document, claimed that the Budniks had been taken "to Colonia Dignidad." That these Jewish prisoners might have been taken to the Nazi colony indeed would have been a sensational discovery. Colonia Dignidad is located outside the town of Parral, more than three hundred kilometers south of Santiago, a good three hours' drive away. Julio Budnik, however, insists that the transfer time from Villa Grimaldi to the final unidentified place of detention was not long.

He is convinced that people had been tortured at the unknown place. "Once, we were alone in there, and I began to explore the premises. There were scalpels and other things near the bathroom that gave me goose bumps to see. There was a small room here, another over there, and beyond that was the office. I knew my way around the entire place. No one else was there but us."

On their last day, "A guy entered the room where we were held, next to the kitchen. He told us, 'There are things I don't understand in this notebook, and I want you to explain them to me.'" It was not the address book Eduardo had been calling about but another smaller notebook with a calendar that he used to jot down his thoughts. The official left the notebook for them to look through and then left the room. Julio began quickly leafing through it and if he found something that could get them in trouble, he tore out the page and swallowed it. "I skimmed through the notebook and if I found something, down it went. I drank water to help me swallow the paper,'" he recalls.

That day they were ordered to sign a statement in which they affirmed that they had not been mistreated. "I could barely keep from laughing," says Julio, "because the guy was writing the statement with my fountain pen, stolen from my office. I signed with my own pen. But I wasn't about to tell him, 'Give me back my pen!'" They were in the process of signing the statement when Eduardo asked about his watch. "Eduardo told them that he had been wearing a watch when we were arrested. He kept insisting, and I turned to him and said, 'You're mistaken; I saw that you were not wearing a watch.' One of the guys, a colonel or something, sitting near me, remarked to me, 'You've got the picture. You have to get out of here fast. Look at your brother, fighting over a watch.'"

Still blindfolded, they were placed into a fake taxi and handed money for cab fare. Another vehicle with DINA agents followed behind. Upon reaching the house, they paid the fare, got out, and the taxi drove off. When they entered the house, the second car left as well.

Twenty-four days had passed. Julio returned home weighing thirty pounds less. "You have to leave at once," insisted Moshe Avidan, Israeli ambassador to Chile. But Kreiman counseled against leaving right away. Julio says that the rabbi advised them not to "go yet or you will give the impression that you are afraid because you are guilty of something. Wait a bit longer before you leave." "If only we had listened to the ambassador instead of the rabbi," he now admits. "Later they extorted us, and we were practically ruined."

A few weeks after their release, Julio received the first phone call demanding money. "They would say, 'We have to talk to you; let's get together at such and such location'; I would go alone. One time I was at work and I had to leave at once to meet the guy at Cerrillos Airport. It cost me a lot of money," he recalls. His wife adds, "I remember twice you told me, 'I have to go meet a guy called Ricardo. If I'm not back by a certain time, let people know.'"

The individual made it clear that they were watching not only the brothers but their children as well. "On the phone, he would tell me, Beatriz drives a car of that color, and Eugenia's car is that other color. To get to the education school where she was in college, she takes the following route. It was an indirect threat in case I did not pay them. Once I was walking along the street, and on the other side I see the guy. He greets me, and I greet him back."

A few days after their release, the brothers went to the Vicariate of Solidarity and the US Embassy to thank them for their efforts to rescue them. But they were paralyzed by fear, and they never reported the subsequent threats and blackmail. "We should have reported it. In that sense, Julio became intimidated. It was strange. He just wanted to erase everything from his mind," asserts Raquel, who has not forgotten the countless nights her husband suffered from nightmares after returning. The extortion reinforced the impact of the brothers' abduction and arrest.

"After I was freed, Angel Kreiman made me a member of the Círculo Israelita board of directors as a way to protect me. He thought no one would touch this person who is so important in the community. All the other board members were diehard anticommunists, but they treated me well. They were Angel's unconditional people," says Julio. Afterward, he was elected vice president of the Vadajinu, the Instituto Hebreo board of directors. Nevertheless, the situation became increasingly untenable. Julio and his family eventually immigrated to Israel and did not return to Chile until the mid-1990s.

All My Bones Shall Speak

Jacobo Stoulman and Matilde Pessa traveled to Buenos Aires to enjoy a few days together, but they never returned alive. By the time their remains had been found, their daughters had grown into adults and six grandchildren had been born. Their absence was a constant presence pounding their family with a thousand questions that for decades were answered with a web of lies, concealment, and silence. It was simply inconceivable that they could have been abducted, and in Argentina.

Matilde Pessa was the daughter of Sephardic immigrants. Her mother came from Yugoslavia and her father from Turkey. She could not finish high school because she was obliged to help sustain the family after her father became ill and died. At twenty-three, she married Jacobo Stoulman, the son of Jewish Russian immigrants. Jacobo and his twin brother, Juan, were born in 1934, the eldest of four siblings. Jacobo was an accountant who worked for the Banco Israelita. He was steadily promoted to positions of greater responsibility in the bank, becoming assistant manager of its accounting department. The family lived in the middle-class neighborhood of Ñuñoa.

Jacobo and Matilde were well known in Santiago's Jewish community. They were members of the Estadio Maccabi recreational and sports complex. Their three daughters' entire school years, from kindergarten to high school graduation, were spent at the Instituto Hebreo. They raised their daughters in an observant but not orthodox Jewish home. The extended family came together at the home of one of the grandmothers to celebrate Passover, and they attended

High Holy Days services at the Sephardic and Bikur Jolim synagogues and, later, the Círculo Israelita on Serrano Street. "My parents were very caring, very affectionate, and very overprotective," said Jenny Stoulman, a psychologist and the second of the three sisters.[16]

In addition to family vacations with their daughters, Jacobo and Matilde had the custom of traveling alone as a couple. In late May 1977, they planned to travel to the Argentine capital, where they would spend a few days with another Chilean couple. In the days leading up to their departure for Buenos Aires, Jenny clearly remembers that her father "looked nervous and was very reserved." He mentioned that he had seen people filming his Cambio Andes money exchange, the business he had founded in 1976.

On Sunday, May 29, the day they traveled, Jenny was in bed sick with the flu. Her mother asked if she would like her to stay home. Jenny, who was sixteen at the time, replied, "No, mama, go with father. Don't worry about me." Those were practically the last words they would share. Whenever they traveled, the couple always would call their daughters upon arriving at the destination to reassure them they had arrived safe and sound. This time, their parents did not call.

The dictatorship headed by Augusto Pinochet had been in power nearly four years in Chile, but the Stoulman family "lived in a sort of community bubble"; they had little contact with the world outside. For that reason, "the context in which they disappeared was totally strange" for the daughters, says Jenny. The dictatorship of which they were barely aware abruptly impacted their lives. Many years would pass before they understood the "context," Jenny adds.

Matilde and Jacobo had been escorted directly from the airplane to a Ford Falcon parked on the Ezeiza Airport tarmac. They were abducted in the most audacious of the joint operations carried out in the framework of Operation Condor, an intelligence collaboration network established between Chilean, Argentine, Paraguayan, and Uruguayan military forces. The arrest of Matilde and Jacobo was the culmination of a series of detentions that had been carried out over the previous fourteen days, affecting a total of sixteen people in Buenos Aires and Santiago.

When family members began inquiring as to the whereabouts of Jacobo and Matilde, the Chilean intelligence apparatus weaved a maze of disinformation to cover its footsteps. The Chilean Foreign Relations Ministry's official explanation, ratified by Argentine dictator Jorge Videla, was that the couple never disembarked in Buenos Aires but allegedly continued on the flight to Montevideo.

Later, Operation Condor's Argentine partners contributed a key element to the labyrinth of disinformation by falsely linking Jacobo Stoulman to the murky story of David Graiver, a financier said to manage funds for the Montoneros, an Argentine left-wing guerrilla organization. In 1974, he arranged for and money-laundered the multimillion-dollar ransom of two businessmen, brothers who were abducted by the organization. Intelligence agents attempted to connect Stoulman to Graiver. Given that Graiver was Jewish and a partner of Chilean José Klein, also of Jewish origin, doubts were sowed among the Jewish community to demonize Stoulman and discourage people from advocating on his behalf.

The Chilean-Argentine military operation was successful, managing to conceal for thirty years that the sequence of arrests of Chileans and Argentines in Buenos Aires and Santiago between May and June 1977 corresponded to a single operation. In failing to grasp the connection to the other arrests, it would be difficult to unravel the circumstances of Matilde and Jacobo's disappearance.

Alexei Jaccard, Ricardo Ramírez, and Héctor Velásquez from Buenos Aires; and Hernán Soto, Enrique Correa, and Jacobo Stoulman from Santiago: each represented spokes of a wheel. They were interdependent parts, each contributing to an operation much larger than each individual's role. If one failed, the others also would fail.

Not all of them were personally acquainted with each other, but they were united by the mission to rearticulate the Communist Party after the debacle resulting from the arrests of its directors in 1976 that practically dismantled the party. Aside from the decimation of party leadership, in the year 1975–76 alone, an estimated 150 party members had been murdered or disappeared by the dictatorship. Party members abroad in exile had to be sent back to Chile to reorganize, but not anyone who had been in prison. In addition to reinforcing the party's human resources, the organization required funding to rebuild party structures. The entry of cadre and the entry of funds were both risky operations.

Jaccard, Ramírez, Correa, Velásquez, and Soto were Communist Party members. But how did Jacobo Stoulman, who was not a member, fit in with them? Probably, the connection was made through Jacobo Rosenblum, a longtime friend and former boss of Jacobo's.[17] Known as Yasha, Rosenblum was director of the Banco Israelita until its nationalization under Allende. He was also known as an outstanding man who was part of the Communist Party's most trusted inner circle. He had been a member since shortly after his arrival in Chile in 1934. After the 1973 military coup, Rosenblum immediately left for exile in France, where he coordinated fundraising under the direction of party finance chief Americo Zorilla, in Moscow, who had been budget minister during the Popular Unity government. In November 1976, Jacobo had traveled alone to Paris, where he met with Yasha, who asked him to help reestablish a financial base for the Communist Party.[18]

Only people who could be completely trusted worked in party finance. The mission Yasha proposed required an absolutely impeccable person who was untainted by Communist Party involvement. Moreover, the candidate for the mission had to be an individual who was trusted by national and international banks, especially the banks of Argentina, where the major part of the party's clandestine financial apparatus was based.

A dire side effect of the military coup was that the party inside Chile had begun to depend almost exclusively on funds raised abroad, which was not sustainable. The party needed more money that it was getting from abroad to operate clandestine printing presses, rent safe houses, acquire and maintain vehicles, and supply a minimum income for members who dedicated themselves full time to party activity. Funding was also needed to help people get out of the country and obtain asylum. David Canales, who worked in Moscow with Americo Zorilla, describes the party's objectives of that moment: "During the first years after the coup, money arrived in the diplomatic pouches of officials who had remained in Chile to safeguard embassy buildings. That way of receiving money no longer worked because they were under intense surveillance. Besides, these were very small amounts. Now we needed a different method, as legal as possible, through financial and banking institutions."[19]

The plan called for a normal bank operation. The party would deposit money in a Buenos Aires bank account administered by Jacobo. The communication of a password or a signal from a party member in Santiago would instruct him as to when to transfer and deliver the funds. Canales, who was Ramírez's brother-in-law, explains how the financial operation worked.

> At the moment the funds were transferred from Europe to Buenos Aires, Jaccard had to make contact with Ricardo Ramírez there to let him know what the mechanism was. He did not need to meet Stoulman or anyone else: Jaccard had to travel from Europe precisely for that reason, so that no one else could learn the identity of the person who received the money. He had a minuscule role but it was the golden key for transferring the information concerning the mechanism that would be used to transfer the funds.[20]

But Jaccard was captured the same day as Ramírez and Velásquez. Therefore, Jacobo did not receive the final information Jaccard needed to give him regarding when to deposit the funds and to whom to deliver them in Santiago.

In Santiago, it was so evident that DINA agents were watching him that Jacobo became frightened, fearing that his participation had been discovered. At one point, he ran into Julio Budnik and confided his fear. With his memory of detention still vivid, Julio insisted that Stoulman leave Chile immediately and go to Israel.[21] But Jacobo replied it was impossible for him to leave Chile at that time.

A few days after May 16, the date the Buenos Aires group had been arrested, a man visited Jacobo in his office, identifying himself as a party member and inquiring about funds. A couple of days later, a different man appeared in his office, employing the same password. Jacobo realized that the second visitor was his genuine contact and that the previous individual had been a military intelligence agent. He had fallen into a trap.

The situation became even more complicated when Argentine intelligence froze his bank accounts, including those belonging to Cambios Andes in Argentina. It appeared that the only way he could retrieve his money was by traveling to Buenos Aires. Well aware that his contact had been arrested, Jacobo was persuaded by infiltrated agents that the bank would only release the money to him in person. The DINA's maneuver succeeded in luring him to Buenos Aires to arrest him discreetly—in Santiago his arrest would have been scandalous—while also enabling it to rob him of his money.

He traveled with bank documents bearing his signature, which was recognized by banking institutions outside Chile. When he was arrested, he was forced to withdraw the entire contents of his checking account, containing not only the funds sent by the party finance group but also personal savings and funds belonging to members of the Jewish community. The DINA and Argentine intelligence divided the cache between them. The court record shows that the DINA continued to demand further funds months later, even charging Cambios Andes debt payments allegedly incurred by Jacobo.

In the case investigated by Judge Mario Carroza, former DINA agents stated under oath that they were sent to the border crossing at what in those years was known as Las Cuevas (today Los Libertadores) to pick up two or more detainees who were being sent from Buenos Aires. From their description of the physical characteristics of these people, it is known that they were Alexei Jaccard and Ricardo Ramírez. The same depositions confirm that they were brought to the DINA's facility at 8630 Simón Bolívar Avenue in Santiago, where more than one agent describes Jaccard, Ramírez, and Velásquez.

In May 2015, forensic anthropologists identified bone fragments discovered in 2001 in an abandoned mine shaft in the Cuesta Barriga area, thirty kilometers southwest of Santiago, belonging to Jacobo Stoulman, Matilde Pessa, and Ricardo Ramírez. The forensic study confirmed that the couple was returned to Santiago and subjected to interrogations at the Simón Bolivar Avenue extermination center. Thirty-eight years after their arrests and disappearances, the relation between the financiers was understood at last. It also became clear that the series of arrests on both sides of the Andes were part of a single repressive operation, jointly coordinated by intelligence forces in the framework of Operation Condor.

As part of his Operation Condor inquest, on June 24, 2005, Judge Victor Montiglio held a hearing at Cordillera Prison to take depositions from former DINA director Manuel Contreras, prisoner at that military base facility. Contreras blamed the Argentine marines for the arrest and disappearance of Jacobo Stoulman and Matilde Pessa, who, he insisted, had been "thrown into the Atlantic Ocean."[22] Contreras added, "It has never been proven that any Chilean individuals arrested in Argentina or in Paraguay were transferred to Chile."[23] But the discovery of the minuscule skeletal remains in Cuesta Barriga categorically refutes Contreras's statement, proving that the DINA did indeed transfer detainees between countries.

Was this just another business deal for Jacobo Stoulman? Attorney Carmen Hertz has thought about this. "In a situation such as the one that existed in Chile in those years—an atrocious dictatorship—of which Stoulman was fully aware, the danger was so great that I don't believe the prospect of making money would have been the factor that encouraged him to risk his life. You will only knowingly put yourself at risk if you have a certain liking for what you are doing." Hertz believes that Jacobo was part of a clandestine operation that "no one—not even his family or business partners—knew about."[24] In those years of danger, it was imperative that people who opted to be politically active kept it a secret. Approximately ten years ago, Carmen Hertz first learned that her father-in-law, Julius Berger, a Jew born in Hungary, had been deeply involved in Communist Party fundraising immediately after the coup.

Of the other people arrested in May 1977, Enrique Correa's family had no knowledge about his clandestine involvement. When, in 1976, he opened a newspaper kiosk, his family did not suspect it might have another purpose. Installed on Santiago's central thoroughfare, Alameda Boulevard, outside the building that housed the Agrupación Nacional de Empleados/as Fiscales (ANEF, National Public Employees Association), the kiosk was strategically located on a busy corner where a great many people circulated, including workers constructing the subway system.[25] Enrique was a longtime Communist Party member who had been banished to remote regions of the country after President Gabriel González Videla (1946–52) outlawed the Communist Party.[26] However, his family did not know that he retained ties to the party. They had no knowledge that the kiosk was in fact a drop box where information and money were handed off and received. Neither did the family know that he was a clandestine leader of his party. On May 27, when he left the kiosk in his wife's care during lunch hour, he was arrested. His lifeless body was found at dawn the next day on the Manuel Rodriguez bridge over the Mapocho River. He had been run over by a vehicle, but the body also clearly indicated he had been tortured as well. The Correa family located his body at the morgue several weeks later. During the following thirty-seven years, they too struggled to understand what happened.[27] Enrique, like Matilde and Jacobo, left three children. Less than ten blocks separated the kiosk from Cambios Andes on Agustinas Street. Enrique and Jacobo were working for the same objective, yet it is likely they did not know one another.

The recovery of Jacobo and Matilde revealed a story of complicity that resulted in their abduction and death as well as in the concealment of the crimes committed against them. As Sara Stoulman, the oldest of the three daughters, exclaimed during the funerals of their parents held at the Sephardic Cemetery on May 29, 2015, quoting the Prophet Isaiah, "All my bones shall speak!"

Student at Heart

In 1973, Sandra Oksenberg was a nine-year-old child. "I don't remember the military coup. I found out about the coup many years later, when I was sixteen or seventeen years old," she says.[28] No one in her house talked about what was going on in the country, and no one discussed it at Instituto Hebreo, where she went to school and her father was a teacher.

"Those were the worst years of the dictatorship, and my family didn't seem to know what country we lived in. We lived in a bubble. Not until I went to college did I learn that we lived under a dictatorship. Throughout my whole life, Pinochet had been there," she adds. When Sandra began studying psychology at Catholic University in Santiago, she was drawn to progressive groups on campus. She joined the Izquierda Cristiana (IC, Christian Left Party) as well as Jews for Peace, becoming a leader in both organizations.

The year 1986 was widely seen as a decisive one for Chile. Three years earlier, people had begun to overcome their fear of participation and organized the first days of national protest. Those were times of increasing openness, with much social mobilization in all segments of the population against the dictatorship and for democracy. It was decisive not only for the country but also for Sandra. In May of that year, she married Juan Flores, a fellow psychology student and leader of the Christian Left Party and Jews for Peace. That year too she was arrested for the first time.

In Santiago, students coordinated university occupations that would take place simultaneously. Sandra was a coordinator for the Christian Left Party occupation at Catholic University. On account of her blonde hair, which in the Chilean imaginary is associated with the upper class and likely to be polit-ically conservative, Sandra was the perfect candidate for bringing in chains for shutting the university gates. She stuffed the heavy chains into her backpack and accomplished her assigned mission, despite her fright.

The students chained the gates shut, with a hundred people inside, and awaited the inevitable appearance of police. Out of respect for the conserva-tive Catholic University, police waited several hours before entering and when they did, they exercised certain restraint, compared to the brutality that char-acterized their response to the student movement at other universities, accord-ing to Sandra. All the same, when the university courtyard filled with armed police, she felt panic rise inside of her.

Approximately eighty students, including Sandra, were arrested, each one of whom received blows as they entered the paddy wagon. At the police station, they received the same "fairly bad" treatment, Sandra notes, and the men were separated from the women. Of the thirty or more female Catholic University students in the same jail cell, two were Jewish: Sandra and Mireya Faivovich, who were also Jews for Peace members. Those days are hazy in Sandra's mem-ory. She is uncertain of the exact date, although she does recall spending six days in jail. Sandra recalls the arrest as occurring after May when she and Juan Flores got married but before September when the assassination attempt against Augusto Pinochet took place. "Fortunately, we were arrested before the attack"; otherwise, her prison experience would have been much worse.

"Previously, I had often visited people in prison, and they treated us fairly well, probably also an effect of classism. Students from other universities were treated harsher. And we had much contact with people outside," says Sandra. One of the visitors to the student detainees was Anamaria Aron, psychology professor at Catholic University and sister of Diana Aron, journalist and leader of the MIR (Revolutionary Left Movement) who was forcibly disappeared in 1974. "It was a difficult experience and quite shocking when the doctor exam-ined me to see if I had been tortured. I am from a family of many doctors, and he seemed to recognize the last name. He was a doctor who assisted prisoners after torture and beatings," Sandra recalls.

Her parents waited in line to enter and see their daughter in prison.

It was terrible for my parents. Although they came to see me, my father didn't say a word during the hour visitation. My parents knew I was politically involved in leftist movements and that Juan was too. They were overcome by fear that we might be tortured, but supposedly this was not happening in Chile. There was this duality. They knew but preferred not to know.

ANTISEMITIC UNDERTONES

In the last few weeks and months leading up to the military coup in Chile, conservative media decried Jewish participation in the Popular Unity government. The most blatant was *La Prensa*'s editorial of August 25, 1973, that charged that members of a "Jewish-Communist sect and cell" held positions as "directors, vice presidents, assistants, administrators, and advisors." Yet in the seventeen years of dictatorship that began less than a month later, antisemitism was a sporadic phenomenon, not a systematic element of the repressive actions.

A source that sounded alarm about possible antisemitic undertones of the recently installed military junta was Klaus Meschkat. The young professor from Germany who taught economics at the University of Concepción was shoved and pushed out of his apartment after the coup. He spent the first night with forty other people in an eight-by-thirteen-foot holding cell at the police station. At Talcahuano naval base, cadets beat the prisoners and threatened to shoot them. On the ferry to Quiriquina Island, administered by the navy, he discovered acquaintances from the university, many of whom had been savagely beaten. What remained etched in Klaus Meschkat's memory was the last question the navy prosecutor asked him: "Are you a Jew?" The German economist is convinced that not being Jewish saved him from much worse treatment. He learned that this prosecutor had punished a Jewish colleague from Belgium, Jacques Silberberg, by placing him in solitary confinement. Meschkat was expelled from the country a few weeks later and wrote a widely published article that caused concern among international Jewish institutions.[29]

José del Castillo Pichardo, a Dominican Republic historian, met Silberberg in 1964 at Santo Domingo University's School of Sociology. "Some leftist students considered him a provocateur due to his scathing style, but others defended him," he says. He and Silberberg met again in July 1968 when both were in Santiago teaching at the University of Chile. "Silberberg was in his element at the university's Macul campus . . . ; he was an intelligent and provocative professor," states Pichardo.[30] His recollection of Silberberg raises a question as to whether he was punished because he was a Jew or because of his "provocative" nature.

It is impossible to ascertain precisely how many prisoners may have been asked whether they were Jewish or how many were subjected to interrogations with an antisemitic slant. A likely conjecture is that former prisoners themselves, if they were subject to antisemitic slurs at all, ascribed little importance to them, likely dismissing such insults as the least harsh of the abuses they endured while in custody. Furthermore, it is probable that few, if any, staff members of human rights institutions that took testimonies from former prisoners would have given second thought to a Jewish last name. Former appellate court judge Juan Guzmán Tapia noted that he never investigated that aspect, and he believed that except for in the case of the Jewish relatives of the prisoners whose identities were expropriated in Operation Colombo, no one raised the issue.[31]

Nevertheless, some former prisoners do associate shades of antisemitism with their detention, and another few experienced outright antisemitic expressions by the repressors. Jorín Pilowsky told very few people about how he was treated after his arrest in Rancagua, immediately after the military coup.[32] Jorín, son of Jacobo Pilowsky, the immigrant from Vilna who fought for refugees from Nazi to be taken in by Chile, was an attorney and an important adviser of the El Teniente copper mine.

"After I was arrested, from the moment the guys started beating me up in Rancagua, they began their anti-Jewish insinuations: 'Where do you keep your money? Do you have dollars at home?' During my first days in prison, antisemitic insinuations and jokes of bad taste were frequent. And when the military had to decide what to do with me—whether to send me to Chacabuco or kick me out of the country—several insisted that I go to Israel."[33]

Jorín was jailed four months. Around Christmas Eve in 1973, he was presented with the two options: the concentration camp at Chacabuco in the northern province of Antofagasta, or expulsion from the country: "They put me on trial before a sort of unofficial military court. What to do with me? I stupidly wanted to remain in Latin America to see what I could do for Chile. But they said that under no circumstances could I stay in Latin America. Either I go to Israel or Europe."

Key to his release was Jacob Kaplan, the grand rabbi of France. Chilean Jewish friends in Paris spoke to Rabbi Kaplan, who had been an active member of the anti-Nazi resistance in Lyons between 1941 and 1944. Rabbi Kaplan sent the Foreign Relations Ministry a formal request to free Jorín. At the same time, Jorín's oldest brother, president of the Valparaíso Jewish community, and his father asked Rabbi Angel Kreiman to insist that General Oscar Bonilla, the interior minister, grant Kaplan's petition that he be expelled to France. Kreiman visited Jorín in jail in Rancagua, where he had been held in solitary confinement a long time. Jorín is convinced that the "Jewish factor" was a critical one in both his arrest and his release.

At the moment of his arrest, on September 11, 1973, psychiatrist Gunter Seelmann was president of Concepcion's Jewish community. After his arrest and transfer to Quiriquina Island, he recalls that his interrogator, a captain, had his "curriculum vitae in his hands" and that he asked Gunter about his "activities in the Jewish community."[34] This line of interrogation did not result in greater hardship, however. Yet, in the weeks after his arrest, *El Sur* published an article alleging that one of the Popular Unity's programs had included a scheme to physically eliminate all opponents. It added that the chosen method would be gas chambers, whose construction had been in the planning stage inside the regional hospital. The person in charge of this project was, the article alleged, none other than Gunter Seelmann, president of the city's Jewish community. "The article was ridiculous," recalls his wife, Hanni Grunpeter.[35]

Jorge T. (who prefers to remain anonymous) was sixteen years old in 1973. The information he received when he asked his father what it meant to be on the "left" or on the "right" is all that contributed to his political formation. The left, his father replied, was with the poor while the right was with the rich. Even though both of his parents were Jewish, they did not instill a sense of Jewish identity in him.[36] In his teenage years, his only encounters with antisemitism had been an occasional "you Jewish so-and-so" from a schoolmate, a commonplace insult. Eight months after the military coup, a classmate proposed an action to express repudiation of the dictatorship. The idea involved throwing flyers handwritten with slogans such as "Down with Pinochet," "End the Dictatorship," and "No to the Military Junta." After writing the leaflets with an ink pen, the two stuffed them in the pockets of their jackets, went to a working-class neighborhood, and began throwing them in the street. Today he sees that action as "totally foolhardy."

Very soon an armed man in civilian clothes arrested them with the leaflets in their hands. Jorge realized too late what a "completely insane impulse" the flyer idea had been. Both adolescents spent the end of that day and the following three days blindfolded, probably in Cuatro Alamos detention center, supplied hardly any food or water, deprived of sleep, and subjected to plenty of blows.

> When we were being transferred to some place, police asked me my friend's name. It was a Spanish surname. "And what's your name?" the police officer asked me. I told him my two clearly Jewish last names, and the guy asked, "Since you are Jewish, at the place where we're going to take you, we'll hook you up to an electric plant." It was a way of saying, because you are Jewish, it's going to be a lot worse for you. We're going to give it to you hard.

Fortunately for Jorge, the threat was mere bravado. Ten days later, he and his friend were released. Yet despite the more than forty years that have transpired, the police officer's black humor is fresh in his memory. Both in the case of this "foolhardy" young man as well as Jorín and Gunter, professionals of long-standing political membership, antisemitism was limited to insults and threats.

While I was talking to Jorge at a popular café in a district of east Santiago, a waitress handed me a napkin on which someone had written the following:

—I am Jewish
—Father exiled 1975
—Uncle tortured 1976
—Doctor
Can I help you?

The waitress indicated that the message had been written and sent by a woman seated at the next table, who had overheard the conversation. However, she had already left the restaurant. On the napkin was a mobile phone number, but repeated attempts on my part to contact her failed.

Jewish and Communist

In 1906, a young man from a family of wood gatherers and peasants near Kiev embarked on a journey. His departure was the direct result of a life of unpredictable jolts of fright experienced by Jewish communities. Brief periods of tranquility alternated with longer periods of abuse. After the most recent attack, Isaac Rosenman was one of the first from his town to leave. He landed on the other side of the globe—in Chile—and promptly added a third "n" to his last name so it would sound more German than Jewish.[37] Nevertheless, the changed spelling of his last name would not provide an invincible shield against the stigma of being a Jew.

His desire to leave behind that hereditary burden appeared to have been fulfilled when his son, born in Chile, married a woman from a Christian family. Yet Jewishness was an ever-present feature of home life. The *zeide*, as his grandchildren called him, visited every Sunday for lunch, and his daughter-in-law learned to cook many Jewish dishes and absorbed other aspects of Jewish culture as well. He continued to speak Yiddish with his son, and his grandchildren learned a few words.

His grandson Igor Rosenmann Becerra was enrolled by his parents in the Alianza Francesa school in 1961. A schoolyard fight that occurred when he was eight years old was a milestone event in his life. "Jewish shit!" his classmates shouted as they kicked him. His grandfather had experienced similar humiliation more than once in Poland; each time he had raised himself up from the ground, biting his tongue to contain the rage that he could not shout back at his aggressors. Isaac had warned his son, Igor's father, "They're going to call you 'Jewish shit.'" Now the phrase had been shouted at his grandson, as if it were a rite of passage that every young Jew must undergo. But this was not Poland; it was Chile. So the grandson got to his feet and in a firm voice responded, "Yes, I'm a Jew! So what?"

Sometimes personal identity is forged in counterpoint to others, because one feels different. That's how it was for Igor: in a boyhood fight, his instinct was affirmation when it might have been denial in order to protect himself from future attacks. "Afterward I said to myself, 'I am a Jew.' That's when it dawned on me that I was Jewish, that I had that identity. That my grandparents and my father had generated something in me that, indeed, was Jewish. That definitively marked me," he said.

The schoolyard beating spurred him to learn more. He began reading every book he could lay his hands on related to Jewish history, Jewish identity, and the Holocaust. At the same time, he began reading about Marxism, delving more deeply into the issue of injustice that he experienced firsthand as a Jew. It was in the Hashomer Hatzair movement where, as of twelve years of age, he started to fuse together two dimensions of his being: his Jewishness and politics.

At fourteen, Igor joined the youth wing of the Communist Party and shortly thereafter was invited to join the Ramona Parra Mural Brigade, an organization of muralists associated with the Communist Party that covered city walls with exuberant and colorful artistic expressions. "The Ramona Parra people were amazing," states Igor. And all of a sudden, this high school junior was one of them, with a construction helmet on his head and paintbrush in his hand. Painting murals for congressional elections and student federation campaigns, he became acquainted with all the vacant lots of Santiago. He also painted the walls of La Chascona, which had been poet Pablo Neruda's home in Santiago. He was with the group when artist Roberto Matta joined it to paint a famous mural in La Granja and others along the walls of the Mapocho River.[38]

Igor painted murals with much talent and energy, but he knew little about art or art history. He did not know that Roberto Matta was one of Chile's foremost internationally acclaimed contemporary artists. Igor asked Matta what he painted. The artist pointed to a cigarette stub on the ground and said, "You see that smoldering cigarette? I paint what's inside the little ember that's left of the cigarette."

"I will never forget that explanation," Igor remarks. "His depth marked me. From Matta I learned who Matta was. Whenever I see a painting of his, I remember: it's inside what's inside."

Within the "Jota," as the Communist Party youth organization is known popularly (the *J* is a reference to the first letter of its name in Spanish, which is "juventudes comunistas"), and generally in the Communist Party, Igor was not the only Jew. He believes there were many, but no one else around him publicly identified as Jewish.

Maybe their last names were not so obviously Jewish, or maybe they just didn't say anything about it. But I know that others wanted to "pass" because Jews were viewed as wealthy right-wingers. There were Jews from poor neighborhoods too, but they practiced self-denial, because they said to themselves, "if I say I'm Jewish, people will think I'm right-wing and that I have money."

In August 1976, Igor was in his third semester studying architecture at the University of Chile. At the State Technical University (today the University of Santiago), he launched a revival of an award-winning play called *Día* (Day) that he had written three years earlier for a theater festival at Darío Salas High School. After the play's successful debut, he had plunged into a dark night, as the military coup had occurred the next day. The theatrical revival of *Día* was about to send him directly to the bottom of an abyss.

The play had just ended, and the applause was continuing, when, from the stage, he saw a man enter the auditorium. The man had been a supervisor at his high school. At that very moment, Igor realized that he was an intelligence agent. Behind him, soldiers began entering the auditorium. They raided the theater and arrested two hundred people from the audience, including his mother and brothers as well as the actors. All of them were forced to get on police buses. They were taken to the police station in Estación Central. Later, nearly everyone was released, with the exception of Igor and six other people.

After his mother was released, she turned to influential people for help in freeing the young people in prison. She spoke to Rabbi Kreiman as well as important police officials. All her efforts to obtain their release were in vain, however, because the DINA had taken over the police station and the police no longer had authority in their own premises.

It was then that the real terror ensued. Between blows and more blows and threats, a tall blond man with a German last name interrogated Igor, shouting: "You're a Jew! You son of a bitch, Jew!" Igor does not know whether the treatment he received in the DINA's hands was different from what his friends experienced, because they were interrogated separately and, apparently, they did not discuss or compare the torture each had endured. The abuse became even more brutal with the incorporation of the use of electric current as a torture device when they were transferred to Cuatro Alamos.

At one point, he heard a great commotion and prison guards running from one place to another from the cell he shared with several other prisoners at Cuatro Alamos, the transitional torture facility within the Tres Alamos detention center.[39] A tall, hefty-built man in civilian clothes and wearing a long tan coat entered the cell. He glanced at all prisoners but stared at Igor, the only prisoner who was on his feet in the cell.

"He looked at me a long time with a very penetrating gaze, and then said, 'shave off that beard, you son of a bitch.' It was something like that, in a very aggressive tone," says Igor. The visitor was Manuel Contreras, director of the DINA. Igor has no way to prove it, but he associates the visit with his mother's ceaseless efforts to release him. He felt as though something had happened and that a protective bubble now surrounded him.

Shortly thereafter, he was transferred to Tres Alamos, the adjacent prison, where he received eighty hearty embraces. "All the prisoners welcomed me, embraced me, and I just cried and cried. As I was entering Tres Alamos, they began singing me a song, and they gave me food. They took care of me." Remembering that moment now, he again feels the incredible sense of relief of transitioning from horror to life again. Soon afterward, on August 18, he turned nineteen years old. Shortly after that, he organized a basketball championship and then a theater festival among the prisoners.

Two months later, Igor was transferred to Puchuncaví detention center, near the coast north of Valparaíso, where the guard towers, coils of barbed wire, and cabin cells that he associated with Nazi concentration camps awakened his inner Jewish self.

> It was shocking to arrive at Puchuncaví. I thought to myself, shit, I'm in a concentration camp. I was living the history that I read about in books, the history I knew about. I was reliving that history. At times, in my imagination, I felt I was imprisoned not because I was a Communist but because I was a Jew. I was in prison, and I knew full well it was because I was a Communist, but I immediately made the association as a Jewish prisoner in a concentration camp. All my life I have felt that I am a Jew-Communist.

His fellow prisoners cracked jokes about Jews and remarked on his last name. "They would ask me things about Jews. And there were many jokes about the fact that I was Jewish. How can you be Jewish if you're a Communist? If you are Communist, you can't possibly be a Jew. That typical way of joking. It was a constant thing; being a Jewish prisoner was a real issue."

"As a nineteen-year-old, it was also like a challenge and I felt proud to be there. It was a childish thing," Igor notes. "I am living this, I thought to myself. I am in a concentration camp, just like the Jews of Europe. It was a sense of ambivalence because the other feeling of fear, danger, worry about what would happen to me was also present. Fear was a constant: at any moment they might take you away and kill you. That feeling never left me," he adds.

The first five days in custody of the DINA had been a horrible nightmare, but the rest were "sheer learning and sheer life, with the sole uncertainty being what would happen to me. That part was terrible." He left Puchuncaví on

November 7 with his aunt, who picked him up in her Citroneta. "I can remember the feeling of freedom. Someone who has never been imprisoned cannot fully know what freedom is," he states.

Igor's parents had everything planned out: after a relaxing vacation, he would go to Canada to study architecture. But Igor was determined to remain in Chile. No argument in the world nor his parents' begging him to leave would convince him otherwise. He was going to stay. He resumed his studies at the University of Chile's School of Architecture, and he returned to the trenches of cultural resistance to the dictatorship through theater as a leader of the Agrupación Cultural Universitaria (ACU, University Cultural Association). That involvement resulted in two more arrests for brief periods of time.

In late March 1985, when he had a daughter who was just fifteen days old, he again experienced terror. The architecture students had set up barricades of flaming tires on the street. They obstructed the road, with Igor in his Volkswagen supplying the students *miguelitos*, or caltrops, a homemade simple weapon used in armed resistance to cause damage to police vehicle tires. But the Central Nacional de Informaciones (CNI, National Information Center) agents blocked the intersection and prevented the students from continuing their protest.[40] Agents got out of a car and put Igor and a fellow architect into what appeared to be a taxi. He could feel his friend's entire body tremble in fear.

Just days before, the death squad known as the Comando Conjunto had abducted José Manuel Parada, Manuel Guerrero, and Santiago Nattino, leaving their bodies with their throats slashed along the road to the airport. The CNI was primarily abducting young leaders as a way to frighten them, but at times they also shot them. "My whole being told me that I was one of those they had decided to kill," recalls Igor. "During the entire time we were in the car, we could tell they were driving on dirt roads. We seemed to be far away, and I was sure they would throw me out of the car and leave me dead right there. It hurt. It was terrible. I began saying good-bye to my daughter. I told myself, okay, I'm about to die for getting involved with the resistance."

Roberto Matta helped him recover a measure of composure. "I began getting into the lines in the [car] seat, in the space for the feet between the front and back seats. I entered deeper and deeper into a line, like Roberto Matta. I entered that space and lost myself inside it. I began thinking rationally about death, how the bullet entering my body would feel, if it would hurt."

In the front seat, the CNI agents spoke in code through a radio transmitter. Igor shouted, "Where are you taking us? What will you do with us? We are architects!" They didn't respond at all. "That was worse. They wouldn't respond, and they spoke in code: X43," he clearly recalls. After about an hour

on the road, the car returned to an urban area. It stopped, and the two architecture students were thrown out in a desolate place. Both remained curled up
on the ground, waiting for the bullets. Igor was able to see a man looking
around in all directions before getting back into the taxi. The car drove away.

Igor sighs. "I was born again," he says. Calmly, he continues his tale. "We
stood up and we began running, running, running, shouting, 'I'm alive! I'm
alive!' We began to see people who had no idea what these madmen were shouting about." They reached a warehouse and asked for a telephone to call the
Architect Professional Society.

It had been no more than one hour of intimidation, but the CNI achieved
its objective. From then on, it became increasingly difficult for Igor to participate in student marches. He was overcome with fear everywhere he went.
His nerves were on edge, and he would jump at the slightest thing. He began
staying at home and writing. "My struggle changed," he says.

When asked if his Jewish being is still present in him, he replies:

> Constantly. I have always felt that what I experienced was marked by the fact
> that I am both a Jew and a Communist. Others make me aware of it, and I do
> too. My grandparents are always present. It is an identity that marks everything
> I have experienced. From the first fights at school when I was beaten up to when
> the DINA tortured me, I always felt it: I am a Jew.
>
> I think I will always be called a "shitty Jew," or else they'll say, "What a fantas-
> tic Jew you are because you belong to the chosen people and are so bright." But
> I have also lived that Jewish identity joyfully and that gives me the strength
> to endure. Just like when I told that boy, "I'm a Jew! So what?" So what! In
> other words, I am a human being, I am happy, and I think. What's the matter
> with you?

You're about to Find Out . . .

Tomás Hirsch went to the Instituto Hebreo school. On Fridays, he and his
classmates took a public bus to practice sports at the Estadio Maccabi recreational center. Whenever they talked about their school, one of his pals would
say, "Shh. Not so loud. Don't let others hear us." That fear of open identification as a Jew resulted from "habits transmitted from each generation to the
next," Hirsch believes. His parents, Jorge Hirsch and Elise Goldschmidt, had
fled the persecution they faced as Jews in Europe and arrived in Chile in the
late 1930s.

Yet throughout his life and political career, he never had been disparaged
for being a Jew. He only experienced antisemitism for the first time in March
1985, when he was vice president of the Humanist Party. Eight Humanist Party

members, including its president Laura Rodríguez, who in 1989 would become the party's first elected congresswoman, were at Maipu Plaza, handing out flyers about the massive earthquake that had shaken the country on March 3. "Our flyers said that Pinochet's economic measures were the equivalent of seven earthquakes. It had a drawing of Pinochet with a fat ass, sitting on top of the country," explains Tomás.

They were handing out the flyers when fifteen plainclothes men and national police with machine guns surrounded them. The group was taken away, forced to lie down on the floor of a large paddy wagon, with police kicking them, to a police station half a block away. There "we were heavily beaten and interrogated" before being transferred to the First Police Precinct in Santiago at the corner of Santo Domingo and McIver Streets.[41]

"During that interrogation, they brought up the subject of my Judaism," he remembers. They told him, "Now you're about to find out what concentration camps are. The concentration camps are nothing next to what you're going to experience!' Many threats. It was a very violent situation, at a time when that day or the next we learned that Manuel Guerrero, José Manuel Parada, and Santiago Nattino had been murdered by members of the Directorate of Police Communications [DICOMCAR]."

Tomás remained in jail for a week. In the period before the 1988 referendum and afterward, he was arrested again, but the most terrifying arrest, and the one during which he received the most blows, was that antisemitic episode at the police station.

I presented my sworn statement at the second session of the Valech Commission. I didn't go to the first session because it was called the Political Imprisonment and Torture Commission. I was subjected to violence, but I wasn't tortured. Torture is something much more atrocious than what I experienced. I went there to provide historic confirmation that we Humanists, who always advocated non-violence, were also arrested, and in some cases, tortured and even disappeared. That's what we did and that's how all of us suffered human rights violations.[42]

Ancestral Hatred

Katia Reszczynski, a psychiatrist who died in January 2006, was arrested in September 1974 was taken to the torture centers at 38 Londres Street, in downtown Santiago, and 1367 José Domingo Cañas Street, in the eastern part of the city. She states:

I met Miguel Krassnoff on the first day I was taken to the torture house, because he made me take off my blindfold in his office, where taped to the wall he had a chart of the MIR political hierarchy. The first thing he did was to introduce himself as the son and descendant of a White Russian. And he asked me if I was a White Pole or a Polish Jew. I answered that I believed we were White Poles because my family was Catholic.[43]

Katia's response did not exempt her from torture, but she survived imprisonment to later become a member of the team of psychologists of the Comité de Defensa de los Derechos del Pueblo (CODEPU, Committee for Defense of People's Rights) that developed a therapeutic practice to help survivors of torture heal.

Miguel Krassnoff is the grandson of Piotr Krasnov, the commander of a battalion of Cossacks who put his anticommunist and anti-Jewish passion at the service of the czars in the late nineteenth and early twentieth centuries. His grandfather Piotr subsequently put that same passion at the service of Hitler as a participant in the German invasion of the Soviet Union in 1941, after which he went on to battle against Yugoslavian partisans until the end of the war. His grandfather, father, and uncle ended up being imprisoned by the Soviets and were executed in January 1947. Krassnoff was born 1945 in Austria and came to Chile with his mother and grandmother as refugees. His grandmother transmitted to her grandson the legendary story of the Cossacks and the martyrdom of his grandfather and father in the struggle against communism and Jewish Bolsheviks. Chile's military dictatorship provided him the opportunity as army brigadier and head of a detachment of DINA agents to recover his glorious family tradition and to vindicate the deaths of his family members at the hands of the Communist Party.

In mid-November 1974, two months after Katia's imprisonment, Diana Aron was arrested. The Cossacks' son exercised his power over a descendant of Russian Jews, the great-granddaughter of Solomon Rotter, founder of the first Jewish cemetery of Santiago, and Marcos Svigilsky, the young man whose mother kept him awake for three whole days to prevent his forced conscription into the czar's army.

In June 1967, at seventeen years of age, despite her parent's opposition, Diana insisted on traveling to Israel to contribute to defense actions during the Six-Day War. She responded to her parents' dismay by saying, "You have taught me, and at the Instituto Hebreo, too, I have learned to defend Israel. Why do poor Argentine Jews have to go fight but not your daughter?" Off she went with a friend, and they were placed serving meals to the soldiers. After coming down with typhus, she had to return to Chile earlier than planned, and by then her Zionist convictions had lost their sheen. Diana had lived in a district populated by Palestine families and witnessed the disdain with which they were treated. Her boyfriend, Luis Muñoz, arrested three weeks after she was, nostalgically recalls Diana and her sister Anamaría strumming a guitar and singing in Hebrew "Erev shel shoshanim," "Shnei javerim," and Sephardic songs such as "A la una yo nací," "Cuando al Rey Nimrod," and others they learned in Israel and at their Jewish high school. The sisters also sang advertising jingles for her parents' radio program. Luis speculates that her vocation as a journalist derived, in part, from the experience on radio as well as *Radiomanía*, the pop music magazine her father Elías Aron published.

Luis remembers the first time he met Diana. He was working in intelligence for the MIR, which needed information about how the truck drivers' strike was affecting different segments of Chilean society. One contact informed him that they could only meet at 7 a.m. Luis went to meet the early riser at Bustamante Park as requested by the contact. A well-dressed young woman arrived punctually at the appointed location, which he later learned was near the Quimantú publishing house where she worked. She introduced herself as "Ursula" and handed Luis a meticulous typewritten report that thoroughly described the spirit of people in the working-class neighborhood of Renca, the mechanics of food distribution there, and the strike's overall impact on that community.

Time passed, and they chanced to meet again in the course of political work and eventually became a couple. "She was always very hard working. She was a strong, assertive, intelligent woman, who was full of life. In meetings, she was vibrant, with her clear, forceful voice. "Her voice came out from inside, conveying confidence and captivating everyone present," says an emotional Luis.[44]

Diana's parents had emigrated to Israel following the presidential election of Salvador Allende. In December 1973, when he was on a short visit to Chile, her father, Elías, asked Luis to meet him. He pleaded with Luis to persuade Diana to leave the country because he had learned that people were being killed. "I got the impression that Elías and Perla were terrified that something would happen to Diana. But Diana was very independent, and was totally wedded to her ideals," Luis notes. Repeated efforts by other relatives to persuade her to leave Chile came up against the same brick wall of Diana's firm conviction that would not allow her to contemplate the idea of abandoning Chile.

During the next few months, Luis and Diana went from house to house, sometimes separately and sometimes together. Once they lodged in a hotel, but the worry that the hotel managers would report a suspicious couple kept them from getting any sleep that night. "The way we fled, the way we sought to escape capture, our furtive glances on the street to see if we were being followed, was reminiscent of the way Jews lived in the Warsaw Ghetto," said Luis.

Diana Aron (*right*) on a radio program with singer-songwriter Víctor Jara (*left*)
(Aron family)

Before the military coup, Diana and Luis had drifted apart politically. Diana adhered to the wing of the MIR that believed they must resist with arms, whereas the intelligence cadres, of which Luis was a member, "knew that would not be possible and would result in all of us being killed." The position that prevailed was the former, sustained by Diana, that held they had to "retreat while striking a blow." She was promoted to the organization's central committee.

On November 18, 1974, Luis and Diana left the house where they were staying near Ossa Avenue. Luis took the bus and Diana planned to take a taxi, having agreed to meet later that evening for tea at the home of Diana's sister Anamaría. "She did not return, and not later that night either. I said to myself, 'This is it, she's been arrested.' The next day I went to our house. I straightened up the place; I washed her clothes. I had been told that after arresting someone, sometimes they went to the prisoner's house to get personal items, like clothes. I took very few things, a few papers, and I left."[45]

Three weeks later, Luis was also detained and taken to the same place, Villa Grimaldi, but did not see Diana.

"On the third day of torture, Krassnoff takes me to the office, and removes my blindfold. He tells me that he knew me from before, that we went to the same school and were in the same grade. He names the teachers' nicknames, and he says to me, 'Since you are a schoolmate, let's make a deal. Miss Diana is seriously wounded in the military hospital. If you cooperate with me, we will proceed with her treatment. If you don't cooperate, she will die, and it will be your fault.'" Luis asked why she was in the hospital, and Krassnoff replied that she was wounded when she was arrested. Luis then asked, "How? She was not carrying weapons and she was wearing high heels." "She was running, and I shot her," Krassnoff said. "How many bullets?" asked Luis. "Four." "I don't believe you. Let me see Diana, and then we'll talk," insisted Luis. Krassnoff answered, "I think that can be arranged." But that night a different person came to torture Luis.

Luis remained at Villa Grimaldi for three months. "Every time they tortured me and asked me about something, I would say, "Show me Diana." Later I understood that probably they had already killed her. It enraged me. That rage helped me survive," he says emphatically. After he left for exile in England, where he now works as a legal assistant and psychologist, Luis married a former prisoner, a Chilean exile who is also Jewish. They named their first daughter Diana.

The former MIR member turned DINA informer Marcia Merino has testified in court that when the wounded Diana was brought to Villa Grimaldi, Krassnoff insisted on personally interrogating her. In her sworn statement, she remarks that "what shocked me most was that Krassnoff left the torture room with his hands covered in blood, shouting 'not only is she a Marxist, the bitch is a Jew. We must kill her.' As he spoke those words, his face contorted. . . . You got the impression that Diana's Jewish origins bothered him more than the fact that she was a Marxist. I found it shocking that his hatred of Jews was so intense. I understood that he hated Marxists due to his family history, but I didn't realize that he hated Jews. I am certain that he killed Diana Aron or at least decided what would happen to her."[46] Following his father and grandfather's footsteps, Krassnoff unleashed his antisemitic brutality, ending Diana's life.

However, Diana was not the only Jew held in Villa Grimaldi's Cuartel Terranova. On February 2, 1975, Gladys Díaz and her boyfriend Juan Carlos Perelman were arrested together and taken to Villa Grimaldi. Gladys was well known not only for her involvement with the MIR but also as a journalist for the program she hosted on Radio Agricultura in 1973. Juan Carlos had returned to the movement after a hiatus in his political activism to study at the University of Concepción. He was not seen nor heard from again after he was taken away from the concentration camp on February 28.

"Honestly, I cannot understand why Juan Carlos is dead and disappeared but I am alive. I have always attributed his death to the fact that he was a Jew," Gladys states.[47] She notes that Juan Carlos was less involved in the MIR than she was. However, other sources close to the movement refute her assertion, and say that Juan Carlos was very politically active.

The Six-Day War heightened Juan Carlos's sense of Jewish identification. He identified passionately with the history of Jewish persecution. "He was quite erudite, and he told me about the different moments in history when Jews were persecuted," Gladys notes. "'We Jews,' he would say; he felt part of a whole struggle for freedom, justice and equality."

Gladys's theory regarding Juan Carlos's death was founded on the conversations she had with Krassnoff in between episodes of horrendous torture during the three months she was held at Villa Grimaldi.

> He attempted to appear like a guy who was not a brute but a thinker. He said he believed the German people's National Socialism had been misinterpreted. They had to cleanse their country of the Communists, Socialists, the Christian Democrats, businessmen, and the Jews. He said Chile needed the same kind of cleansing. I heard him speak disparagingly about Jewish comrades of mine. I believe he was the only true fascist of the lot. The rest were power-hungry brutes.

Did other Jewish prisoners encounter antisemitic treatment at Cuartel Terranova-Villa Grimaldi or at other detention and torture centers? It is logical to assume that the few recounted here were not the only ones.

At Colonia Dignidad

Before the war, Viktor Shtrum never had ever given any thought to the fact that his mother was Jewish and that he too was a Jew. His mother never spoke to him about it, not even when he was a child, not even when he was growing up. Despite never having regarded himself as a Jew, the dramatic occurrences in the life of this prestigious physicist—accused of being anti-Soviet and then expelled from the scientific institute, cast out, jailed, his life destroyed—were inexorably shaped by the sole fact of having been born the son of a Jewish mother and having grown up in the Soviet Union in the 1940s and 1950s.

Shtrum is the main character in Vasily Grossman's semiautobiographic book *Life and Fate*. However, it offers an accurate portrait of many real people of Jewish origin, including Boris Weisfeiler, who was arrested and subsequently disappeared in the vicinity of the Nazi enclave Colonia Dignidad in 1985. Boris, who was born in Moscow on April 19, 1941, the son of Dyula Weisfeiler and Anna Bernstein, had a life marked by his origins. "We were not religious Jews. We did not practice anything Jewish. Basically, you know you are a Jew because your parents and grandparents are. And you know you are Jewish because you suffer on account of it," notes Olga Weisfeiler, Boris's sister.[48]

Anna Bernstein was a brilliant doctor who was fired from Moscow hospital as a consequence of a climate of paranoid suspicion in the early 1950s when Stalin believed that Jewish doctors were confabulating to assassinate him. In 1953, when he was twelve years old, Boris was savagely beaten, left unconscious with his face bleeding, sprawled outside the apartment building where the family lived. The attackers had beaten him because he was the son of Jewish doctors. The same year, Olga, too, was attacked, although not as severely as her brother.

In the Soviet Union, every citizen had a passport-style identification document bearing the carrier's name, date of birth, and nationality. The passport belonging to all Jews indicated as nationality "Yudiye," Jew. To apply for university entrance—for which Jewish students were allotted a quota of 2 percent—or a job, stay in a hotel, or obtain any legal document, a person had to exhibit the passport. "When we lived in Russia, we were never Russians. When we came to the United States, people would hear our accent and remark, 'So you are Russian.' No, I would say, I am Jewish. After leaving Russia, I become a Russian for the first time in my life!" Olga laughs.

In 1963, after he had graduated from Moscow University and was focusing on finishing his doctoral thesis in mathematics on the subject of algebra, Boris was accused of being anti-Soviet and expelled from the Komsomol, the Communist youth organization, membership in which was key in the practice of any profession. Two years earlier, he had refused to sign a letter charging that a certain professor was anti-Soviet; now the same accusation was being leveled at him. Once again, many of the people accused of anti-Soviet views were Jews.

Foreseeing that his professional ambitions would be stifled, Boris decided it was time to leave. It was 1974, midway through Leonid Brezhnev's term, and approximately two hundred thousand Jews had been authorized to leave the country. In June 1975, Boris Weisfeiler arrived in the United States with refugee status. He began working at the Institute for Advanced Studies and later accepted a teaching position at Pennsylvania State University.

Boris got along well with all his colleagues, but he found a special affinity in his life as an immigrant with a circle of Russian Jews, refugees like him. He kept in touch with his sister Olga, who remained in the Soviet Union. He

Boris Weisfeiler, the only US citizen still disappeared in Chile (Olga Weisfeiler)

was a frugal man, not attracted by consumer goods, but he had two passions: the challenge of solving complex mathematical problems, and traveling. With a backpack over his shoulder, he traveled throughout Europe and places of astounding natural beauty, such as Alaska, northern Canada, and Peru.

Time and time again, Olga has studied the route her brother took on his last excursion, which began on December 25, 1984. Boris's route took him through forests of cypress, beech, and *coigüe* trees in the Chilean foothills of the Andes. Beginning at El Abanico in the southern province of Ñuble, he circled Lake Laja, near the Argentine border, and then turned north, following the Ñuble River. Perhaps Boris sat down on the rocky banks of the river to enjoy the serenity, unaware that he was approaching the outer perimeter of Colonia Dignidad. In fact, he was completely unaware of the existence of such a sinister place in the midst of stunning natural beauty.

A current tourist website describes the bright turquoise color of the Ñuble River's turbulent waters as optimum for white water rafting and recommends kayaking downstream in the cold, narrow Los Sauces River. Chile today has become a prime destination for international adventurers. But in the 1980s, it was not, especially not for people who were aware of the military regime that ruled with an iron fist and that had called on citizens to report suspicious foreigners. A local resident who saw and spoke to Boris did just that. He reported the presence of an unknown foreigner to the police station of the hamlet of El Roble.

Boris felt protected by his US passport. However, what would likely stand out for a policeman in a military dictatorship was his place of birth: the Soviet Union. He had encountered the paradoxical situation of being regarded as a Russian only once he had left his native country. Now he would be excoriated for his past, in a place where and a time in which "Soviet" was synonymous with subversive and enemy.

In July 1987, a mysterious informant appeared for the first time at the Santiago Archdiocese's human rights defense institution, the Vicariate of Solidarity, and later at the United States Embassy, claiming to having participated in a military patrol that arrested Boris and took him to Colonia Dignidad. The witness, who identified himself only as "Daniel," reappeared at the same office in March 1990. Between 1987 and 1997, on different occasions, he supplied information to the US Embassy in Santiago, to Socialist Party politician Maximo Pacheco, and finally to journalist Ricardo Israel and Senator José Antonio Viera-Gallo.

Olga is convinced that "Daniel" did not act on his own initiative but rather was sent by Colonia Dignidad to carry out a mission for the German hierarchy with a plan supplied by it. Former Vicariate of Solidarity staff agree that while the witness who voluntarily offered information did have military bearing, it is likely he was sent by military intelligence. Regardless of what the informant's underlying motives may have been, Olga emphasizes that he provided the first clues concerning Boris's possible destination, enabling her to initiate a criminal complaint.

The indictment issued on August 21, 2012, by Santiago Court of Appeals judge Jorge Zepeda represented a major breakthrough in the case. His indictment of four retired national police officers and four former military men constituted recognition that the crime was committed by state agents and therefore was a human rights violation. However, on March 4, 2016, Zepeda reversed his decision, dropping charges against the eight defendants, and concluded that Boris had been victim of a common crime, although the judge did not provide any answers concerning his whereabouts or his fate.

The ruling was a serious setback for Olga and incomprehensible to her. In 1993 and again in 2011, the National Truth and Reconciliation Commission failed to reach the conclusion that Boris was a victim of human rights violations, that is, in other words, that he was forcibly disappeared by agents of the state of Chile. Olga's personal mission has been to strive for that recognition. She has declared her intention to keep fighting to achieve that objective, "as long as I have strength" to do so.

What happened to Boris after his arrest has not been discovered. And there is an another element Olga considers key that has never been investigated, namely, "the fact that Boris was a Jew." This, she thinks, "points directly to the involvement of and cover-up by the military and national police in Colonia Dignidad."[49] She always found it odd that the informant "Daniel" had noted that Boris, according to Colonia Dignidad officials, was a "Jewish spy," "a Mossad agent looking for Josef Mengele," and that "he was treated like a Jewish dog."[50] Such allegations by the anonymous witness and police planted a seed of doubt in the human rights qualifiers regarding Boris's condition as victim.

Yet these and other references to Boris's Jewish origins were perplexing, given that nothing about him could possibly have identified him as a Jew. He did not wear a Jewish symbol of any kind, and he was not circumcised. The persistent question that nags Olga is how "Daniel" knew Boris was a Jew. She has her own hypothesis. "Boris himself had to have said it. When? Perhaps he had revealed it when he was being tortured at Colonia Dignidad, or maybe earlier, they brutally beat him before arresting him by the riverbank, and he told them then." She adds, "It is clear to me that only for a German settlement linked to Nazis, as is the case with Colonia Dignidad, would Boris's nationality or religion have any relevance. And only Paul Schaeffer and his 'special' friends, the Nazis, would exploit that fact."

The Jewish dimension of this case might also be key in disproving statements issued in 1987 that CNI agents allegedly killed Boris beside the river where they had first found him. Had this occurred, the "agents would not have known anything about the religion or nationality of Boris and, more importantly, it would not matter to them," stresses Olga. This reinforces her belief that her brother entered Colonia Dignidad alive and that there he was recognized as a Jew. That question of how they could have known that Boris was a Jew occurred to her as soon as she began to study the declassified documents in 2001, when she received them. She attempted to convey the significance of this issue, but she feels that no one lent it any importance.

In his life, Boris lived somewhat as a foreigner in a strange land, his identity defined by others. It is likely that for this reason—suspicion toward a foreigner, a Russian Jew, to be exact—he was deprived of his life. His sister hopes that Boris's status as foreigner may eventually contribute to removing the layers of concealment that obscure his fate.

Four Names

In the first fourteen months the military junta was in power, already more than fifteen hundred people had been summarily executed or forcibly disappeared. Thousands more remained in detention in either official or clandestine prisons.

The urgent and terrible reality of Chile led the UN to introduce human rights monitoring mechanisms that had been approved eight years earlier but never before activated. On November 6, 1974, the UN General Assembly approved Resolution 3219, which urged Chile to take measures to restore and protect human rights and fundamental freedoms. The resolution also recommended that the UN Human Rights Committee conduct an on-site inspection.

The multiplier impact of Resolution 3219 was felt less than a month later. For the first time in its history, the US Senate voted that US military support to another country would be conditional on the country's respecting fundamental rights and freedoms. Known as the Kennedy Amendment owing to the driving force behind the measure, Senator Edward Kennedy, it resulted in military support to Chile being cut off for the next sixteen years.

Still another reason for optimism in those days when repression was reaching a peak was the UN Human Rights Committee's creation of a work group in 1975 that would carry out the General Assembly's mandate to investigate Chile. "You cannot imagine how we celebrated in the Propeace Committee!" attorney Roberto Garreton said. "It was a spectacular step against the dictatorship."[51] To conduct its examination, the work group required Chile's authorization, and the country's response was long in coming. Meanwhile, Augusto Pinochet devised a plan that sought to give an explanation to these international inquisitors as well as to family members inquiring about the whereabouts of loved ones who disappeared subsequent to arrest.

The plan called for strategic support from the military on the other side of the Andes that would capitalize on the presence in Argentina of thousands of Chileans who had fled the dictatorship. Among those was Julia Concha, who came to Buenos Aires with her three children in March 1975. She recalls being advised to say the family was from Mendoza and to never admit they were Chileans. She was also advised not to seek political asylum or refugee status, which would alert authorities. "Rumor had it that the Chileans coming to Argentina were all a bunch of terrorists," she says.[52] In Buenos Aires she reunited with her husband and brother, who had left Chile a month after the military coup. Luis Concha, her brother, was a union activist and member of the MIR who coordinated the distribution of material documenting the abuses of the Pinochet dictatorship among eight solidarity committees in Buenos Aires. He turned a warehouse in the town of William Morris, in the western part of the greater Buenos Aires area, into temporary housing for Chilean refugees. Up to fifty people at a time, including families, found shelter there, where they were also provided with information on how to begin their lives as refugees. "You had to be careful. You couldn't say where you had come from or why," says Julia.

Ten months before the Southern Cone dictatorships formalized their collaboration in Operation Condor, Chile and Argentina were already coordinating closely in the military intelligence sphere. On September 30, 1974, Argentine and Chilean agents had collaborated to assassinate General Carlos Prats and his wife, Sofia Cuthbert, in Buenos Aires. And in May 1975 the first arrest coordinated by three countries took place when Paraguayan police at the Argentine border removed Amilcar Santucho, an Argentine, and Jorge Fuentes Alarcon, a Chilean, from a bus. Fuentes was tortured in Asunción by agents of Paraguay and Chile.[53] Subsequently, he was brought to Villa Grimaldi in Santiago, where he continued to be tortured until, on January 12, 1976, he was taken away to an unknown destination, never to be seen again.

In February 1975, a year before the Argentine military coup, thirty military units under the command of General Acdel Vilas, with full official backing from President Maria Estela Martínez de Perón, unleashed Operación Independencia in northern Tucuman province. The armed forces sought not only to annihilate the Ejército Revolucionario del Pueblo (ERP, People's Revolutionary Army) guerrillas in the hills of that province but also to perfect practices they would soon extend throughout the country: abductions carried out by men in plainclothes dress, detention in clandestine prisons, the systematic denial of these arrests, torture, and the concealment of bodies of people murdered. It is estimated that more than three hundred people were forcibly disappeared or summarily executed in Tucuman prior to the military coup in March 1976.[54]

To these practices, already routine on the other side of the Andes, the Argentine military added a component of its own. Since the early years of the twentieth century, antisemitic undercurrents that correlated between being Jewish and being a Marxist had been widespread in Argentina, the result of the marked presence of Jews in socialist unions and antifascist movements as well as in political parties of the left. During the era of the last Argentine military dictatorship (1976–85), this latent native antisemitism was harnessed to suggest a connection between Jewishness and subversiveness.

What Pierre Vidal-Naquet has called the "Jewish-Marxist syntagma" that in 1942 and 1943 drove Hitler's hosts to wage war in the east—"indissolubly against Jews and Marxists, considered a single entity"—regained vitality in the so-called dirty war of Argentina.[55] Embrace of this idea was apparent in Argentina through differentially cruel treatment of Jewish prisoners and the fact that Jews represented a proportionately greater number of the forcibly disappeared relative to the overall population.[56]

However, in Chile the perception of Jews as synonymous with the left was not culturally rooted. Indeed, it was quite the contrary; Jews were more likely to be associated with the community's known institutional support for the military junta. Therefore (and notwithstanding the cases noted of antisemitic treatment of some Jewish prisoners), the view that equated being Jewish with leftist ideology was absent from the discourse and repressive practices of the Chilean military junta. In this context, Argentina provided a propitious setting for an orchestration through which Chile aimed to derail scrutiny into the fate of people whose detention was being systematically denied. For the Argentine military, the story would reinforce the perception that its national territory had been invaded by international subversives who plotted with nationals to produce a dangerous destabilization that required the state's iron fist.

Chilean DINA agent Enrique Arancibia Clavel would be the principal liaison in Buenos Aires. Years later Arancibia Clavel, the only defendant indicted for the assassination of Carlos Prats and Sofía Cuthbert, collaborated with his Argentine counterparts via the Secretaría de Inteligencia de Estado (State Intelligence Administration). After his arrest, a handwritten document listing the names of thirty-two disappeared Chileans and the border crossings through which they allegedly had entered Argentina was found in his house.[57] Jaime Eugenio Robotham Bravo allegedly entered by way of Tromen (today Mahuil Malal), along a gravel road fifty kilometers from San Martín de los Andes, on February 29, 1975, while Juan Carlos Perelman Ide supposedly entered through Las Cuevas (today Cristo Redentor) on March 29 of the same year.

The names of Jaime Robotham and Juan Carlos Perelman in addition to those of David Silberman and Luis Guendelman, both graduates of the Instituto Hebreo, were used for a macabre prelude to the hoax that came to be known as Operation Colombo, or the list of the 119.[58] These four are the only Jewish last names or at least Jewish-sounding names—as the Robothams are unaware of Jewish ancestors in their family—associated with Operation Colombo.

Arancibia Clavel's partners belonged to the Argentine Anticommunist Alliance, known as the Triple A, who began circulating in green Ford Falcons in the streets of Buenos Aires. In light of the group's notorious antisemitic slant, it is probable that their operatives selected the four Jewish-sounding names to launch the ruse.

Argentine journalist Stella Calloni, author of two books on Operation Condor (which followed Operation Colombo), is convinced that Argentine intelligence agents had the job of choosing the names. "I am certain that those here who participated in the operation did so enthusiastically. My theory is that the Chileans reached an agreement with a group of nationalists, Nazis really, and so appeared four bodies that happened to have names of Chilean Jews. We still don't know whose corpses those were. The Argentine agents did this as a favor to Chile and then Chile probably paid back that favor to the Argentines, by giving them people or names. They exchanged favors for other favors."[59]

Laura Elgueta, eighteen years old at the time, lived in Buenos Aires with her Chilean parents, who had been exiled since 1974. She has studied the Chilean-Argentine intelligence structure in an attempt to understand the circumstances of the abduction and subsequent disappearance of her brother Luis, a music student and member of the MIR; her sister-in-law, Clarita Fernandez; and Clarita's sister, Cecilia, on July 27, 1976. "It is not a coincidence that they chose Jewish-sounding names." Laura notes that "extremely antisemitic views were entrenched in traditional sectors associated with the most orthodox wing of the Argentine Catholic church" and associated with the Triple A.[60]

Laura witnessed firsthand the antisemitic bias that tinted the Argentine repressive apparatus. Nearly a year after the disappearances of Luis, Clarita, and Cecilia, around 11 p.m. on July 12, 1977, she was abducted together with another sister-in-law. "They enacted the classic kidnap operation that was being carried out throughout 1977," she points out. They were forced into a car and taken to a clandestine center that, years later, she identified as Club Atlético. When they were taken out of the cars, "the first thing we heard was the voice of Chileans who were waiting for us. I think there were more than two."

> They followed the customary procedure. They took away our IDs and gave us a letter with a number. At the moment of the interrogation we were forced to undress. My sister-in-law was taken away first for interrogation. I was left waiting my turn, naked and blindfolded. At one point I hear them bring in two kids, who they were roughly beating. The woman was terrified. When they are stripped, the agents realize he is a Jew. They have great fun: "Oh, this one's a Moishe; look at you, so you are a Jew; we're going to give it to you real good; how great to have another one in our hands!" At one point there was silence. I realized that the three of us were alone, and so a lovely gesture was possible. I coughed, he coughed, and then she too coughed. We communicated with each other that way. I never heard anything more about them. Surely they are disappeared, dead.

When it was her turn to be interrogated, she realized that at least one Chilean was present, listening, while they interrogated her. Benito José Fioravanti, who belonged to a group of fundamentalist Catholics of Nazi persuasion, has been identified as the head of the Atlético torture center. "Fioravanti's participation in conjunction with Chileans was proven through my case in 1977," Laura confirms. She reiterates, "I don't believe it was a coincidence that those characters" who inflicted special cruelty on Jews participated in Operation Colombo and chose people with Jewish-sounding names to detain.

The scheme began on April 16, 1975, with the discovery in an underground parking garage of Buenos Aires of a corpse that had been burned and mutilated to the point of being unrecognizable and that was accompanied by a handwritten sign with the words "Dado de baja por el MIR" (Decommissioned by the MIR) on the ground, intended to suggest that the death was the result of a settling of scores among leftist combatants. Beside the body was found a Chilean identification card, intact, bearing the name of civil engineer David Silberman, manager of the Chuquicamata state copper mine. Six months earlier, Silberman had been abducted from the Santiago penitentiary, in a dramatic maneuver described by the interior minister as an operation by the MIR. Subsequently, witnesses testified having been held with him in the torture center at 1367 José Domingo Cañas Street in Santiago in October 1974.[61] This modus operandi would be repeated in July with the appearance of three more bodies, also charred, once again accompanied by signs referring to the MIR and the Chilean identification cards of Luis Guendelman, Jaime Robotham, and Juan Carlos Perelman.

On July 12 and 16, 1975, family members read in horror and with incredulity the first-page headlines of Chile's leading daily newspapers *El Mercurio*, *La Tercera*, and *Las Ultimas Noticias*. With the title "Bloody Internal Vendetta within the MIR," *Las Ultimas Noticias* described how Luis Guendelman and Jaime Robotham were "sought after by international agencies such as Amnesty and other supposed humanitarian groups. . . . But now it turns out they were killed by their own extremist comrades in the neighboring country."

Architect Luis Guendelman, arrested on September 2, 1974, in his home, was seen in the secret detention center of José Domingo Cañas the day after his arrest, and on September 26, he arrived at Cuatro Alamos. At Cuatro Alamos he told fellow prisoners with whom he shared a cell that he had been tortured at Villa Grimaldi. In November and December 1974, Guendelman was taken to the military hospital, only to be returned to Cuatro Alamos, where in October, a prisoner heard him sing the tango "Adiós muchachos compañeros de mi vida."[62] He was last seen alive at this place.

On December 31, 1974, sociology student Jaime Robotham shared tea with his friend and fellow Socialist Party member Claudio Thauby. Later that evening, as the friends walked along Sucre Avenue, a car stopped abruptly, and Fernando Laureani Maturana jumped out of the car onto the sidewalk. Laureani was acquainted with Claudio because both had been cadets at the military academy. Seventeen survivors of the concentration camp that operated at Villa Grimaldi testified before Judge Alejandro Solis how Jaime Robotham was brought there bleeding from a wound to his head that was inflicted at the moment of his arrest.

As previously noted, Juan Carlos Perelman had been arrested together with his girlfriend Gladys Diaz on February 20, 1975, and both were brought to

Villa Grimaldi. A week later, they were placed in a line of prisoners who were about get into a vehicle. Gladys was taken from the line while the last image she had of Juan Carlos was of him entering the vehicle.

Family members of the Chileans had the horrific experience of having to travel to Argentina to view the corpses. In the case of Luis Guendelman, his mother, Sara Wisniak, and wife, Francisca Hurtado, traveled to the morgue of Pilar, in Buenos Aires province, carrying X-rays of Luis's hip. Luis had a metal plate implanted in his hip when he was ten. Neither of the bodies the authorities showed them had a metal plate inserted in their bones. The dental X-rays likewise did not match the characteristics of the teeth of the body they viewed in Pilar.

"The situation was completely absurd," states Alejandro Guendelman, a cousin of Luis's.

> The corpses were so scorched that you couldn't even count the fingers on their hands. Yet amid the remains of burnt clothing they found plasticized identification cards intact. These were little green plastic books, issued by the Identification Bureau, printed by the corresponding governmental agency. In those years identification cards were handwritten, and this one was too. However, the photo of Luis was the one used when he received his first identification card, when he was ten years of age. Moreover, the surname was spelled with a *W* instead of a *G*. It was as if someone handed Lopez Rega or Arancibia Clavel a blank identity card, and he phoned to ask, how do you spell that? And he wrote a *W*. Do you think the Chilean Identification Bureau would make that kind of mistake and put a *W* instead of a *G*?[63]

The maneuver was so crass that merely on sight it betrayed itself as a fraud.

In February 1975, detectives had gone to the Robotham home in Santiago, requesting a photograph of Jaime. Four months later, the same photo appeared glued to an identification card with Jaime's name found next to one of the bodies. Moreover, as in Guendelman's case, the last name was misspelled, Robostam.

In early July, the UN work group had arrived in Peru and was awaiting approval from the military junta to enter Chile. As a way to pressure Chile, the delegation stationed itself in the neighboring country. Finally, on July 8, the Foreign Relations Ministry conveyed its reply to the UN Group. "The situation in Chile was at its worst moment, and the work group was in Peru. We were happy this group was going to visit," says Roberto Garretón. "Chile's response was unreal. In light of the danger to the nation, states Pinochet, entry is prohibited. And since it will not be allowed to enter, he says the UN work group should dissolve! There they came up with the idea of the list of 119."

On July 18, for the first and last time, newsstands in Buenos Aires carried a new magazine called *Revista Lea* that featured the headline "Sixty Chilean Extremists Have Been Eliminated in the Last Three Months by Their Own Comrades in Arms" and that printed a list of sixty Chileans alleged to have been killed by their own in Argentina. On July 24, for the first time since ceasing publication in 1923, an edition of the newspaper *O día de Curitiba* appeared in Brazil featuring a list of another fifty-nine names of "Chilean extremists" who allegedly died in confrontations with police in Salta, Argentina. The total number of names from both single-issue publications, whose news was widely disseminated by Chilean media, was 119.

On May 28, the family members of many disappeared persons had filed a collective habeas corpus petition before the Santiago Court of Appeals, and on July 8, they filed it with the Supreme Court. Now the Chilean press pointed to the roster of names published by the press in an effort to allege they had never been arrested. Consequently, the habeas corpus was denied.

In the Puchuncaví detention camp, political prisoners recognized the names of people who had been held with them at Villa Grimaldi, Cuatro Alamos, and other secret prisons. Their indignation on realizing that the dictatorship was killing their comrades surmounted their fear, prompting ninety of them to undertake a hunger strike.

"A great number of humans rights violations cases in Chile carry a message, a message of state terrorism. Generally, the message is 'this is the way we treat enemies,' in other words, with great cruelty," notes Juan Guzmán Tapia, a retired Santiago Court of Appeals judge who investigated and brought Augusto Pinochet to trial in 2000. In all likelihood, the message of Operation Colombo and its prelude also was addressed to Chilean opponents of the Pinochet regime residing in Argentina, such as Luis Concha. At seventy-nine years of age, Concha, who still lives in Argentina, said, "We knew that if we were nabbed here in Argentina, we would have a bad time." Guzmán Tapia underscores that "the second message is an order to the army and all the armed forces concerning how to deal with enemies: no compassion and no mercy. I don't think it is a coincidence that this disinformation maneuver began with Jewish names."[64]

In September 2004, Guzmán Tapia indicted sixteen former members of the DINA for Operation Colombo. In November 2005, Judge Victor Montiglio indicted Augusto Pinochet for his role in Operation Colombo, and in May 2008, he indicted ninety-eight DINA leaders and former agents for the abductions and forced disappearances of sixty victims of Operation Colombo. All had been abducted and held in various clandestine detention centers in Chile. The judge proved that none of the 119 missing could have been in Argentina at the time they were purported to have died. He also established the participation of the DINA agents who had drawn up the lists of names and falsified identification cards.

Pinochet, emphatically and angrily, charged accusers with defamation when they said the military regime had killed these people. Yet, according to Guzmán, the Operation Colombo case was the easiest of all to prove.

David Silberman, Luis Guendelman, Juan Carlos Perelman, and Jaime Robotham had Jewish-sounding last names, and they were selected for the hoax in order to derail the truth. Yet the ruse backfired: the usurpation of their identities unmasked a colossal lie, and justice prevailed.

5

Rescuers and Bystanders

In his book *Camisa Limpia*, the Chilean writer Guillermo Blanco described what he imagined to be the real-life experience of six-year-old Francisco Maldonado da Silva in 1601, after the Inquisition in San Miguel de Tucumán, Argentina, arrested his father, Diego Núñez da Silva, accusing him of being a secret Jew.

> San Miguel abruptly became alien to us. I discovered, for example, that when any of us approached someone, the neighbors suddenly had a very urgent need to do something else, always somewhere else. Or our "good morning" became inaudible to them. . . . Occasionally, I felt a gaze upon my skin, but if I turned my face to see from where or from whom, I encountered a fleeting glance. But before they looked away, I perceived fear in their eyes.[1]

Twenty years later, the physician Maldonado da Silva would be denounced by his own sister and arrested in southern Chile, in the city of Concepción, for "keeping the law of Moses" and transported to the Inquisition's secret prisons in Lima. He endured twelve years in prison, never denying or relinquishing his faith. On January 23, 1639, he and eleven other Jews were led to Lima's Plaza Mayor to be burned at the stake in the largest, as well as the last, auto-da-fé held by the Inquisition in Latin America.

Authoritarian regimes have long deployed the strategy of instilling fear of contagion and stigmatization by association in the masses as a means of controlling them. It was employed effectively by the Inquisition and five centuries later by the Nazis as well. As of September 11, 1973, many Chileans experienced a similar feeling of marginalization and isolation when a family member was arrested.

When the days of her husband Gunter Seelmann's imprisonment on Quiri-quina Island turned into weeks and then months, Hanni Grunpeter felt increasingly alone. While she took charge of their three children and undertook countless efforts to obtain Gunter's release, the people who came forth to support her could be counted on the fingers of one single hand. Even though at the time of his arrest, he was president of the Jewish community of Concepción, members of that community, Hanni recounts,

> with few exceptions, never asked me about him. They acted as if Gunter were vacationing somewhere. People would cross the street opportunely to avoid having to greet me. They acted as if nothing had happened. . . . The reaction within the Jewish community was no different than that of society as a whole. My youngest child, David, played with the next-door neighbor's granddaughter. We enjoyed good neighborly relations. "You can borrow some salt." "I can lend you the ladder." And from one day to the next, they stopped talking to me. She forbade the little girl from playing with David [and] spread the rumor throughout the neighborhood, starting at the beauty parlor that at night—the walls were quite thin—I listened to Radio Moscow and that I was a spy.[2]

In northern Chile, the Caro family had the same experience after Samuel Caro's arrest in October 1973 and subsequent two-months' imprisonment. He too felt abandoned by his old friends of the Jewish community. He was highly respected in La Serena as a man with a deep social commitment. His membership in the Lions Club and his election as the organization's president on several different occasions were signs of his standing in the community, as in a provincial city like La Serena, the Lions Club was an influential institution.

His daughter Sara still remembers his loneliness. "After the military coup, my father was left on his own. The only Jewish community leader who went to visit him was Isaac Bitran. Not long ago, however, I learned that another gentleman, who was Jewish community president at the time, collected money to pay the bond. But no one came to our house to visit us while he was in prison. Total indifference. Where were all his lovely friends?"[3] A couple of months later, Samuel came home from prison, but he continued to feel a great sorrow that resulted not only from the privations he suffered in prison and the murder of his cellmates but also from a sense of having been abandoned by people who had been his closest friends.

The isolation Hanni and Samuel experienced can perhaps be attributed to the nervousness generated by an environment in which the military junta had outlawed the Popular Unity's political parties and their supporters. The fact that Hanni had been a Socialist Party city councilperson, that Gunter was a well-known Socialist Party leader in the Biobío Region, and that Samuel, although he did not belong to any political party, was a close associate of Communist Party congressman Cipriano Pontigo, who represented La Serena and a business consultant for the regional governor, may have been factors in their ostracization.

Yet even Perla and her husband, Elías Aron, who had applauded the coup, and were widely known and respected by the Jewish establishment, had the same experience. When their daughter Diana was arrested in November 1974, no Jewish institution or members of any such institution offered support, made inquiries on her behalf, or offered a word of consolation: "Everyone kept silent. No one said a word. I can't remember anyone saying 'Perla, I'm with you.' People talked just like I am telling you: 'They took the Arons' daughter,' but as far as doing something, asking about her, at least no one ever mentioned having done so. I always look for a reason for everything. The community didn't want to oppose the regime, because after all, there were another fifteen thousand Jews. And the girl was Jewish. So, they did nothing, no one would do a thing."[4]

Marcos Svigilsky, Perla's father, had been vice president of the Círculo Israelita synagogue, and Elías had been a board member of that synagogue before he and Perla immigrated to Israel. The couple spoke with Angel Kreiman, who as rabbi of that synagogue had seen three generations of the family grow into adulthood. The rabbi expressed concern and promised to do all he could to locate Diana and take her out of the country. But a week later, we received a letter from him: 'The community prohibits me from getting involved in this matter.' You know, I understand how they felt. They were afraid. Maybe I would have reacted the same way."

When asked whether the Instituto Hebreo, where Diana and her siblings went to primary and secondary school and her father had been a board member, tried to locate her or supported the family, Perla replies, "I can't recall anyone moving a finger at all or anyone calling me on the phone. The community had marginalized us because one of our children had openly declared herself against Pinochet. It was like the time of the Nazis. If a brother of yours was in a concentration camp, you would not even say he was your brother. Understand? Exactly the same."

Hanni agrees.

Yes, people were afraid. The element of fear was something we recognized when we were in exile in Germany. People told us how afraid they had been to help, even though they were not fascists. They were afraid something would happen to them. Afraid of being denounced. And some thought, "Maybe they did something; that's why this is happening to them now. Better not to get involved." The attitude among Aryans in Nazi Germany was like that, not wanting to know very much.

Sara Caro recalls being upset about the lack of support from their community after her father's arrest in La Serena but also notes that eventually she came to understand the difficulty of the community's position.

> When I was younger, I was greatly disappointed at what I viewed as a betrayal against my father. Now that I'm an adult, I try to put myself in their shoes, and the fear they experienced in those years. At the time, I called them cowards for not coming to see us. Today I understand that fear was immense. Their relatives, as Jews, had experienced persecution; this made them relive that experience. I believe that in their memory they must have been reliving many things. It was very powerful. I no longer bear any resentment. I entered into another state of mind.[5]

Gladys Díaz thought the Jewish community would be able to save her boyfriend, Juan Carlos Perelman, from disappearance at Villa Grimaldi, where both were being held. When her captors ended her solitary confinement, after three months at Villa Grimaldi, Juan Carlos's father, Simon Perelman, came to visit her. She had thought the fact that Juan Carlos was Jewish would readily persuade the Jewish community to come to his aid. However, she says, his father

> did not find support in the Jewish community. It greatly disappointed him. He even went to talk to a Jewish judge of the court of appeals. The judge told him: "Forget about that matter, because nothing can be done. And I believe your son left the country." Simon insisted that the information had come from a woman who had been held with Juan Carlos at Villa Grimaldi. The judge replied: "That's your truth. There is another truth; that of the commander of the armed forces, General Pinochet. He says there's no torture here and the disappeared people are an invention, and I'll stay with his truth." Simon said to me: "He couldn't care less that we are Jewish."[6]

In 1948, Simon, an architect, and his wife, Elisa Ide, had sheltered Pablo Neruda in their home when the poet was persecuted by the Chilean government for his membership in the Communist Party. As a young boy, Juan Carlos played with Neruda, whom he already knew from the literary get-togethers his parents hosted. Never was he told why Neruda was living with them; he thought the poet was simply spending some time with them. Neruda found the protection he needed, but twenty-five years later, as an adult, Juan Carlos did not.

Fear explains many things such as passivity and complicity. However, some people manage to overcome their fear and do not remain indifferent or passive regarding another's suffering. Héctor Shalom, director of the Anne Frank Foundation of Argentina, puts this dilemma in context:

> If Anne Frank lived two years in hiding, it is because she had protectors. To understand the phenomenon of the Shoah, four roles must be considered: the victims, the perpetrators, the protectors, and the bystanders. The fourth role is very important because Nazism employed a strategy geared to achieve adherence and passivity. For us, working with the concept of protectors is key. Who takes responsibility for another? Not a hero but someone whose life ethically incorporates responsibility for others. We can see that Miep Gies and the other protectors in Anne Frank's story defended others, as did those who sought to defend victims of human rights violations in Argentina. A protector is someone who takes responsibility for the other.[7]

A Chilean Partisan

The night of July 16, 1942, was the last one Betty Friedman slept in her own bed in Paris.[8] The panic that overcame her in the daytime and compelled her to hold her mother's hand tightly in the street regularly prevented her from sleeping peacefully. Next to Betty, her little brother Marcel often whimpered in his sleep, as he had done ever since their father had been taken away. That night, however, he slept soundly, as if his body sensed he would soon need the rest. When the first rays of light began lighting up the bedroom, boots echoed over the cobblestones down below. Betty could hear a voice speaking through a megaphone ordering all Jews to assemble on the street: "All Jews out! Just one blanket, one sweater, and two shirts per person. Nothing else! Quickly!"

Beginning at 4 a.m. on July 16 and continuing through the next day, 13,152 Jews, including 5,802 women and 4,051 children, according to police records, were arrested in a massive roundup ordered by Nazi occupation forces in which the Paris police wholly collaborated. The two initial destinations of the thousands of detainees were the D'Hiver Velodrome and the Drancy detention camp, both transit places en route to Auschwitz.

Betty, Marcel, and their mother were among the seventy-five hundred people brought to the Velodrome. The glass roof, painted dark blue to avoid attracting bomber planes, increased the temperature inside the stadium. The stadium bathrooms had been closed because their windows might offer an escape route, and there was but a single faucet. In this unsanitary setting, many detainees became ill. Marcel broke out in scabies, and his mother fell sick with dysentery. Both were taken to Rothschild Hospital, and Betty went with them.

The children were placed in the contagious disease ward while their mother was taken to another section of the hospital. The children were allowed to visit their mother, but one day they found her bed empty. Their mother had recovered her health; therefore, she had been transferred to Drancy and from there to Auschwitz. Rothschild Hospital was not an ordinary medical facility. Some of the wards had been cordoned off with barbed wire and converted into detention camps. Patients in these barbed wire hospital wards faced a malignancy much worse than any fever. At any moment they might be sent to a concentration camp.

At this Jewish medical center, priests, doctors, and other hospital staff had formed a network that coordinated with people outside to hide and rescue as many Jews as possible. They obtained false identification documents to create a new identity for persecuted people and found places for them to hide. Two hospital social workers, María Edwards and Claire Heymann, rescued Betty and Marcel and sent them to the town of Château du Moulinet, where families were hiding at least twenty children in their homes. They also cared for the children after the German defeat and the Allied forces liberation.

Betty always would remember "aunts" María and Claire. Aunt María was Chilean María Edwards, youngest daughter of Agustin Edwards Ross, Senate president in 1948 and owner of the *El Mercurio* newspaper. María had lived in Paris since the 1920s, when her husband had been appointed to a diplomatic post at the consulate. During the German occupation of Paris, she worked as volunteer nurse and was a frequent collaborator with the French resistance. In 1944, French police apprehended her and tortured her with what is known as *bain glacée*, a method that consisted of submerging the prisoner's head in freezing cold water until he or she nearly drowned. Intervention by the Spanish ambassador secured her freedom, and María returned to Chile after the war.

On October 27, 2005, Yad Vashem, the Israeli memorial to Holocaust martyrs and heroes, posthumously awarded María (December 11, 1893–June 8, 1972) the status of Righteous among the Nations. María was the first Chilean and the second Latin American honored with this distinction conferred to non-Jewish persons who risked or gave their lives to save thousands of Jews marked for extermination by the Nazis.[9]

RIGHTEOUS AMONG THE NATIONS

The Righteous among the Nations are individuals like María Edwards who were driven by "human instinct, the voice of conscience, and belief in the value of human life to risk their own lives and those of their families on behalf of another who was in mortal danger" from Nazi persecution.[10] The designation of Righteous among the Nations underscores the extraordinary spirit of solidarity that leads some people to selflessly place themselves at great risk in order to save the life of a stranger to whom they are connected only by virtue of the fact that he or she is a human being.

The Yad Vashem Museum was founded in Israel in 1953 as the international documentation and education center on the Holocaust. It honors not only the victims but also those people who risked everything to save a life, the few people who "in a world of total moral collapse . . . mustered extraordinary courage to uphold human values. These were the Righteous among the Nations."[11]

Many people dared to save a single person persecuted by the Nazis, providing food or indicating where to find help. Others sheltered Jews for a night but warning that they would have to leave the next morning. Few, however, Yad Vashem found, "assumed the entire responsibility for the survival of a Jew or groups of persecuted people. It is these mostly who qualify for the title of the Righteous among the Nations." The Righteous among the Nations hid Jews in their own houses or other properties they owned for a prolonged period of time; they provided false identity documents and helped them escape.

By January 2009, Yad Vashem had recognized 22,765 individuals from forty-four countries as Righteous among the Nations. One was the Chilean María Edwards. The origins of the concept can be traced to the biblical precept that "lo tujal l'hitaleim" (you shall not remain indifferent) outlined in Deuteronomy 22:1 and 3: "If you see your fellow's ox or sheep gone astray, do not ignore it; you must take it back to your fellow. . . . You shall do the same with his ass; you shall do the same with his garment and so too shall you do with anything that your fellow loses and you find: you must not remain indifferent."[12] The next verse employs the same expression, "lo tujal l'hitaleim," in regard to the ass or ox that has fallen on the road: "Do not ignore it; you must help raise it."

While the mandate here is motivated by the importance assigned to private property (in both ancient and many contemporary civilizations, property has had greater value than human life), another biblical verse unequivocally emphasizes that one must not remain indifferent when your neighbor's life is in peril. As Elie Wiesel, writer and survivor of the Auschwitz concentration camp, noted when he addressed the Summit for the Emergency in Darfour in July 2004: "One of the main tenets of my life has been 'Do not stand by idly while your neighbor's blood is shed; do not abandon him when he is in danger' (Leviticus 19:16)."[13] Who counts as a "neighbor," and whether the idea of a neighbor includes non-Jews, has been the subject of debate and controversy. Wiesel indicates that the Hebrew word employed in this verse is not "aheeha," which means "another Jew," but rather "reeha," which is properly translated as "neighbor," or any human being of any cultural identity, whose life is in peril.[14]

The underlying theological principle is that of *pikuaj nefesh*, which demands suspension of all other biblical laws when it comes to saving a human life, whether Jewish or Gentile. The Jewish tradition teaches that destroying a human life is the equivalent of destroying the world. On the other hand, saving a life is like saving the world, given that we are all descendants from the first human beings created on earth.

Active resistance, despite the danger such resistance poses to a person's own life, contrasts with the passivity that results from fear, the convenience of ignoring what is happening, or affinity with the persecutors, which is ultimately an accomplice to terror and persecution. Such commitment to protecting human lives is activated by individuals or members of a network, motivated by deep ethical or religious values, or undertaken as a clear political position of resistance. The same dichotomy of passivity-complicity may be observed in institutions and countries.

The danger was real and latent. Adhering to the concept of collective blame, the Germans took brutal reprisal not only against individuals who dared help a Jew but also against the protector's family. Moreover, they maintained meticulous records of Jews and punished entire families if a member escaped from the ghetto.[15]

When Primo Levi was deported to Auschwitz, in February 1944, he was assigned as helper to two Italian bricklayers who had been hired for a construction job at the concentration camp. Lorenzo Perrone, one of the bricklayers, began bringing Levi a can of soup he stole each night from the kitchen leftovers. Levi comments that the five hundred additional calories Perrone supplied him every day and other gestures, all of which meant Perrone taking great risks over the course of the six months he was at the camp, were fundamental to his ability to survive until the camp's liberation in January 1944. In his book *If This Is a Man*, Levi notes that the gesture of giving him hot soup nurtured him way beyond the vital calories it contained: "I believe that it was really due to Lorenzo that I am alive today; and not so much for his material aid, as for his having constantly reminded me by his presence . . . that there still existed a just world outside our own, something and someone still pure and whole . . . for which it was worth surviving."[16]

THE RIGHTEOUS AMONG CHILEANS

During the Chilean dictatorship, too, refuge, false identity papers, and safe passage out of the country constituted the most pressing needs for persecuted persons. Many people made small gestures or undertook great actions to protect lives during the years of terror under the military regime.

In every institution that arose to protect lives during the dictatorship, the staff included Jews. Rabbi Angel Kreiman was a member of the Propeace Committee; Dora Guralnik was director of the Vicariate of Solidarity's medical assistance program; Washington Domb and Lorelei Friedmann were members of the Vicariate's legal department; psychologist Judith Horowitz worked at the Fundación de Ayuda Social de las Iglesias Cristianas (FASIC, Christian Churches Social Assistance Foundation); psychiatrist Gunter Seelmann worked at the Fundación de Protección a la Infancia Dañada por los Estados de Emergencia (Fundación PIDEE, Program for Children Injured by States of Emergency); and Eliana Bronfman worked with the United Nations High Commissioner for Refugees (UNHCR).

After the murder of her husband in 1984, Kathy Castro, who was an enthusiastic participant in Hashomer Hatzair in the mid-1970s, also was at risk. "There was a Jewish family, a man who was a good friend of Luis Guendelman, who helped and hid me a long time. They took care of me emotionally, financially, and in every way. They were very important for me. They extended their solidarity to me because they were friends of my older brothers. They were lovely people. They not only helped me but many other people as well."[17] Kathy prefers not to identify her protectors without their permission.

Remembering the Jewish household that protected her also stirs emotions for the journalist Gladys Díaz. During the initial weeks after the coup, several foreign correspondents brought Gladys, sought by agents of the dictatorship, to the homes of diplomats of their respective nationalities.

> One time I stayed with a foreign Jewish family associated with an embassy; I believe they were Dutch. I will never forget them. They were very concerned about feeding me well. They constantly gave me food. I was wearing a blouse with a large pocket. In my pocket they placed a large sum of money. . . . An aunt of theirs had been killed in the Holocaust. Their parents were survivors. I stayed in that house a week in September 1973. In other houses I usually stayed no more than twenty-four hours; in that house I stayed the longest. I never found out their names. And they did not know mine. But I know they were Jews.[18]

Protectors and the protected generally did not know each other's identity. Today, when the fear of those years has subsided, it is possible to give those protectors the recognition they deserve. Some were Jews who did not remain indifferent and put their lives on the line to save others.

A Family Network

A network consisting of a daughter, father, grandmother, and other members of the Friedmann Maskivoinic family protected many persecuted people. On the maternal side of Sonja Friedmann's family, the Maskivoinics came from a village near Odessa. Her great-grandfather was the first to arrive in Chile, in the early twentieth century, after completing many years of mandatory military service. Once he arrived, he sent his wife two tickets, but she was nursing their newborn baby and was unable to travel. In her stead, she sent their two other children, her eleven-year-old daughter and her fifteen-year-old son. In 1908, the children, who had never been outside their village, traversed the Atlantic on their own. In Argentina, they discovered that their tickets ended in Mendoza on the Argentine side of the Andes, instead of the Chilean port city of Valparaíso, where their father was waiting for them.

"Then, a gesture of solidarity occurred," recounts Sonja. "A man who happened to be passing by heard them talking in Yiddish, probably crying, and he bought them the tickets. That is the story about how *bubbeh* traveled by train, and was one of the first Jews in Valparaíso."[19] That eleven-year-old girl who came to Chile alone with her brother thanks to the concern of a stranger was Elisa Basis, Sonja's maternal grandmother. Sonja recalls:

> She was a lovely elderly lady of eighty. She hid many people. She told the neighbors that the lodgers in her apartment near Bustamante Park were her nephews or grandchildren. Everyone adored her. My grandmother lived alone, and since we often visited her, no one found it unusual that once in a while someone else was at her house. One of them was Juan Carlos Villar, my secretary's son, who was arrested and tortured at seventeen years of age. When he got out, he went walking to his house only to discover that no one was there. He was so skinny and filthy that when he rang the neighbor's bell, they didn't recognize him. We brought him to our grandmother's house. On the average, people stayed with her a few weeks. She made sure they ate. She regarded them as children. At night, she would give them candy, "for a sweeter life," she would say.

Furthermore, Sonja's paternal grandfather, José Aron Friedmann Cohen, a cantor (Jewish liturgical singer), was known in Bessarabia as a generous individual who evinced a great sense of solidarity.[20] People called him *der ziganer*, a nickname meaning "the gypsy," in reference to his trade as traveling salesman, one of few professions permitted to Jews. It is likely that the nickname also stemmed from his frequent treks to help other Jews obtain passports and accompany them to the border to leave Romania. José Aron Friedmann bequeathed this vocation for solidarity to his children and grandchildren, who were born in a distant continent. In the first years of the military dictatorship, his son Marcos Luis Friedmann (Sonja's father) was also a member of this family rescue network.

Marcos, who lived in Valparaíso, brought women to Santiago using Sonja's identification card. Father and daughter both helped them obtain asylum in embassies. Sonja describes what they did.

> Women would come to my house with their hair dyed and the same style of glasses I wore. One, Olga Morris, was with us two months. We had a sewing machine in the loft, and whenever someone we didn't trust came to the house, she would be up there sewing. In 1974, we were able to get her into the German Embassy, then on Presidente Errázuriz Street. Police permanently guarded the perimeters. The first time we went with her, without a suitcase but carrying a large purse, it did not work. We returned another time and organized a maneuver involving many people. A street vendor, right outside the embassy, spilled a basket of oranges. One or two policemen began helping him gather up the oranges. Precisely at that moment, a woman passed by walking two dogs on a leash. The mother of one of my sisters-in-law approached the police, asking about an address. It all happened at the same time. The police were distracted, and Olga was able to enter the embassy grounds.

When Sonja is asked what motivated her to risk her own safety for others, she replies, "I never thought about the risk. I only thought that I had to help."

Hajnasat orjim

At more than eighty years of age, Frida Sharim has not lost the grace and poise of the ballerina who in the late 1940s was the only Jewish member of the University of Chile School of Dance. Frida has a crystal-clear memory of the Shabbat candles her grandmother lit on Friday evenings. "I loved those candles! It was such a beautiful thing to behold, how the flame climbed higher and higher. My grandparents Elías Sharim and Fortuna Paz always invited guests— sometimes gentlemen who happened to be traveling in Latin America—to share the ample Shabbat meals." Also they would kill chickens and give them to poor Jewish families. "I noticed those things," she says.[21]

Frida felt pure exhilaration during Allende's presidential campaign. She participated in marches and sold Popular Unity coalition newspapers. She was enchanted by the songs associated with those exciting days. Her day job was as secretary to the director of the Facultad Latinoamericana de Ciencias Sociales (FLASCO, Latin American Faculty of the Social Sciences) in Santiago, and three nights a week she worked at Peña de los Parra, the music coffeehouse founded by singer Violeta Parra's son and daughter.

In early September 1973, she was preparing to leave FLACSO to accept a position of great responsibility as secretary to President Allende. Her seven-year-old daughter, Karina, begged her not to take the job. "You're going to get killed, Mama!" she cried. She was on the verge of moving to the office in La Moneda when the coup took place. Foreign students studying at FLACSO were detained and several were killed. Her first work of solidarity consisted in taking testimony at FLACSO from Argentine and Colombian prisoners who had been tortured.

In 1974, her nephew David, her sister Sara's son, was arrested by the DINA. When he was transferred to Tres Alamos, his parents, his aunts and uncles, and his grandmother took turns each Friday to wait in line outside the prison to bring him cake, baked chicken, and other things to eat.

In those same years, Frida revived her grandparents' custom of showing generosity toward strangers on Shabbat. That tradition of hospitality, known as *hachnasat orjim*, had been a common practice among Jewish communities of Europe. Since Jewish villages might be geographically distant from each other, travelers and traveling salesmen could not always reach their home before sunset on Friday afternoon, after which, in traditional Jewish households, working was prohibited for the next twenty-four hours. It was a common custom for families to receive travelers in their homes on Shabbat. The Talmud quotes some rabbis who regard offering hospitality to the stranger as more important than praying on Shabbat. The seeds of this tradition were sowed in Frida, and she transformed it into an imperative to save lives. From 1973 to 1978, Frida sheltered many people in the house she shared with her mother and daughter on a short, dead-end street in well-to-do Providencia.

Jorge Müller and Carmen Bueno were two of those people who spent a night—their last in freedom—in Frida's house. The evening of November 28, 1974, was the premiere of Jorge and Carmen's film *A la sombra del sol* at a Las Condes movie theater. Following the ceremony, she remembers that "Carmen came up to me and asked, 'Frida, may we sleep at your house tonight?' I did not ask her anything, not a word. I just told her yes." After the premiere, someone brought them to Frida's house.

> They were brought to my little house that was quite small but had a spare room. Jorge was so sweet with my daughter Karina. He talked to her. He was a love. The next day, my brother Lalo insisted, "Don't go." Carmen insisted, "No, I'm going with Jorge. Jorge has to go to Chile Films today." "Stay one day more; please stay," Lalo implored. They would not listen. They left. And they were

never seen again. That day they were arrested. Before leaving my house, Jorge said, "My situation is clear to me: if they catch me and I talk, they will kill me. And if I don't talk, they will still kill me. So I won't say a word." And he did not say a thing about where he had been. Otherwise I would have been arrested too.

Frida goes on to describe how, also in 1974, she helped people enter embassies so they could seek asylum.

I would go into the embassies with them. At the Honduran Embassy on Ricardo Lyon Street, I pushed people over the fence. I also went to the Embassy of Venezuela once. And I helped several people enter and get asylum in the German Embassy, on the eighth floor of the building facing the Municipal Theater. There I would go with a friend who was a doctor. I'd phone him and say "Hey, we have to get somebody in." "Okay, let's go," he would reply.

   It's not that I looked for people to help. They just came my way. I'd bring them to the entrance and then leave as fast as possible. Once there was a dentist who was with the MIR. Because his father was a police general, he allowed himself the luxury of helping people too, until the DINA began looking for him. The first thing he did was go to FLACSO and crying, he said, "Help me Frida!" because he was sure they were about to kill him. Well, we helped him too.

To the same question—what drove her to act?—Frida replies, simply and unwavering, "I just had to do it. You don't think twice about it."

Every Youngster Reminded Them of Jorge

From childhood, Rodolfo Müller had always been diligent and studious. On the ship crossing the Atlantic, he studied Spanish with books he found on board, and by the time they docked at the port of Valparaíso, on January 12, 1937, he had a good command of the language. Once settled in Santiago with his parents, Adolfo and Lotte Müller, and brothers, he found the Chilean public school quite basic and easy. When he turned fifteen, he left school, preferring to learn a trade. In a small mechanic shop in downtown Santiago, on Santo Domingo Street between Morandé and Bandera streets, the German technician Otto Meiser taught him how to work a lathe. They built Santiago's first observatory on Gran Avenida, adjacent to land belonging to the air force, and at night they observed the stars. With the boom of talking movies, around 1940, the shop used French machinery to manufacture sound equipment and installed this equipment in two hundred movie theaters throughout Chile, many in small towns. As an adult, he would tell his two children that one of the happiest moments of his life was the time he was a young apprentice because "I learned everything." With that vocational base, he opened a Citroen repair garage, with which he supported the family.

Irma Silva, Rodolfo's wife, created a warm family atmosphere. The household she managed was generous and open, and they enjoyed bounteous afternoon teas and Sunday lunches with family and friends. She was efficient and detail oriented, characteristics discernible in her household management as well as in her meticulous paintings.

On November 29, 1974, Rodolfo's and Irma's lives changed forever. That morning, their son, Jorge, and his girlfriend, Carmen Bueno, left Frida Sharim's house. Jorge had told his mother that he and Carmen would be stopping by the house to pick up material for Chile Films. As they walked along Los Leones Street near the corner of Bilbao Avenue, a squadron of heavily armed men in civilian clothes arrested them. Their parents would keep waiting for them the rest of their lives.

As of that moment, Rodolfo and Irma began directing their talents outward, to the search for their son. They reported the arrest to the Propeace Committee—the first of countless steps they took to locate the whereabouts and ascertain the fate of Jorge and Carmen that radically changed their daily routine. The couple opened to the world. They became a team of two, each strengthening and encouraging the other to continue. According to their

Irma Silva and Rodolfo Müller in El Quisco, 1962 (Müller family)

grandson Carlos Arriagada, "They experienced a conversion, they became activists in processes that helped shape the fight against the dictatorship."[22]

At the height of their panic, neither the Müller nor the Silva extended families were there for them. Rodolfo, with a tone of bitterness in his voice, notes that his family, who fled from Northeim in 1937, "did not do a thing for Jorge. Not my parents or my brothers. Nothing."[23]

Rodolfo's and Irma's efforts not only focused on the search for Jorge. In their new house, purchased a few months before Jorge's disappearance, they gave refuge to other people, so that what happened to their son would not happen to them. "Jorge always hoped that someday we would have a house with a garden, where he could sit on a bench underneath a tree and read," recalls his father.[24] The house's beautiful garden features a magnificent leafy tree underneath which is a bench, just as Jorge dreamed of. His mother prepared a room for her son, with his belongings, clothes, and books waiting for him. Many people, especially during the years 1975 and 1976, were welcomed into this house in middle-class Ñuñoa. Rodolfo remembers that

> at times we had one or two people here who needed a place to stay before leaving the country or going elsewhere. It was not wise for them to stay a long time because security agents might follow their tracks. They might even be found here. They had to move from one house to another quickly. Once a couple with a child stayed at our [beach] house in El Quisco. Since few people go to the beach in the winter, two strangers might attract attention. They had to be very careful. Thank God we never encountered a major problem. Sometimes we were asked to bring food to people who lived in Lo Hermida before curfew. Since I had a car, we offered to go. We became very familiar with Lo Hermida in those days.[25]

Carlos Arriagada, born in 1973, the first of Jorge's sister's three children, has gradually learned about the people who stayed at his grandparents' house in Santiago and at the summer house. "The El Quisco house had a separate room and bathroom that one could only enter from the outside. I was surprised to see strangers staying in that room. We played with their children and shared with them, but when we had to return to Santiago, they stayed there. I didn't understand why they stayed. Many years later I found out that those people were in hiding there." He is certain that at least up until 1983 other "strangers" spent a night, a couple of days, or sometimes more at his grandparents' house.[26]

In addition to opening their home and their hearts to shelter people, they continued their daily efforts to find out where Jorge was. They didn't know what happened to the detainees. Were they at some police station? At a military base? Or maybe at the civil police building? Like all relatives facing the same situation, they thought that in time Jorge and Carmen would be released, like any prisoner. Rodolfo and Irma certainly believed that later on there would be a trial, and they would be set free. At the German Embassy, they obtained a visa for Jorge in the hope that as soon as he reappeared they would fly him to his father's native land. They also left clothing, cakes, soap, and personal hygiene items at Tres and Cuatro Alamos detention facilities, where Jorge and Carmen were rumored to be held.

Every place they went, they met other people on the same pilgrimage. They ended up joining the new organization of family members of disappeared people, and later its offshoot of relatives of people whose names appeared on the Operation Colombo list of 119. Irma represented Carmen, who was included in the Operation Colombo list, even though it did not include Jorge.

Often, members met in Irma and Rodolfo's house, despite the distance from the Vicariate of Solidarity where the association was housed. The spacious living room seemed small with all the people, many sitting on the floor. All heartily enjoyed the copious afternoon tea Irma prepared for them. Afterward they addressed the issues on the agenda. When the meetings ran late, the people would leave the house in small groups as a security measure to avoid attracting attention: first, three or four people, then another three or four, walking together to take the bus on Irarrazaval Avenue. "They were such a united couple," recalls María Pilquín, a friend and organization member from those years.[27] "They always arrived together for the organization's assemblies. Some husbands ended up separating because the wife devoted all her time to the search and somewhat abandoned things at home. We would go to the association and wouldn't be home until nighttime. Irma was always very systematic. She participated but always set an hour for when she would return home."

Another facet of Irma's meticulous nature is evident in her *arpilleras*, patchwork art that portrays Chile's reality, expressing desolation but also hope, and that has been exhibited around the world. Her *arpilleras* are particularly detailed and have special touches. Irma thought about the subject she wished to portray and designed each *arpillera* before embroidering the bits of cloth. She was quite demanding and did not like it when some organization members hastily completed their *arpilleras*, resulting in a sloppy product.

In 1978, Rodolfo and Irma contributed to the creation of the folk dance and music group Aydar, made up mostly of young family members of prisoners, disappeared, and executed persons. Carlos, their oldest grandchild, spent many weekends at his grandparents' house. If his parents thought he shared a quiet time at home with his grandparents, they were mistaken. In fact, by the time he was six they were already taking him to Aydar's performances and sing-alongs. Carlos remembers his grandmother teaching Chilean folk dances and singing while his German-born grandfather, wearing a thick woolen hat and socks from the large southern island of Chiloe, accompanied on accordion.

The Aydar group functioned under the auspices of Vicariate of Solidarity's eastern zone department. Various churches in eastern Santiago, such as the one on Plaza Ñuñoa, as well as a school on Macul Avenue and Rodrigo de Araya Street, lent the group facilities, the goal being to rotate locations each week so that more people could be incorporated. Aydar spawned several other folk groups in southern Santiago. The groups performed Chilean folk dances at the Vicariate's various events and tributes.

His grandparents stayed in touch with those "youngsters" who today are approaching fifty years of age. Carlos remarks,

> When my grandfather was hospitalized, many of those kids, who now have families of their own, came to see him. The nurses always remarked, "My! You sure have a lot of children, sir!" They saw this man surrounded by younger people, and they thought all were his children. On February 1, 2012, we celebrated Opi's ninetieth birthday, and many guests were those kids with their families. Somehow through that avenue my grandparents channeled the dreadful pain they endured. My grandmother always said that those youngsters reminded her a bit of her own son.

Integrity in Vulnerable Times

During the ten years before the military coup, Eliana Bronfman worked as a lawyer in the Foreign Relations Ministry. During the Popular Unity government, she worked alongside diplomats as a technical assistance director in charge of establishing scholarships and joint training programs between Chile and countries such as Sweden, England, and France. "I was raised and grew up in a democratic, republican tradition, and all of a sudden they set La Moneda on fire," she says.

Eliana returned to the ministry offices a week after the coup. "A list had been drawn up of supposedly seditious people who were forbidden from entering the building. I was not immediately forbidden from entering. From September to December, I was retained simply because treaties had been completely burned in the bombing of La Moneda. They needed to reconstruct them, and only a few of us were familiar with the content of those treaties."[28]

Eliana was obliged to go to various embassies to request copies of the treaties and agreements in order to reinstate them. "The situation was paradoxical. I spent several months working on that task, strictly guarded by security personnel. In December 1973, I got a phone call from the personnel director, who did not mince words. He told me straightaway that my good performance evaluations meant nothing because the military junta did not trust me." The official ordered Eliana to leave the Foreign Relations Ministry and gave her half an hour to gather her belongings and get out of the building. "I remember perfectly well the feeling I had of being born again. I had become just another citizen in this country, but I felt I was under surveillance with no possibility of finding another job."

It occurred to her to speak to G. J. Malik, ambassador of India for Argentina and Chile. Eliana had known Malik for many years. She knew Malik was democratic and opposed the dictatorship. Together with Ida Weinstein, Eliana's mother, Malik had founded the Society of Friends of India in Chile. She asked him for not only work but also a protective environment. The ambassador offered her a position with the embassy's Culture Department, but his budget was so limited that he told her he would have to pay her in Indian rupees. Unfazed, she accepted the job at once.

After some time, Ambassador Malik sent her as an emissary to the Swedish embassy, where she would assist Ambassador Harold Edelstam. From 1942 to 1944, Edelstam, who was in Berlin at the time, protected Jews persecuted by the Nazi regime as well as members of the resistance, earning the name Black Carnation. In 1972, Edelstam was appointed Swedish ambassador to Chile for the Popular Unity government. Edelstam is credited with having saved an estimated one thousand people during the first three months after the military coup.

The Swedish embassy was authorized to accord political asylum to Chileans who were persecuted and facing serious risk to their lives. He needed a Chilean to interview asylum applicants and evaluate their suitability for political asylum in Sweden. Eliana listened to the testimonies of men and women in very deteriorated physical and psychological condition who had been intimidated, persecuted, and tortured. "I felt useful, and I was becoming increasingly involved in human rights," she says. When Edelstam was expelled from Chile in December 1973, Eliana returned to the Embassy of India until Ambassador Malik was transferred to another diplomatic post.

In those days, Eliana became acquainted with Belela Herrera, a Uruguayan diplomat and director of the UNHCR, which was launched in Chile. In 1976, she began working as the UNHCR local assistant in a small office facing the court building. There she remained until 1985.

Eliana's acute consciousness of the critical situation that forced people to flee their country to protect their lives had its roots in her childhood. Her father, Samuel Bronfman, was about five years old when the first pogrom took place in his city of Kishinev. It was April 19, 1903, Easter Sunday, when hordes led by priests reached the Jewish neighborhood, shouting hysterically "Death to the Jews!" Samuel's family did not witness how a man who was a humble glassmaker was dragged from the hut where he had tried to hide and beaten and kicked until he died. But what happened next—three days of terror resulting in forty-seven Jews dead, ninety-two seriously injured, and seven hundred houses in shambles—became engraved in the memory of all Jews who lived in that city. Two years later, another pogrom occurred in the same city, prompting the Jews of Kishinev to search for more peaceful lands. At fifteen, Samuel and his older brother left for England, where they embarked on a ship to Buenos Aires, escorted by the British Navy. These were the months immediately before World War I, and one transatlantic vessel had already been bombed. The two brothers crossed the Andes over to Chile. Much later, Samuel married Ida Weinstein, the first member of her family born in freedom, in the town of Moisesville founded by Russian Jewish settlers in the Argentine pampa. Weinstein was a dentist and later in life became a fervent pacifist and follower of Mahatma Gandhi.

Eliana Bronfman, the eldest of two sisters, was born from this union and this story. During World War II, she went to school at Manuel de Salas, the first coed primary and high school in Chile, where the teachers were very attuned to what was happening outside the country. Eliana, already known in those years as Nana, remembers a teacher whose lessons shaped the rest of her life. "She opened our eyes to a different world, she awakened social concerns in us. One day a girl, Rose Marie Sternberg, whose family had fled Germany, joined the class. She spoke little Spanish. Her parents had been prosperous in Berlin. The teacher introduced her to the class and asked two girls—Lorelei [Friedmann] and I—to take care of her. We regarded it as an important responsibility. We became her friends. We were quite close. We became aware of what it meant to live in a strange country."

Eliana's solidarity had been nurtured from her earliest years, which may explain why she describes her ten years with the UNHCR as "the best years of my working life." Moreover, she adds, "humanitarian work and the experience of working with a person of the human qualities of Belela Herrera enabled me to understand the characteristics of a dictatorship that murdered and made people disappear with total impunity and that reigned through fear and terror." Through their work with the Vicariate of Solidarity, FASIC, and the UNHCR, she and her colleagues were able to protect people who otherwise would have faced death like so many others, enabling many to attain asylum status. Working closely with FASIC, they were also able to reunite families with people who had secured asylum and were living outside Chile.

Eliana mentioned the UNHCR's intervention in the issue of the *l* passports. As a result of international pressure, after a few years, the Pinochet regime began allowing some of the people it had expelled to return in the case of circumstances such as the death of a family member. But this largesse was a trap. Many passports had been stamped with a small letter *l*, whose meaning was not clearly understood. The UNHCR discovered that it meant "list." Someone with an *l* stamped on the passport was liable to be arrested at the airport, imprisoned, or immediately forced to leave Chile again. It was a secret list administered by the Interior Ministry, whose undersecretary at the time was Alberto Cardemil.

"We had to negotiate each case with him to get the *l* removed so the person could return to Chile for a few days for humanitarian reasons," Eliana notes. Furthermore, Cardemil consulted with the CNI as to the regime's perception of "the degree of danger the returnee represented before responding to the UNHCR. There were people whose father or mother was dying. They just wanted to see their parent a last time or be there for the funeral. Sometimes we managed to obtain permission for a person to enter for only forty-eight hours. But, other times, we couldn't even obtain that."

At a critical moment, she transitioned from the role of protector to that of victim, and her capacity as UNHCR became vital in protecting and saving her own family. On July 15, 1981, Coronel Roger Vergara, director of the Army Investigation Academy, was murdered by members of the MIR. Military forces combed the city searching for the perpetrators, taking reprisal by abducting people who had absolutely no connection to the Vergara murder.

At six that afternoon, her husband, Sanson Berlagoscky, phoned her at the UNHCR offices to let her know that the CNI had raided the rural property in Macul where the extended family lived. The house was across the street from a working-class neighborhood where their daughter held literacy classes and where Sanson's daughter from his first marriage administered vaccinations.

Eliana's daughter lived in a small house on the same spacious premises with her baby. When she arrived, Eliana says, "I encountered a Dantesque scene, with a hundred soldiers at the place. Not only had they raided our property. Along a wall where all the cars were parked, I found my children standing with their hands behind their neck. Even our cook, who was around seventy years old, was there with her hands behind her neck. A young man we hired to repair some cushions had chosen that day to come, and he, too, was arrested. The auto mechanic also was arrested. All of them were blindfolded."

More than thirty years had passed since that day, but the anxiety and indignation she felt remained, evident in her as she narrated what happened next.

I entered the house to find the place in disarray. Then I entered our bedroom and found the chest of drawers turned over and clothing strewn on the floor. When I had to go to the bathroom, a female soldier entered with me. . . . They took away several people, including the cook, still blindfolded and scared to death. They did not take me because I was from UNHCR. I shouted that I was with the UN and they could not take me away. Sanson was spared because of his crutches, and my seven-year-old boy too was left in the house. Around midnight, some of our family returned, but my daughter Franci and her partner, Benado, remained in custody quite some time. Later they cut the telephone lines. The worst part was that we had to live with those people occupying our house. We had to serve breakfast to the military commander. We had to sit at the same dining table with them. Finally, UNHCR and the embassy intervened, otherwise who knows what would have happened.

After this personal experience with repression, Eliana continued working several years more with UNHCR. Many years later, in 2003, she coauthored, with the writer Luisa Johnson, *De enterezas y vulnerabilidades*, a book of reflections from a broad range of people of her generation on how the dictatorship affected their lives.[29] The book led Eliana to dedicate herself to the transmission of the historic memory of those years to the next generations by teaching university classes and holding workshops. She died on October 18, 2013. Her life is itself an eloquent testimony of ethical integrity in vulnerable times.

A Healer with an Aching Soul

In 1971, the National Health Service sent teams of four or five young health professionals, fresh out of college, for three months into the industrial districts to solve workers' dental problems. The program, known as the Basic Health Groups, had as its director dentist Dora Guralnik, who in 1930, at eight years of age, had arrived in Chile with her family from Ukraine. They transported portable dental chairs to the factory area along Vicuña Mackenna Avenue, in south central Cerrillos, and to other places in Santiago. "There was Dora in charge of that whole crew of young dentists. Working three months, full time, they treated the dental problems of workers in those factories. It was an incredible undertaking," recalls dentist Mario Tapia.[30]

September 10, 1973, was their last day at work. The military junta's health authorities dissolved the teams. Some were expelled from the National Health Service, while others found work elsewhere.

In northern Chile, Dora's oldest son, Carlos Berger, director of Radio Loa and public relations director for the Chuquicamata mine, was arrested and imprisoned in the Calama public jail. After that, things moved quickly. Eighteen days after he entered the prison, a war council sentenced him to sixty days in prison, yet on the night of October 19, he and twenty-five others were removed from the prison and savagely killed by the Caravan of Death.

When Dora was told about her son's execution, a piercing scream erupted from deep inside her. A Midrash (rabbinical interpretation of Torah texts) describes how the matriarch Sara broke out in a similar piercing wail upon learning that Abraham almost sacrificed their son, Isaac. After letting out her scream, Sara immediately died. For Dora, whose son was murdered, after the scream came out, it settled back inside her, lodging there for years. Outwardly, she quickly pulled herself together. As soon as the Propeace Committee was created, she joined its staff, using all her strength to carry out her work as a health care professional. Subsequently, she did the same at the Vicariate of Solidarity as director of the medical center it ran in the southern zone of Santiago.

"My mother-in-law, Dora, would have worked there even if Carlos had been alive," notes Carmen Hertz. "The medical centers basically served defenseless people. By late 1976, when the concentration camps were closed, there were thousands of political prisoners in Chile. The victims' families were priority concerns. They had nowhere to go; there were no health centers they trusted."[31] In 1975, Dora organized a neighborhood clinic in Santo Cura de Arce Catholic Church on Gran Avenida as part of a Vicariate of Solidarity program to bring social and medical assistance to victims of repression.

In a small book published in tribute to Dora, Haydée López writes, "At night, threats were painted on the health center's walls, telling us that we'd better get out of there, that they would kill us. It was not a relaxing environment. Dorita had to work with a nun, a dental assistant, who didn't like us. Eventually, she overcame her mistrust."[32] In the same book, social worker Victoria Baeza describes the afternoon teas, known as *onces* in Chile, that Dora organized for people just released from the concentration camps. "Despite her own deep pain that never left her, I saw her share the happiness of all those mothers and wives of former prisoners," Victoria notes.[33]

In 1980, when lack of funding obliged the Vicariate of Solidarity to end its health outreach program, the Centro Integral de Salud (CIS, Comprehensive Health Center) was founded with Dora as its director. In the midst of the dictatorship, they replicated the Popular Unity's basic health team model. Mario Tapia had worked for five years with Dora as an enthusiastic collaborator under the wings of the Vicariate of Solidarity by the time he began working at the Comprehensive Health Center. "From 1980 to 1990, under a full-fledged dictatorship, we undertook solidarity-oriented work. We built a health system that we even extended to include health education and prevention. We had agreements with many agricultural organizations to provide medical assistance in outlying rural areas of Santiago. We brought doctors, nurses, midwives, and dentists to places where there was nothing at all, not even running water: Calera de Tango, Batuco, Paine, La Florida Alta. We provided medical assistance and diagnosed diseases for referral to the public health system, problems that people often did not know they had."

A group of health professionals providing free care in working-class neighborhoods would not go unnoticed by the repressive intelligence apparatus. Security agents kept watch on everyone who entered and left the old rambling house in Ñuñoa, which was the Comprehensive Health Center's central office. The building was raided more than once. Mario Tapia recalls one such occasion: "One day we went to conduct health check-ups in La Florida, near the mountains, when that [south Santiago] area was still rural. Someone came in to tell us that guys outside were filming with a video camera. When we finished our work and left that afternoon, they were still there. My car was filled with people and even a gynecology table. It was just harassment to intimidate us." He added, "But we never said, 'We'd better close this up.'"

"We were pretty bold," Mario admitted. "I can remember how a few days before the national strike of 1986, a large group of us went to the corner of Irarrazaval Avenue and Chile-España Street to hand out flyers calling on people to join the strike and bang pots in protest. Suddenly, a group of plainclothes guys got out of a car and threw themselves on us. Two or three people were arrested. Dora went to the police station to get them released. She had a very terse conversation with the police lieutenant. She insisted on seeing the detainees because they were her employees. 'Calm down, lady, you have my word they are okay,' the officer replied. She told him that his word was not enough, 'because my son was shot. I know what I'm talking about.'"

In late 1987, a witness revealed to *Apsi* magazine the brutal way Carlos Berger had been murdered. "You always hope that your loved one suffered as little as possible; that they killed him right way. When you find out it was not like that, it's too devastating for a mother," notes Carmen. Dora had been in Canada visiting the family of another son, but the chilling news compelled her to return to Chile. She traveled north to Calama to join the wives and daughters of the men killed with her son by the Caravan of Death. With these women, she combed the desert, digging the hard ground with their shovels, gusts of wind in their face and hair, searching not just for fragments of bone but especially for truth and justice.

Back in Santiago, she fell into a deep depression. Dora, the pillar who sustained her colleagues, who encouraged others to take heart, who was outraged by others' suffering, could not withstand another blow. Near three in the afternoon of June 24, 1988, Eva Mateluna, an administrative coordinator at the health center and a person very close to Dora, received a telephone call. It was Dora calling to let her know that she would not attend the staff meeting scheduled for three that afternoon. She did not feel well and was a little dizzy. "I immediately called a doctor friend. He called Dora, and then at 3:20 I called her again to let her know the doctor was on his way. At 3:30 she made her decision," Eva said.[34]

The matriarch Sara's despondent cry killed her instantly. Dora's asphyxiated her for fifteen years. That day in June, Dora launched herself into the void from a towering building, penetrating the country's complicit indifference.

PART 3

ROADS TRAVELED

6

Echoes of Anne Frank

From Amsterdam to Concepción

263 Prinsengracht Street, a narrow four-story building built in 1635, is typical of the homes seventeenth-century merchants built for themselves facing the canals of Amsterdam. The building's wide double doors at one time opened onto a horse stable. Later, in the twentieth century, it was converted into a warehouse. The left door of the double doors opened directly onto a staircase that led to the main floor, elevated above the street level to protect the place from frequent flooding. Behind each canal house is often a second building, separated by a garden or courtyard and connected by interior passageways. At 263 Prinsengracht, an interior courtyard measuring four meters wide separates the two buildings. On the rainy morning of July 6, 1942, four people quickly entered this *achterhuis*, or "back house," soon to be followed by another four, where they remained until their arrest on August 4, 1944.

A book that has impacted several generations the world over was written in this place. In 1947, a copy of what came to be published in English as *The Diary of a Young Girl* arrived in the mail in Concepción, a city in southern Chile. Home from work one afternoon, Frederick Seelmann, excitedly commented to his son Gunter, "I got a letter from my friend Otto Frank who's in Switzerland."[1] Frederick Seelmann and Otto Frank were from Aachen, Germany. Otto Frank married Edith Hollander in 1925 in the synagogue of Aachen, the same one Gunter as a boy saw reduced to rubble and ash after the pogrom of November 9, 1938. By that time, the Frank family had been in Amsterdam since the summer of 1933. The Seelmanns left for Chile in 1939.

Gunter knew his father was well acquainted with the Franks when they all lived in Aachen. During several years, Frederick played tennis with Alice Frank-Stern, Otto's mother and grandmother of his daughters Margot and

Anne. Later, the Frank family moved to Frankfurt and they lost touch with each other.

Gunter recalls that when his father received the letter, which was the first indication he had that Otto was still alive, his father "lost his customary composure and cried tears of joy. Sitting together with my parents and sister, we listened as my father read the letter aloud."

Frederick had in his hands a copy from the first Dutch edition of 3,036 copies that Otto Frank published in June 1947 of the diary written by his youngest daughter. After the arrest of the eight people hiding in the secret annex and before the Gestapo returned to arrest them too, Miep Gies and Bep Voskuijl, Otto Frank's two secretaries who collaborated with the rescuers, found pages of the diary scattered on the floor. They gathered up the pages, and Miep placed them in a safe place. When Otto returned to Amsterdam in June 1945, Miep gave him the diary. "We were tremendously moved to tears," says Gunter.

However, the Seelmann family was unaware of a special link between the drama they read in the diary and Chile. Fritz Pfeffer, a German dentist who shared the small room with Anne Frank, wanted to go to Chile. On January 13, 1939, Pfeffer, who is described in mocking and indignant tones by this girl who was nearly forty years younger than him, wrote the Santiago Israelite Protection Committee expressing his desire to immigrate to Chile with Charlotte Kaletta, whom Nazi laws forbid from marrying because she was not Jewish. In his letter, Pfeffer states that since 1919 he had been working with horses and wished to engage in agriculture in Chile. He also stated that he possessed 4,000 Netherland florins in savings. The following day, Pfeffer wrote the Dutch Justice Ministry requesting permission to remain in the Netherlands while waiting for a response from Chile. Pfeffer remained in the country without the authorization he sought, and in 1942 had to hide in the "back house." It is known that during the time he was in hiding, Pfeffer studied Spanish, presumably because he still had hopes of going to Chile. Pfeffer died in 1944 at the Neuengamme concentration camp.[2]

Long after the Seelmann family first read *The Diary of a Young Girl*, the University of Concepción Theater prepared to present the teenager's life on stage, and Frederick was an advisor to the theater production and attended the rehearsals. Gunter, who many years later joined the professional staff of the Fundación PIDEE, wrote the following in an essay he published in 1992: "The dramatic fate of this preadolescent Jewish girl, who was born in Germany and became a refugee in Holland, moves us even more today, at the dawn of the second millennium. In a rapidly changing world, in which old paradigms are ruptured, humans have been incapable of assimilating the past in a positive way."[3]

Scandal at the Achterhuis

In 1947, when *Het Achterhuis: Dagboekbrieven 14 Juni 1942–1 Augustus 1944*, which is the way its author Anne Frank referred to her diary in Dutch, was published, people began looking for the building facing one of the most beautiful canals of Amsterdam. They wanted to see the forty-six-square-meter space where the teenaged Anne dreamed of freedom and spent the afternoon hours writing her journal. In 1955, the building was about to be demolished when human rights activists rallied and saved it. In October 1957, the real estate firm that had bought the property donated it to the new foundation that had been created by Otto Frank.

The name Anne Frank was already widely known in the United States after the 1955 performance of a Broadway play based on the book. The diary was eventually translated into sixty-five languages, and since May 1960, when the restored building opened to the public as the Anne Frank House, the building has drawn thousands of visitors each year. Among the people who waited in line to see the "back house" one day in early January 1974 was the Chilean Héctor Precht, a journalist for the newspaper *El Mercurio*. In his column published on January 6, 1974, Precht described his visit and the feelings it evoked in him.

After visiting the reconstructed hideout and then going down the stairs to the main house-museum lobby, the journalist was astonished to find an exhibit of photos taken in his own country: soldiers burning books, military aiming guns at people lying on the ground on Morande Street outside La Moneda. Four months after the military coup, the Chile Solidarity Committee had mounted an exhibit to denounce the repression that featured a photo of the army commander-in-chief who had directed the coup. The photo had the caption "Pinochet, the Hitler of Chile."

Indignant, the journalist complained to museum staff and the representative of the Chile Solidarity Committee, castigating what he referred to as a "politically biased" and "Communist propagandistic" display. He did not deny the veracity of the photos; rather, he charged that they were taken out of context "because they do not show that this is Chile's response to Communist aggression," adding that it was "an offense to Anne Frank, who yesterday was persecuted by brown-shirted right-wing Fascists and today is capitalized on by red, leftist fascism."[4]

Ten days after Precht's column presented his opinion, the Jewish Representative Committee conveyed its own protest to the director of the Anne Frank House in Amsterdam and sent a copy to Otto Frank as well. Published in *La Palabra Israelita* as an open letter, its signers Gil Sinay and Robert Levy, president and secretary general, respectively, of the Jewish Representative Committee, stated:

> We believe that your Foundation must never get involved in the terrain of political conflict through slogans in favor of or against any system of government; this would prevent an interpretation similar to Mr. Precht's based on evident facts of intervention and that unfortunately damages Judaism as a whole and this Community in particular. In fact, neither this Government nor any previous ones ever practiced a policy of racial or religious discrimination and that is why we enjoy absolute freedom in our community, religious, and cultural affairs without the equal rights of Jewish residents having ever been in question. Consequently, nothing could be more unfair than to compare our current leader with Hitler.[5]

At the moment Precht and leaders of the Jewish Representative Committee penned their messages of protest, more than twelve hundred people had already been murdered or disappeared in Chile. The DINA's repressive machinery was in full operation, and torture had become routine in the secret detention centers throughout the country. That the Anne Frank Foundation pointed out these facts, according to those critics, was a distortion of what was happening in Chile and a "deviation of fundamental principles" embodied by the figure of Anne Frank.

Isaac Caro, a Chilean from a Jewish family, also visited the Anne Frank House in early 1974 and saw the exhibit mounted by the Chile Solidarity Committee. He had a different reaction. The university professor recalls:

> When I visited the Anne Frank House, on the first floor there was an exhibition in favor of human rights in Chile, featuring photographs of victims. The first thing that caught my eye was that this event had been organized in such a symbolic place, thereby associating the Holocaust with human rights violations in Latin America, where several countries, including Chile, were under a military dictatorship. Then and still now I think that the subject of Holocaust should be approached as an emblematic example of genocide but at the same time must be an example for memory to spur us on to fight against all kinds of violations, genocides, ethnic cleansing, and discrimination in any region of the world.[6]

A CRY FOR FREEDOM

In a quiet tree-lined neighborhood of Belgrano, an urban suburb of Buenos Aires where skyscraper condominiums do not yet dominate, a three-story house has been the South American headquarters of the Anne Frank Center since 2009. Its administrative offices and a permanent educational exhibition about the development of the Shoah are on its first floor. On the second floor, visitors enter a reproduction of the hideout of the famous house in Amsterdam. Upon leaving the replica of the "back house annex," schoolchildren and other visitors enter a room with a permanent exhibition that shows the consequences of human rights violations committed during the last Argentine military dictatorship. It is quite similar to the controversial display on the Chilean dictatorship seen in the Anne Frank House in Amsterdam in 1974.

Testimonios para nunca más: De Ana Frank a nuestros días, a book published by the Argentine institution, employs photos and texts to chronicle the Nazi rise to power, its genocidal policy, and the history of the Frank family. It also narrates the stories of three children of disappeared Argentines and their fight for truth and justice. The last third of the book highlights twelve examples of "diversity and discrimination in our days."[7] All institutional publications of the Buenos Aires Anne Frank Foundation adopt this approach, highlighting both the story of the Shoah as well as the disregard for life that characterized Argentina under the military dictatorship.

Héctor Shalom, a psychologist and the director of the Buenos Aires Anne Frank House, defines the foundation's mission as that of "recovering the value of memory in order to move people to action and provoke reflection regarding all forms of oppression."[8] Shalom points out that the "Shoah is a unique phenomenon" but not an isolated one.

> There is a risk of undermining its value as a great school for humanity. If Auschwitz existed, it can be repeated. The risk lies in isolating the phenomenon. We are concerned about the story of Anne Frank and the story of the Shoah being regarded as events only of the past, because its mechanisms continue to be repeated. Our aim is to identify the mechanisms that built and consolidated Nazism and that were emulated by genocidal regimes in subsequent decades.

During the Argentine dictatorship, Héctor Shalom collaborated with the Israeli Embassy and international organizations to help get persecuted people out of the country. The building where Shalom has his office and that houses the foundation, previously known as "Hilda's house," was donated by the family of a woman of Italian descent married to a Jew, known for their solidarity. During forty-five years, they sheltered people who needed a place to sleep and eat, who had lost their homes due to flooding and economic crisis. During the last military dictatorship, they hid persecuted people, much as Miep Gies and the other four protectors did when they protected and sustained the Frank and van Pels families as well as Fritz Pfeffer during a year and a half at the annex house at 263 Prinsenstrach Street.

Military personnel have also visited the Anne Frank House in Belgrano, expressing outrage over the Nazi genocide of the Jews, but when they see the exhibition on the Argentine dictatorship, they say those events were the consequence of a legitimate war. Shalom believes that the views of those military officers exemplify the risk of regarding the Shoah as a singular event that will never be repeated.

> You'd think that whoever repudiates the Shoah could not support any other genocide. By isolating the Shoah, it becomes possible to condemn what happened there because it happened a long time ago, and the Nazis were very bad people. But the Nazis bear no relation to the Pinochet army of Chile or with Videla's army in Argentina. These are the risks of isolating the Shoah. In other words, it is possible to repudiate Nazism while also supporting other dictatorships. For us, that is not a valid option. Whoever repudiates Nazism must repudiate Milosevic and Pinochet and Videla.

Shalom believes Anne Frank's legacy, embodied in her diary, represents nothing less than a "cry for freedom" that resounds in all continents and in every era. He rejects the interpretation of her diary that emphasizes "the pain and sadness of a girl who suffered very much and died at fifteen years old" while "depriving it of all ideological and political components." By focusing on her individual suffering, he notes, it becomes impossible "to make a connection with events in the future, with subsequent events or events of our days. One fact is the pain and tenderness. Another is to say that the *Diary* is an act of resistance that questions the Nazi genocide and all acts of genocides."[9]

EXEGESIS OF THE DIARY

Published two years after the end of the war, Anne Frank's diary was for many years practically the only narrative on the personal impact of Nazism and the Shoah for Spanish speakers. In 1955, when the first Spanish translation, titled *La habitación de atrás*, was published, Elie Wiesel, the prolific author of testimonies about the Shoah, published his first book, *Night*, in Yiddish, but it was not translated into Spanish until 1975. In 1957, Primo Levi, an Auschwitz survivor like Wiesel, published his first book, *If This Is a Man*, which was not translated into Spanish until 1987.

No testimonial book concerning the Shoah has achieved the massive influence of *The Diary of a Young Girl*, which was not only turned into a Broadway play but also made into a movie in the United States in 1959. The book is included in the mandatory reading lists of classrooms of Chile, the United States, and many other countries. For many students, this is likely their first contact with literature about the Holocaust. Therefore, the way they interpret and read the book shapes their knowledge and approach to the Shoah.

Teenagers can completely relate to the teenaged Anne, who describes having a good time with her schoolmates, falling in love for the first time with Harry Goldman and coming to prefer his company to that of her girlfriends, and then experiencing an exhilarating first kiss—although not during a romantic stroll with Harry but rather in the attic with Peter van Pels, her companion in clandestine life, on a Sunday in April 1944. These kinds of experiences are common in the adolescent world. At the same time, Anne speaks to the universal idealism of youth when, for example, she wonders, "Why are people so stupid that they devote money to war?"

Only her own family and the four other people who shared the hideout witnessed Anne's growth, both physical—all her clothing became too tight for her—as well as intellectual. She entered the refuge as a capricious girl who delighted in candies, skating with her friends, and fights with her older sister. But this girl who shows how similar she is to many adolescents when she bitterly complains to her "Kitty" journal confidant about how unfairly everyone treats her, increasingly matures. She herself recognized this change in her March 7, 1944, journal entry: "When I think back to my life in 1942, it all seems so unreal. The Anne who enjoyed that heavenly existence was completely different from the one who has grown wise between these walls. . . . I'd like to live that seemingly carefree and happy life just for an evening, a few days, a week. At the end of that week, I'd be exhausted, and would be grateful to the first person to talk to me about something meaningful."

Anne came to understand and analyze with keen intellect the roots of the intolerance that culminated with her family's need to seek a clandestine living space and that would prematurely shorten her life, preventing the achievement of her dreams. A marked social conscience and sense of solidarity is evident when she writes on January 13, 1943, that "terrible things are happening outside. At any time of night and day, poor helpless people are being dragged out of their homes. They're only allowed to take a knapsack and a little cash with them, and even then they're robbed of these possessions on the way. Families are torn apart; men, women, and children are separated. Children come home from school to find that their parents have disappeared. Women return from shopping to find their houses sealed, their families gone."[10]

The Amsterdam described by Anne Frank was similar to what thousands of Chilean boys and girls experienced thirty years later, when, as of September 1973, they were deprived of their parents.

When, in a letter printed in *El Mercurio* on May 27, 2009, Senator Carlos Larrain stated that Anne Frank died only because she was born a Jew and that President Michelle Bachelet had no right to complain about "her stay at Villa Grimaldi," the then president of the Renovación Nacional (National Renewal Party) employed the mechanism of negation to justify political imprisonment and torture during the military regime he supported. Anne Frank was an "innocent victim," but Bachelet "was an adult and already expressed her political choices before 1974," the year of her "stay" at Villa Grimaldi. The implication is that Bachelet was not an "innocent victim" but simply paid the consequences of the political choices she made.

On April 4, 1944, Anne wrote in her journal: "I want to go on living even after my death! And that's why I'm so grateful to God for having given me this gift, which I can use to develop myself and to express all that's inside me."[11] Anne continues living after her death to the extent that her memory and conscience continue to have force and as long as her martyrdom is not disassociated from the political and social principles that gave rise to the violence and genocide of the Nazis' actions or those of the military dictatorships of Latin America and throughout the world.

THE ANNES OF CHILE

In every continent of the globe, countless girls and boys have suffered persecution and death in different wars that have been waged in the sixty years since Anne Frank's death. Gunter Seelmann, who arrived in Chile as a child refugee and later returned to Germany as an adult refugee of the Pinochet dictatorship, is deeply moved by Anne Frank's story and the trauma of so many children like her.

> How many children of other nations and other generations, including our own, could have represented themselves like she did if they could have left us their written testimonies? Let's think about the children born under Apartheid, the Kurdish children persecuted in Turkey, Iraq, and Syria. Let's remember the Palestinian children in refugee camps and the Israeli children threatened by Saddam Hussein's missiles. All of them and so many more would have something to transmit to us about their suffering and their severed dreams. The recent history of our country also documents the unfathomable suffering of children and young people mistreated by the state security apparatus.[12]

Yes, in Chile, some children and adolescents died due to "stray bullets"; however, in many other cases repression took direct aim at them, making no allowances on account of their young age. The very day of the coup, September 11,

1973, Sergio Gómez Arriagada, a twelve-year-old boy, was arrested in front of the bread shop near his house in San Joaquin. To this day, Sergio remains disappeared.

Carlos Fariña Oyarce, thirteen years old, was arrested October 5, 1973, in the La Pincoya neighborhood, located in northern Santiago. His family learned that he had been taken to the San Felipe military base in Quinta Normal, but they never saw or heard from Carlos again. He remained disappeared until his body, with twelve bullet holes, was located in the year 2000.

During the afternoon of October 13, 1973, Elizabeth Leonidas Díaz, a fourteen-year-old schoolgirl, was arrested along with seven people outside Los Sauces, a neighborhood pub in Puente Alto in south Santiago. All were taken to the Fourth Police Precinct of Santiago. The next day, at dawn, they were put in a jeep and taken to Bulnes Bridge, in central Santiago. At that place, Elizabeth and the other people were forced to run, and then the police squad fired on them. Her body was found along the Mapocho riverbed.

In the National Stadium, Pedro Hugo Pérez Godoy, who was fifteen years old, was last seen alive in November 1973.

The National Truth and Reconciliation Commission report documents 329 cases of children and adolescents killed, just like Sergio Gómez Arriagada, Carlos Fariña Oyarce, Elizabeth Leonidas Díaz, and Pedro Hugo Pérez Godoy, as of September 11.[13] Of these, thirty-two children of the same age as Anne Frank or even younger had their lives ended in the first four months after the coup.

Abducting children as a means to pressure their parents is regarded as an especially repugnant practice of the DINA, the Servicio de Inteligencia de la Fuerza Aérea (Air Force Intelligence Service), and the CNI. The cases of 102 children who were arrested have been documented, and in June 2001, attorney Hiram Villagra filed a criminal complaint on behalf of 5 such children before Judge Juan Guzmán Tapia.[14] Some of these minors were taken to punish and pressure families who were politically active, as in the case of Hugo Chacaltana, nephew of Atilio Ugarte Gutiérrez, a victim of the Caravan of Death. Other children were taken to serve as hostages, a tactic employed by the DINA, as in the case of the sisters Lena and Cassandra Parvex, who were three and six years old, respectively.[15]

Villagra, who was for many years a member of the legal staff of the Comité de Defensa de los Derechos del Pueblo (CODEPU), states, "Beyond the extreme cases of children forced to listen to their parents being tortured, I am absolutely convinced that the sole fact of having a child in the environment of Villa Grimaldi is a form of torture. Even if they are not touched, that child will hear screams, will see people with wounds, will see people with hoods over their head pass along the hallway."[16]

At a commemorative event held in Villa Grimaldi in December 2006, Rodrigo del Villar, at the time director of Peace Park Corporation, remarked that "several Anne Franks passed through Villa Grimaldi between the years 1974 and 1978: children and young people endured here the horror spewed by those who converted this site into a place for torture and murder."

Macarena Aguiló was one of them. She was three years old in 1975 when DINA agents abducted her and initially brought her to Villa Grimaldi. From there, ignoring the habeas corpus writ filed by her family, her captors took her to a children's home run by police, where she remained for twenty-two days. Her mother had been arrested, and the DINA wanted to force her father, a leader of the MIR, out from hiding in order to arrest him as well. When she became a party to Villagra's lawsuit, she declared that her son, who at the time was the same age when she was abducted, "was important in helping me fathom what happened to me." Today Macarena Aguiló is a film producer. Her documentary film *El edificio de los chilenos*, which won first prize in the Santiago International Documentary Festival in 2010, explores the impact a parent's exile and arrest can have on their children.

Beyond the extreme cases of children taken into custody or killed during dictatorship, behind countless thousands of men and women arrested, disappeared or executed, there were children. It is impossible to determine the precise number of children who witnessed their house being raided, their family under surveillance, their father or mother beaten and arrested.

Raúl was three years and ten months in 1979 when he witnessed the raiding of his house and the arrest of his father, who was held for eighty days in jail.[17] Sara was almost two in 1974 when her grandfather died as a consequence of torture, and she was eight when an aunt was forcibly disappeared a few years later. The grandfather and aunt lived in the same house with the little girl and her family.[18] Rodrigo was eight when his home was raided and both parents arrested. His mother was released soon afterward but his father remained in prison for several years.[19]

Between 1979 and 1992, an estimated twelve thousand children like Raúl, Sara, and Rodrigo were treated for psychological disorders by the Fundación PIDEE. Under the direction of María Eugenia Rojas, the foundation provided support and emotional containment for children and their families of Santiago and in eight provinces. In 1980, the team of psychologists began working with children of disappeared persons. Of the total 1,847 families it assisted, 267 had a member forcibly disappeared. As of 1985, it sheltered children in its Casa Hogar, a house it owned, where more than once the staff had to hide children in danger of being kidnapped by intelligence services who sought to pressure their parents.[20]

The children assisted by the foundation grew up but did not leave their traumas behind; many relived various episodes. Psychologists observed "extreme passivity and inhibition," loneliness, sadness and anger, as well as persistent nightmares. Moreover, their fears intensified each September, with the approach of the anniversary of the military coup, worrying their parents might be arrested again or killed.[21]

Two siblings cared for by the foundation were the children of Alonso Gahona, who was forcibly disappeared on September 8, 1975, when they were six and seven years old. The lives of Evelyn and Yuri changed dramatically; various uncles and aunts raised them. When they were young adults, they spoke about the implications of the absence of their father and their need to bear witness to their father's ideals through their own lives. Yuri remarks: "I would think to myself, how can there be so much injustice done to people who never hurt a soul? It is something that affects you forever. Despite everything, although I know he is dead, I feel that he is alive in me."[22]

Yuri keeps his father alive through his own activism in the cause for human rights, justice, and historic memory, a path that has led him to join the Association of Families of Disappeared Detainees as well as the organization of children whose parents were disappeared called Hijos e Hijas por la Identidad y la Justicia contra el Olvido y el Silencio (Sons and Daughters for Identity and Justice against Forgetting and Silence). In the introduction to his master's thesis ("Reparation for Human Rights Violations"), Gahona thanks not only his faculty advisors but also "all those men and women who persevere despite pain and difficulties."

A Natural Next Step

In 1968, a group of six Dutch Oblate seminarians came to Chile for the first time, accompanied by priest Martin Schram, their spiritual guide and professor in mission practice. In Chile, they believed, there was a receptive and modern climate in which to forge a new form of mission work. Oblates of Canada and Belgium had been in Chile for a long time, but these young Dutchmen "followed their own road," says Joop Kaldenhoven, who joined the group in January 1970.[23] The methodology they designed combined Paolo Freire's concientization with pastoral service in working-class segments of society.

They requested and received permission from the Catholic bishop that authorized them to work in Chile and support themselves on their own. They shared a small house in the working-class neighborhood of Jose Maria Caro, in south Santiago. Joop, like his other Oblate brothers, worked in a factory. "In this way we hoped to coexist, share, and learn from each other. Between Chileans and the Dutch missionaries, there arose a shared aspiration and work for a more just society," he explains. Several of the young Oblate seminarians thus supported the Popular Unity government when Salvador Allende took office.

In the Netherlands, people followed the Allende administration with great interest, and many Dutch citizens traveled frequently to Chile to witness the process firsthand. Schram began a newsletter called the *Inca-Bulletin*, one of the major sources of information in the Netherlands about the situation in Chile. When Santiago hosted the third session of the UN Conference on Trade and Development from April 13 to May 21, 1972, there was "a great invasion of Dutch politicians, union leaders and activists" who traveled to Chile.[24]

Schram was born on December 14, 1924, in Afferden, a small town in southern Holland. He "felt very close to the less fortunate and tried to help people materially, morally, and politically."[25] When he was twelve years old, he entered the seminary, where he studied for eleven years. After that, he remained at the seminary as a professor of Latin and Greek. He was sixteen years old when the Germans invaded the Netherlands.

A close friend of his, Els Nicolas, describes his early life: "His father was a member of the civil guard and—like everyone in the family—had a very strong sense of justice. He discreetly disobeyed orders from the occupying forces to turn in 'subversives' and helped many people escape."[26] His oldest brother, Henk Schram, later an Oblate in Sri Lanka, was an active member of the local resistance against German occupation.

After the military coup, at noon on September 15, 1973, a patrol of soldiers and police arrested him and the Dutch theologian Albert Bolk, at the house they shared in Lo Vial, a neighborhood of the municipality of San Miguel in south Santiago. After spending the entire day and night in a San Miguel police precinct jail cell, their destination was the National Stadium, which had been converted into the country's largest prison.

They were left in a locker room measuring twelve meters long by six meters wide, which was already crowded with approximately 150 people. There they encountered four other men of Dutch nationality, including their fellow seminarians. One night the agents detaining them opened the locker room door to force them to witness a chilling scene: people with their hands and feet chained, unable to stand up, were facing a firing squad with rifles aimed at them. From the locker room they could hear the order to shoot, but there were no bullets.[27] It was a fake execution, designed to strike terror. On September 28, the Dutch embassy was able to get them out of the National Stadium. Three days later, the seminarians were boarding a jet, but the echo of the rounds of machine gun and the shouts and cries they had heard during their twelve days in prison continued to haunt them.

Twenty years later, Schram remarked that "crammed in the catacombs [of the National Stadium] together with thousands of others, I learned the meaning of dictatorship and repression: fear, arbitrariness, cruelty." He added, "Those adherents of Pinochet were simply Nazis. They repeatedly told us: 'Here we're going to do the same thing that Hitler did.'"[28]

The military coup shocked Holland, and several thousands of people turned out on the streets to protest against the atrocities committed every day in Chile. Upon his forced return to the Netherlands, Schram and Bauco van der Wal, international secretary of the Anne Frank Foundation, revived the Chili Komitee Nederland that had been formed in late 1972 in support of Salvador Allende's government. After the coup, this committee, with support from the government of the Netherlands, ceaselessly denounced the crimes committed by the military junta and became a mainstay of solidarity with persecuted people. The four seminarians who had been in prison in Chile were active members of the Chili Komitee. The magazine *Inca-Bulletin*, started by Schram during the Popular Unity, now became the *Chile Boletin* and served as an organ for denouncing the repression. At the same time, Schram became one of the coordinators of Fondo de Lucha por Chile (Chile Resistance Fund), which raised much-needed money for community organizations in Chile that opposed the military regime.[29] The Chili Komitee was part of the Dutch Movement for Chile that coordinated activities nationally, including a major event on September 11, the anniversary of the coup, each year. The Anne Frank House also participated, represented by its director Bauco van der Wal, who at one point became Dutch Movement president.

Hernán Leemryse, a Dutch priest at Santo Cura de Ars Church located in the municipality of San Miguel in southern Santiago, was also forced to leave Chile in 1973 and only was able to return in the early 1990s. In Holland, he participated in activities organized by the Chili Komitee. "One concrete action we carried out," he notes, "was to boycott the arrival of Chilean apples at the port of Rotterdam. We stood in front of the ships with signs saying 'There's blood on those apples! Don't buy Chilean apples!' We also protested outside grocery stores, asking consumers not to buy Chilean apples."[30]

In mid-1974, Schram was invited to become a member of the Anne Frank House staff and was vested with the task of creating a documentation center. He devoted twenty years to the documentation center until he retired in 1994. His work consisted of compiling historic archives about the Shoah, subsequent genocides, and contemporary manifestations of fascism and repression throughout the world. In conjunction with his archival work, Schram continued to participate in Chile solidarity activities.

Journalist Peter Gelauff, who participated in the Chili Komitee Nederland and knew Schram, notes, "I believe that for Martin's generation, the experiences of the Second World War and of solidarity with the Jewish people in those years contributed significantly in endowing a deep sense of solidarity, I would say with practically inevitable, impact on the rest of their lives. Now, I am speaking about a specific generation and within that generation I refer to those people who learned that lesson during the war."[31] In Els Nicolas's opinion, "people who were actively solidarity during the war . . . formed the nucleus of solidarity and actions for human rights. For Martin, as well as his brother Henk, it was a natural step."[32]

MEMORY STONES

Another thread in the fabric connecting Chile with the Anne Frank Foundation is Chilean Boris Vildósola. A Socialist Party member, Boris worked at the State Technical University in 1973, was president of his neighborhood council in the Valdivieso-El Salto area of north Santiago, and was vice president of a federation of unions that represented workers of the Mapocho-Matucana factory district. On September 8 of that year, his oldest daughter had turned four years old. Three days later, when soldiers ransacked their house, it was still decorated with garlands and a piñata. Boris had left for work early that morning, and so when the soldiers raided the house, he was gone. He was wanted both for his union activities as well as his neighborhood leadership role. Initially, the trade representative for the Embassy of Finland protected Boris in his home. Later he was transferred to an office of the Dutch Embassy. Shortly later, he and his family left Chile for the Netherlands, which accorded him political refugee status.

Zaandam, the Dutch city where the family ended up living for nearly twenty years, was "a marvelous place." There on February 25, 1941, the residents held the only general strike in protest against the deportation of Jews that Germans ever encountered in an occupied country. In the neighborhood where the Vildósola family lived, they met the children of resistance members shot by the Nazis. His neighbors showed tremendous solidarity with the Vildósola family and other Chilean exiles, solidarity that derived from the fact that "Chile was experiencing forms of repression similar to what the Dutch people had experienced," says Boris.[33]

As director of the Central Unitaria de Trabajadores (CUT, Chilean Federation of Workers) in exile and participant in solidarity activities, Boris entered the Anne Frank House many times. "One of the world's major centers for human rights advocacy was that building on Prinsengracht Street," Boris remarks.

"The Anne Frank House constantly posted information and mounted visual exhibits regarding the contemporary barbarities being committed in different corners of the world. It was their practice. It was logical that we would have close working relations with the Anne Frank Foundation."[34] Chileans exiled in Holland would give the foundation material that they used to maintain the bulletin board in the building's lobby. One such exhibit included the series of photos the journalist from *El Mercurio* saw in January 1974.

In order to foster and disseminate Anne Frank's universal message, in the late 1980s, the foundation's international office organized a traveling photographic exhibition, in English and German, that traveled the world. Boris was so insistent about not forgetting the Spanish-speaking world that the exhibit was also translated into Spanish, and the foundation asked Boris to be its representative for Latin America.

The inaugural exhibition in Latin America was held in 1991 at the University of Chile to mark the return of democracy. Over the next four years, Boris traveled throughout Latin America with the exhibition. In each country, he contacted three major entities for support: the German Embassy, as the country where Anne Frank was born; the Embassy of the Netherlands, the country that provided refuge for the Frank family; and the Embassy of Israel, because of her Jewish heritage. "We showed the world this exhibit so that the events that occurred during the Holocaust would not occur again in any other country," he says, adding that he personally "felt very close" to the story he presented.[35]

In 2006, Peace Park, a site of conscience constructed on the premises of what had been the Villa Grimaldi detention and torture center, developed a program to teach human rights and historic memory in the schools. The program's focus was the traveling exhibit *Ana Frank, a Contemporary Story*, which was presented alongside another exhibit, titled *Villa Grimaldi: Past, Present, and Future.*

During the program's first year, more than eleven thousand students, teachers, and parents from eleven schools of the municipality of Peñalolen viewed the joint exhibitions, guided by young people from the same schools who had been trained in holding special daylong sessions. High school teacher Mario Rojas commented on the experience at his school, the La Reina Educational Complex: "It is gratifying to see how the students have absorbed this activity that underscores transversal values such as respect and tolerance that should exist between people."[36]

Although Anne Frank's story unfolded in geographic and cultural latitudes distant from Chile, it is more accessible for Chilean children than the more recent story in their own country. Margarita Romero, president of the Peace

Park Corporation Board of Directors in 2012, indicated that the Anne Frank exhibition enabled Peace Park to address the story of the serious human rights violations in Chile. "Anne Frank represents something that is somewhat familiar to Chileans; yet Villa Grimaldi is not known," says Romero. "The essential association between the two is the right to life and the right to think differently and how that was repressed both during the period of Nazi domination in Germany as well as in Chile under the dictatorship."[37]

Anahi Moya, coordinator in 2012 of the Peace Park's itinerant educational program, notes another aspect that connects both stories. "Just as there are people who aided those persecuted for their leftist political thinking, there are people who aided Jews persecuted in Germany and other countries of Europe. The students saw that always there are people willing to risk danger in order to aid others who are persecuted."[38]

Margarita adds that "the Anne Frank exhibit enables children to better understand that in order to stay in power Pinochet used repression as a state policy of terrorism in which not only individuals but society as a whole were victims. That was also the case in the Second World War. There the entire society suffered; it was a practice that denied all freedom of expression, only permitting a prescribed culture, prescribed education, and even certain values. That happened in Chile too."

In the context of the *Ana Frank, una historia vigente* exhibition at Peace Park, on December 6, 2006, the Jewish Progressive Center coordinated a commemorative event called "Remembering Anne Frank and Diana Aron," for which Gunter Seelmann served as master of ceremonies. With an estimated three hundred people in attendance, the event honored Luis Guendelman, Jorge Müller, Juan Carlos Perelman, and Diana Aron, all of whom had been last seen alive at Villa Grimaldi. Attorney Roberto Garreton, an active member of the UN Commission for the Prevention of Genocide, underscored that Anne and Diana shared not only a common Jewish descent but also a similar worldview: "Both Diana and Anne, despite the latter's young age, were politicians in the best sense of the word. Anne's diary is a constant expression of solidarity, a vision of a country different than the one she was living in at that moment. . . . Diana embraced a just cause and chose to continue, knowing full well the risks she would encounter." Lastly, Garreton pointed out, "to this day both Anne and Diana are still disappeared persons."

The event closed with Rabbi Daniel Zang of the Sephardic Synagogue of Santiago inviting people to come to the Peace Park wall of names to participate in the traditional Jewish ritual of leaving small stones in memory of the deceased, normally on a tomb. Rabbi Zang explained the significance of the ritual in the context of those remembered at Villa Grimaldi.

When a person goes to a cemetery and finds a little stone on a tomb, you know that someone else remembered that loved one. Not only are they remembered in the cemetery but also in our hearts, especially when there is no cemetery or tomb or even known place of burial. Our prayer says, "Tzureinu tzur hayeinu" [God is the rock of our life]. Memory is associated with a rock; it endures forever.

At that moment, Rabbi Zang took a small stone and placed it by the wall of names, noting that "just as we say that each one of us must feel as though we have left Egypt, today we say, remembering Anne Frank, that each one of us must feel as though we have left Auschwitz. And, remembering Diana Aron, we must also feel as though we have just left Villa Grimaldi."

7

Selective Memory and
Its Lessons

In 1988, Archbishop Marcel Lefebvre, founder of the Society of Saint Pius X, for which antisemitism is a foundational pillar, consecrated four priests as bishops with authorization from the Vatican. The following year, one of them, the new fledgling bishop Richard Williamson, emboldened by his ecclesiastic promotion, delivered a sermon at the Church of Notre Dame in the city of Lourdes Sherbrooke, Canada, in which he stated that "not a single Jew died in gas chambers. Those are all lies, lies, lies."[1] His homily represents the most extreme form of Shoah negation. In denying that the Jewish genocide was planned and systematically carried out by the Nazis, he confirmed his affiliation with a group of individuals who are virulent antisemites and apologists for the atrocities committed by Germany.

In 2009, twenty years after he had delivered this hateful sermon in Sherbrooke, he was interviewed by the Swedish television station SVT. The view he expressed in the interview was only slightly different from the one he expressed in his sermon. At the time, he was director of a Lefebrist Seminary at La Reja in Argentina. Bishop Williamson affirmed: "I believe there were no gas chambers. I believe that 200,000 or 300,000 Jews perished in the Nazi concentration camps, but none died in gas chambers."

The internationally broadcast interview prompted President Cristina Fernández de Kirchner to order that the bishop's visa be revoked. His words, she declared, "offend the deepest heartfelt feelings of the Jewish community, all of Argentine society, and humanity."[2] At the time of the interview, Williamson was in the German city of Regensburg, which authorized a German court to file criminal charges against him. In 2010, on the basis of his remarks on Swedish television, the court ruled that Bishop Williamson was guilty of Holocaust denial, and sentenced him to pay a fine of 10,000 euros. In mid-2011, the court lowered the sentence to 5,700 euros (approximately US$7,200).

The "Final Report of the International Commission on the Holocaust in Romania" (the commission was established in October 2003 and chaired by Nobel Peace Prize recipient Elie Wiesel), which was published in 2004, defines three forms of negationism. The first is the complete negation exemplified by Williamson, which it calls "integral negationism."[3] The second is what it identifies as "deflective negationism."[4] This is a defensive modality that acknowledges the existence of the Shoah but ascribes responsibility to others. In the case of Romania, Germans are held as wholly responsible, while Romanians are represented as innocent.

The second negationist modality consists of acknowledging the facts but justifying them. This approach blames victims for their mishap, such as in the suggestion that the slaughter "was the price Jews paid for having killed Christ." A variation of this modality is the argument that Jews represented a threat to German society and that Hitler was simply forced to take measures to defend the country in light of the danger.[5]

The report also identifies a strategy it calls the "comparative trivialization" of the Holocaust as separate from negationism, a position that has gained ground since the 1990s. Revisionists adopting this approach engage in relativism by comparing violent events such as wars in world history and arguing that brute force has always characterized relations between human beings and therefore that the Nazis are no different from those that came before them. Negationists who trivialize the Shoah accuse Jews of monopolizing suffering to serve their own ends.[6]

In Germany, laws enacted in line with the concept of *Volksverhetzung* prohibit inciting hatred against a segment of the population and have been used in trials against Holocaust negationism, such as the case against Bishop Williamson. Article 130 of the Criminal Code of the Federal Republic of Germany, amended in 2002 and 2005, sanctions punishment of, with a maximum of five years in prison, "whoever publicly, or at a meeting, denies, diminishes, or approves of an act committed under the regime of National Socialism . . . [that disturbs] public peace."[7] It also penalizes, with a maximum of three years in prison, "whoever publicly . . . violates the dignity of the victims by approving of, glorifying or justifying National Socialist tyranny and arbitrary rule."[8]

Austria, Belgium, Spain, France, Hungary, Luxembourg, and Switzerland all have laws that address genocide negation in general. In Bosnia and Herzegovina, the Czech Republic, and Poland, laws penalize not only crimes against humanity committed by Nazis but also those perpetrated by Communists.[9]

Germany, as a defeated nation occupied by three armies after the war, had to submit to observation of its political, ethical, and educational conduct under the tutelage of the occupation governments. Laws such as those that penalized Bishop Williamson for his remarks were included in the set of conditions Germany had to agree to in order to receive the assistance from the Marshall Plan, which reactivated the economy and created the so-called German postwar miracle. Laws that penalize Shoah negationism face a broad contingent of critics, ranging from historians Raul Hilberg and Pierre Vidal-Naquet to linguist and philosopher Noam Chomsky, who contend such laws limit freedom of expression.

Karl Bohmer, a Chilean of German descent and former director of Amnesty International Chile's Education Department, finds it worrisome that a society should need this type of law. It suggests, he says, "the majority has not internalized or taken possession of the issue as a human ethical concern. Laws against trivialization repress but do not educate. In fact, if a society needs such laws, that should be a warning to us that we have failed as educators," Bohmer contends.[10] According to Bohmer,

> It represents the deep failure of a society that holds responsibility for these events. It is the failure too of all human rights institutions that only make wounds visible but fail to create a human rights–centered culture. In the 1950s, when homosexual survivors, on whom Nazis performed experiments, demanded reparation, the German judiciary responded with these laws. And homosexuality continues to be criminalized, so your punishment was well deserved. I hope that Chile never has to legislate against defamation of events that occurred in the dictatorship.[11]

Alejandra Morales Stekel, creator of Foundation Memoria Viva, an organization that gathers testimonies of Shoah survivors living in Chile and that has created an oral archive, observes the following:

> Laws against negationism are meant to foster the existence of a national historic memory. Many people today did not experience these events. We can debate about them but not deny them. In Germany, laws against negationism address the resurgence of Nazism. How would we do that in Chile? It is risky to make comparisons. In Germany, it is against the law to be a Nazi; a Nazi can go to jail. Here you can be a diehard Pinochet supporter and go out into the street to celebrate what he did.[12]

The People Won

Is there nothing you question the Armed Forces about regarding abuses?

Honestly, I do not believe those were institutional actions; I think that, like everything, a few people abused their power and overstepped their authority.

Ambassador, I asked you about the coup in itself as an alteration of the institutional order.

If the military pronouncement had not existed, today Chile would be another Cuba. The economic behavior that changed Chile from a mendicant nation to a dignified country, that led us to business freedom is another thing . . .

You say "we wanted more democracy" but you had a dictatorship.

Let me explain something. Most of Chile didn't feel the dictatorship. On the contrary, they were relieved. Because, before, you couldn't buy import goods, you had to buy expensive, bad quality goods, what was produced in Chile. Practically overnight you began to find what had not been available. The people won. The streets got cleaned, and there began to be work again. We found out about the repression much later on. People judge without understanding the situation lived in Chile.

—*Clarín* (Buenos Aires), June 6, 2010

The June 6, 2010, interview with Miguel Otero, Chile's ambassador to Argentina, that appeared in the Buenos Aires newspaper *Clarín* cost him his diplomatic post.[13] An analysis of his remarks reveals that his views fit within the categories of negation defined by the Wiesel Commission.

In response to the journalist's first question, Otero does not recognize that the dictatorship was indeed the result of "an institutional act." Instead, he pretends that what happened was merely that certain "people abused their power and overstepped their authority." This outlook, which suggests that the Chilean state and the collaborators with the military dictatorship have no responsibility, exemplifies one aspect of the negationism, namely, deflection. It is a recurrent strategy employed most notably by the armed forces and the Chilean political right.

In response to the journalist's second question, whether the coup was "an alteration of the institutional order," Otero again deflected. This response exhibits another modality of negationism, namely, the attempt to justify human rights violations, which Otero avoids naming, as the cost required to transform Chile "from a mendicant nation into a dignified country." This too has been a common recourse for apologists of the Chilean military dictatorship.

Similar to the way Williamson denies the systematic massacre of Jews and others, when the journalist refutes Otero's claim that "we wanted more

democracy" with "but you had a dictatorship," he minimizes the magnitude of
the situation. When Otero says that "most of Chile didn't feel the dictatorship," once again, he attempts to justify it.

"What Otero does is deny, first, the magnitude; second, his responsibility;
and third, its meaning for society," notes the psychologist Elizabeth Lira, advisory member of the National Truth and Reconciliation Commission as well as
the National Commission on Political Imprisonment and Torture.[14] She adds,
"But it is impossible for him to deny it one hundred percent after the reports
of the Rettig and Valech commissions. It is hard to allege that nothing happened here. He has to say that what happened is unimportant, that most of
the country was untouched. In terms of statistics, it is relatively insignificant
to have three thousand people dead or disappeared in a country of a population of nine million people." With respect to both the Shoah and the systematic violation of human rights in Chile, there is a mindset that "directly
discredits the victims and denies their experience," notes Lira. Even worse, "it
casts doubt on the validity and veracity of what people say happened to them."

In March 1991, President Patricio Aylwin formally presented the Rettig
Report to the nation during a television broadcast and asked for forgiveness
on behalf of the state of Chile, a gesture that all branches of the armed forces
as well as the Supreme Court rejected. However, they did not question the
report's veracity. Instead, they maintained that the report ignored the fact that
the armed forces had saved the country and that the facts contained in the
report should be interpreted in that context. "The context is the explanation
for the conspiracy to overthrow Salvador Allende and the role exercised by the
military," Lira underscores.

> When things are explained in terms of context, it means no one is responsible.
> Context is an abstract category. Pinochet never steps forward, nor does Matthei
> acknowledge the military's role. The Supreme Court does not come out to say,
> "You know, everything the report says is the truth," instead they say, "we would
> do it again; we did for the sake of our country because we had a different vision
> and a different belief." This response is culturally quite common in this country,
> where people avoid taking responsibility for their actions. They can't deny the
> facts, so they justify them.

The psychologist's explanation suggests that if Miguel Otero had made the
same remarks to a Chilean newspaper, he would have attracted little attention
and there would have been no major consequences for him.

On November 28, 2004, the day the National Commission on Political
Imprisonment and Torture handed its own report to President Ricardo Lagos,

the reaction was different. Before the report was issued, General Juan Emilio Cheyre, the commander in chief, acknowledged that the army held responsibility and announced the elimination of the army's intelligence battalion. One may question the sincerity of the gesture, but the general publicly acknowledged the army's wrongdoings and expressed regret before the nation.[15] However, the Supreme Court decried the report, stating that the document unfairly criticized the judiciary.

"Between the time of the Rettig and the Valech reports, attitudes changed," Lira says. The focus, she explains, is now on a strategic vision, not morals: "The army has to distance itself from Pinochet and the dictatorship. The right too has to distance itself from Pinochet and the dictatorship. To do so they are obliged to drink from a bitter cup, and admit 'yes, we were involved.' The focus changed from total negation to, 'well, yes, it happened but let's not argue about it anymore, and let's look to the future.'"

CALLING A SPADE A SPADE

Hitler said, "I don't kill people, I kill Jews." In Argentina, General Camps said, "We didn't kill people, we killed subversives."

—HÉCTOR SHALOM, director of the Anne Frank Foundation of Argentina

Not only in its practice but also in its use of language, the military dictatorship that dominated Chile over sixteen years concealed facts, later cultivating the negation and minimization of the serious human rights violations it committed. Up until the beginning of the administration of Patricio Aylwin, the first democratically elected president after the dictatorship, the media commonly employed expressions such as "alleged disappeared" and "self-proclaimed political prisoners." Only after the National Truth and Reconciliation Commission issued its report, in March 1991, when the truth concerning the victims was positioned as truth of the entire Chilean society, did the national press abandon the adjectives "alleged" and "self-proclaimed" in reference to irrefutable acts of barbarism.

The interview Miguel Otero gave to the Argentine newspaper *Clarín* is an indication of how deeply rooted in Chilean politics and culture the phrase "military pronouncement" is in referring to what the world outside Chile recognizes as nothing short of a coup d'état. The use of the phrase can be traced back to the Supreme Court's legitimization of the military action on September 28, 1973. On that date Enrique Urrutia Manzano, president of Chile's highest court, welcomed the four members of the military junta into judicial chambers to express his "satisfaction with the military pronouncement and the change in government."[16]

A segment of Chilean society that includes many civilians like Otero and other officials of the government of President Sebastian Piñera, who appointed him ambassador, habitually employs the phrase "military pronouncement." Their intention is to uphold, without hesitation, the bombing of La Moneda and subsequent brutalities committed against Chileans and others, while also justifying or minimizing the scope of the repression.

"Pronunciamiento" is a Spanish term associated with a series of military revolts against monarchies led by Spanish generals during the nineteenth century that sought to install a government attuned to their own interests. From 1814 to 1820, the Spanish military staged nine *pronunciamientos* in an attempt to overthrow Fernando VII. In contemporary times, when the Honduran army took its troops into the streets of the capital city of Tegucigalpa to remove the chief of state on June 24, 2009, the Spanish daily *El País* referred to this action as a "pronunciamiento militar." Four days later, when the military forces arrested, abducted, and then expelled President Manuel Zelaya, the Spanish newspaper replaced its initial nomenclature with the word "coup."

In Chile, another confrontation in the minefield of language broke out on January 4, 2012, when the Education Ministry, with approval from the National Education Council, announced that new history textbooks for the country's primary schools had replaced the word "dictatorship" with "government" and military "regime." Education minister Harald Beyer explained that the goal was to use "a more general" term to refer to the period from September 11, 1973, to March 10, 1990. Alberto Cardemil, a congressman for the Unión Demócrata Independiente (UDI, Independent Democratic Union) and a former military regime cabinet minister and unconditional supporter of Pinochet, stated that the change was intended to "give a more balanced version of our history."[17]

In a January 5, 2012, press release, the Association of Families of Disappeared Detainees expressed concern that Chilean children would learn a distorted version of their nation's history.

> During many years, the practice of forced disappearance was denied, it was absent from language; the word was not used in oral speech or in writing to acknowledge that there were secret detention centers and agents in the country who pursued and tortured at the behest of the state or that civilians were informants. This did not exist; it was simply erased from our language. Now that we have made progress in this regard, . . . they intend to remove the word "dictatorship" from primary school textbooks.
>
> This Association, which has always been known for saying things as they are, demands that the measure be repealed. Our boys and girls have a basic right to get accurate and objective information using the tools the government has the

obligation to give them. Tomorrow they will be the ones to judge the dark episode experienced by the country in the period of DICTATORSHIP between 1973 and 1990.[18]

Elizabeth Lira, a member of the National Education Council, also expressed her opinion concerning this controversy: "The term 'dictatorship' has symbolic meaning for all Chileans, but especially for those who suffered its consequences. That explains the strong reaction to the term 'military regime,' if we understand that change to represent a future threat to attenuate, erase, or modify the way that period is taught in schools."[19]

In a geographically and culturally different country, a similar linguistic process that had unfolded over the last forty years might have implications for or offer lessons to Chile. In 1940, General Ion Antonescu implanted himself in Romania by force and remained in power for four years, during which he emulated Hitler and in certain ways surpassed him in brutality. Antonescu enacted laws along the lines of the Nuremberg model to marginalize the Jewish population and very quickly forced the country's Jews to live in ghettos. He created concentration camps, and his Iron Guards massacred an estimated 280,000 to 380,000 Romanian and Ukrainian Jews.

The Commission on the Holocaust in Romania, headed by Elie Wiesel, detected a change in language that occurred in the 1970s, nearly thirty years after the events, accompanied by official historical revisionism. Whereas official documents had previously referred to the period under General Antonescu as a "fascist dictatorship," the Romanian government began replacing that term with "military-fascist dictatorship." This replacement was believed to have been motivated by the idea that the brutalities had been politically motivated actions imposed under military circumstances rather than antisemitic policies that associated Romania with Nazi Germany.[20]

In the late 1980s, the commission notes, another linguistic change was effected. Because the term "military-fascist dictatorship" suggested that the Romanian army had supported the dictatorship, from then on, the preferred expression was one that referred to Antonescu as the leader of "a personal dictatorship" or "totalitarian regime." This change was meant to absolve the military "of any responsibility."

Jewish historian Nicolae Minei states the following in relation to thousands of Jews who, on July 25, 1941, the Romanian army forced to cross the Dniester River, where they were handed over to the Germans who occupied Ukraine:

The deportations beyond the Dniester carried out by the Antonescu authorities were never motivated, explicitly or secretly, by the intent to exterminate those affected. That some would nevertheless perish was due to three main reasons: abuses committed by some representatives of the authorities, who embezzled funds allocated for food purchasing; criminal excesses by degenerate elements belonging to the surveillance and supervision organs; the intervention of the Nazi *Einsatzkommando* assassins who, while withdrawing from the East, forced their way into the camps and exterminated the inmates.[21]

Gheorghe Zaharia and Ion Cupșa recognize 50,741 survivors. Everyone else, together with the Romani, supposedly died at the hands of the Nazis "by epidemic, by malnutrition, and by harsh work conditions." The Wiesel Commission noted that Zaharia and Cupșa's book underestimates the number of victims but is an exception among Romanian historians.[22]

Negation and its corollary, historic revisionism, both in Romania and Chile, form the foundation for a society that by refusing to honestly confront the past fails to shoulder corresponding responsibilities in the present.

Education for "Never Again"

Negationism persists in Chile despite volumes of legal documentation and graphic proof and despite depositions by survivors and witnesses because former officials of the military dictatorship and their collaborators have never expressed the commitment to human rights that would enable a human rights culture to take root. Unlike Holocaust deniers, people who minimize the serious human rights violations committed in Chile are not peripheral characters. They are academics, businessmen, military, and politicians who hold prestigious public positions, and many are well-known figures.

Alejandra Morales Stekel, the director of the Memoria Viva Foundation, believes a significant segment of the population in Chile still lacks sufficient awareness regarding the atrocities: "'Gee! A few people died,' they say. The Rettig Report has never been widely disseminated and the Valech Report even less so. Political segments of the right take advantage of public ignorance, enabling negationist ideas to flourish. If people had a better understanding, they would not be able to not voice such opinions."

The most effective and long-lasting defensive strategy against negationism and oblivion is, as Karl Bohmer notes, education. Beginning in the mid-1950s, German students studied the history of genocide carried out by their country, a condition imposed by the Allies, and beginning in the 1960s, the Ministry of Education and the Ministry of Culture made the history of the Holocaust part of national curriculum policy. The subject of the Holocaust is incorporated in history, civics, literature, and religious or ethics classes. Visits to a memorial at the site of a former concentration camp are routine for high school students.

According to the German Human Rights Institute, teaching about the Shoah strives not only to inform German pupils about historic events but especially "to develop competencies to prevent such acts from ever happening again."[23]

In Chile, since the mid-1990s, teaching about the Holocaust has been incorporated into curricula programs for eighth graders. To assist teachers in presenting this subject matter, Abraham Magendzo, a well-known academic and specialist in human rights, and Marcela Tchimino, a specialist in peace and human rights education, developed an education resource tool. Launched in 2007 with the support of Isaac Frenkel, the product was a CD-ROM titled *Let's Learn about the Value of Life, Nondiscrimination, and Peace from the Holocaust*. Through music, images, and interactive features, this multimedia tool teaches students from second grade to high school about the historic development and consequences of the Shoah. Marcela explains how they approached the issue.

> Even though this is a historic event that apparently has no connection to the personal lives of the students, when we analyze the story and see who the victims were, who the perpetrators were, who helped save Jews, and who informed on them, many lessons can be learned related to tolerance, nondiscrimination, acceptance of the other, and the value of diversity. In that way, we open an entire field about human rights that indeed is connected to the students' lives.[24]

Abraham adds, "Certainly, the memory of the Holocaust . . . will not only recall the violation of fundamental rights committed in our own country . . . but also the struggles to end the violations, recover human dignity, denounce illegalities and abuses."[25]

Marcela underscores another dimension.

> For us, the most important thing is that they not see this as something that occurred many years ago but instead make the connection as history that affects our daily lives today. It is important for us to be familiar with history not because learning dates by heart matters but because people evolve through history, If we don't learn from our history, we can't say "never again." If we fail to learn from history, those crimes will be committed again.

Under the auspices of the Education Ministry, ten thousand copies of the CD-ROM were distributed to Chile's public schools. Abraham and Marcela, with support from B'nai B'rith, trained facilitators to train other teachers. However, the program came to a premature standstill when the ministry decided it did not want to continue it. The ministry likewise decided it did not want to support teaching on human rights and the history of the military regime in Chile.

Human rights education as the building block of a "culture genuinely respectful of human rights" was one of the recommendations the National Truth and Reconciliation Commission proposed in 1991. Later, the same institution published the Human Rights Library, a three-volume book that outlines a human rights curriculum. The use of this curriculum, which is included as part of transversal curriculum objectives such as drug abuse prevention, conflict resolution, and human rights, is subject to the discretion and methodology of each teacher.

In 1994, human rights organizations formed the Forum of Human Rights Education Institutions with the goal of persuading the Chilean government to incorporate human rights as part of school curriculum. Verónica Romo, Universidad Central early education director, represented Amnesty International in the forum. She remembers that "the government's response was positive, but we had the impression that our proposals ended up in a desk drawer of some Education Ministry office."[26]

More than a decade later, in 2005, Patricio Oyarzun, then director of the Education Ministry's Human Rights Department of the Transversal Support Unit, stated, "Only now, fifteen years after the inauguration of the first democratic government, is Chile at a more propitious and less conflictive moment for teaching human rights in the classrooms."[27]

In practice, because human rights is presented as a transversal elective, many schools and teachers are reluctant to teach this subject matter. "Human rights violations were not a truth accepted by the country as a whole. Consequently, teachers were not trained in human rights doctrine. This has meant that some teachers, who in theory would include it in their own class material through the principle of transversality, are not trained to teach about the issue of human rights," stated Jaime Prea in 2005, at the time, director of the Human Rights Department of the Santiago Teachers Union.[28]

The fact that human rights and Chilean history under the dictatorship are not widely taught in the public schools owes not only to a lack of trained teachers but also to the contentious nature of the issue. Many teachers who have taught these subjects in their classrooms have informed the teachers' union that some parents and school directors view human rights as political and put pressure on them to prevent them from speaking about it. In other cases, the teachers themselves chose not to bring up the subject of human rights and the military dictatorship in order to avoid conflict.

A study conducted in 2006 and 2007 on the teaching of this subject matter found that only 41 percent of Chilean students, most in public schools, had studied these subjects, despite their having been incorporated in the curriculum as a subunit. At the same time, the study found that students wanted to learn more. This, the researchers indicated, is "highly promising," and it should motivate educators to "fully meeting that interest."[29]

Teaching about the Shoah and Chile's recent history should be associated with shaping citizens who are conscious of the importance of human rights and committed to respect for life. Achieving that objective is what guides María Eva Bustos in her classes on Chilean twentieth-century history at SEK University and University of the Americas. Several years ago, Bustos attended a course at Yad Vashem, in Jerusalem, on Shoah teaching methodology, and she has close ties to Generations of the Shoah of Buenos Aires. Her course always opens with case histories, showing photos of disappeared persons in Chile, often of Juan Carrasco, who was last seen at Villa Grimaldi, alongside an unknown prisoner at Bergen-Belsen. She then invites students to imagine and reconstruct the stories of each, to reclaim the individual from anonymity and from the annulment of identity, which captors in both concentration camps attempted to carry out by depriving prisoners of their names and reducing them to a mere number. The photos become alive, and the history both of two countries as well as the two men emerge, producing empathy.

"It is very hard for people to understand that this happened here," says María Eva, "but when you show them that it doesn't matter if you're not a Communist—you could be arrested all the same—and it doesn't matter whether or not you are Jewish—this still could happen to you—the kids want to learn more."[30]

María Eva is not Jewish, and although she helped protect people persecuted by the military dictatorship, she was never arrested, nor did any family member directly suffer from repression. "I have an ongoing personal battle. No one can tell me, 'You are breathing through your wound; you are in this because you are the daughter or granddaughter of a victim,'" the educator underscores. She adds that she doesn't "want the Shoah to be a Jewish issue" or for human rights to be an issue that is the sole province of the Communist Party, the Revolutionary Left Movement, or the Socialist Party. "Just as the phenomenon of the unicity of the Shoah keeps it within the Jewish community, so too the issue of human rights in Chile is viewed as if it pertained to victims and their families. The belief is that we don't all have the right to talk about it. But, in my opinion, these are issues that belong to everyone."

Only if "everyone," as María Eva suggests, recognizes the larger truths as well as the smaller more subjective and personalized truths associated with the genocide known as the Shoah committed in another continent and atrocities against life committed in Chile can Chileans fight against negationism: that

veiled attempt to justify the unjustifiable, to blame the victim, and to turn the
page instead of establishing truth and justice as the scaffolding for the future.
People knowledgeable about their own history is the first line of defense
against negationism.

KILLING THE DEAD

When a noted Jewish community leader is asked whether a point of comparison exists between the military dictatorship's policy of human rights violations
and the genocide of the Jews carried out by the Nazis, he lifts an index finger
in caution and, in a serious tone of voice, says, "Careful! Do not trivialize the
Shoah!"

Trivialization is but a step away from denial and negation is akin to killing
someone already murdered. This has led to the installation of a virtual fence
around the Shoah, and Jewish officials are quick to thwart any attempt to
diminish the magnitude of the genocide. Trivialization and negation of the
Holocaust are regarded in contemporary times as covert antisemitism.

The valley of death through which six million Jews traversed was so enormous that it constitutes a unique chapter in the history of humankind. The
Holocaust is unique by virtue of the sheer quantitative dimension—six million exterminated. It is also unique in terms of the genocidal technology
employed—an industrial-scale death machinery—and also due to the underlying objective: to erase all vestiges of a people and its culture from the face of
the earth.

Philosopher Miguel Orellana Benado energetically takes issue with the idea
of constructing parallels between the Shoah and the policy of systematic human
rights violations in Chile: "It seems to me that there is no point of comparison. From the beginning of the active stage of the 'final solution,' in four years,
three out of every four Jews had been eliminated, as the Nuremberg trials concluded. Pinochet did not kill three out of every four members of the Communist Party in sixteen years. I don't think the facts hold up in this comparison."[31]

Nevertheless, as Argentine sociologist Daniel Feierstein remarks, "the weight
of the authority and . . . the uniqueness of the Nazi genocide against the Jewish population . . . has produced a disregard—indirectly but no less serious—
of all other victimized populations in different historic junctures. This was
achieved through the gradual process of degradation and inferiorization of
others' conditions of suffering, the delegitimation of others' suffering."[32] Thus
we paradoxically end up trivializing other acts of genocide and minimizing the
severity of others' suffering by emphasizing the uniqueness of the Shoah.

Writers and Nazi concentration camp survivors Bruno Bettelheim, Elie
Wiesel, and Primo Levi also contend that the extermination of the Jews of

Europe was unique. At the same time, however, they do not ignore the fact that other nations and peoples have also been victims of genocide. If we take it as a given that the Shoah was a planned, large-scale, and extreme act of repression that gradually but systematically affected all aspects of life, including life itself, then we should not conclude that what occurred in Rwanda, Cambodia, Bosnia, or Chile is less serious or less monstrous.

Marcela Tchimino underscores the singularity of every historic event: "I think that what happened in the Shoah is neither comparable nor analogous to other instances of extermination of other peoples. And what Chile's dictatorship did is not comparable to what happened in the Shoah." However,

> What is comparable are the shared characteristics associated with discrimination, segregation, torture, and crimes against humanity. A torturer is the same in Chile and China. If we fail to carry the human rights banner everywhere, we are negating history. This is also a lesson for us as Jews. To the extent that we fail to continually remember what we endured during the Shoah and before that during the Crusades and the Spanish Inquisition, we too negate our history. If I, as a Jew, who belong to a people subjected to discrimination, discriminate against others, I too negate my history. It is a lesson not only for Jews but for all peoples whose ancestors have endured discrimination or persecution, or who have had crimes committed against them.[33]

It has been postulated that comparison diminishes and relativizes the Shoah as a unique historical episode. But comparing highlights not only the similarities but also the differences. Comparing the systematic violations of human rights committed in Chile with those carried out by regimes in other countries enables us to work through their meaning and put those experiences in perspective. Although the Shoah, as the greatest crime of the twentieth century, is not analogous, it has become a reference point, and "Holocaust" has become synonymous with modern-era barbarism.

In Chile, the Shoah is a reference point that facilitates working through the experience of systematic human rights violations committed by the dictatorship as part of its policies of repression. In many forums and seminars related to Chile's recent history, it is commonplace for at least one speaker to refer to the "Jewish Holocaust," and frequently Chilean authors turn to it as well in search of clues that may help explain the rise of the systematic terrorism enacted by the Chilean military.

Paz Rojas, a neuropsychiatrist and cofounder of CODEPU, explains that Jewish writers who were concentration camp survivors helped her map a route for healing victims of repression in Chile: "In no text, either medical or on human rights, did I find anything to help me understand what happened in Chile from the standpoint of the crimes. It did not exist. What helped me understand? I read copiously about Jews and non-Jews who had survived the concentration camp experience, who describe what they went through not only from a material perspective but also psychologically and intellectually. How they lived through it and survived. And what happened."[34]

She read everything written by Primo Levi, Hannah Arendt, and many others, but the author who helped her the most was Bruno Bettelheim. The writing of all these authors pointed out for her analogies between what happened to a person imprisoned in a Nazi concentration camp and a person held in a Chilean detention center. "Both universes of people are subjected to a system that has the power to tyrannize them, to torture them, to make them disappear," she says. "It is a human relationship that occurs between a person who is absolutely powerless, defenseless, and another who has complete power to humiliate, destroy, rape, make them disappear. It is a perverse human juxtaposition. Each one was absolutely in the hands of another person. Of course, in any concentration camp in any part of the world, whether it be right or left, such as North Korea, this perverse relation exists." Moreover, when a survivor left Auschwitz and, thirty years later, a prisoner left Villa Grimaldi, each faced a similar experience. "Both were exposed to not knowing anything more about life," she explains.

In her book *La interminable ausencia*, Rojas traces the history and impact of the crime of forced disappearance as institutional policy of the Pinochet regime. She explains that this policy was a technique conceived by high-ranking military as a way to conceal crimes, a technique whose key element was negation. She observes that the closest ancestor of this crime, whose objective was to construct "a perverse subjectivity of reality at the individual, family, social and cultural levels," was the Nacht und Nebel (Night and Fog) decree, developed for the same purpose by Nazi Germany.[35] Through a decree issued on December 7, 1941, Marshal Wilhelm Keitel implemented the first measures designed to circumvent international public scrutiny. Opponents and resistance fighters of the occupied countries—mainly, France and Belgium—and Soviet soldier prisoners were rapidly deported in secret to Germany. Keitel gave the following instructions as to how to carry out such operations: "a) The prisoners will disappear without a trace; b) No information shall be given regarding the individual's place of detention or destiny."[36]

A few days later, Keitel, in his capacity as commander in chief of the German Armed Forces, explained the grounds for these operations. "Efficient and enduring terrorization can be achieved only either by capital punishment or by measures to keep the relatives of the criminal and the population in the dark as to the fate of the criminal. This aim is achieved by transferring the criminal to Germany."[37]

Prior to the Nacht und Nebel decree, the Germans treated prisoners in accord with existing national and international law, such as the Geneva Convention. Nacht und Nebel deviated from international norms on humane treatment of prisoners. There would be no more letters notifying governments or families concerning the whereabouts of the person or even the fact that the person was imprisoned. In the concentration camps, those prisoners had a tag pinned to their shirt with the letters NN. Up through April 1944, an estimated seven thousand persons, most from France, were captured in Nacht und Nebel operations and taken to concentration camps.[38]

Explicit instructions from Chilean military dictatorship hierarchy have not been found concerning the practice of forced disappearance. However, the intermeshed responses from the Interior Ministry, the courts, police stations, and the intelligence apparatus that systematically denied arrests, and even the existence of the clandestine detention centers such as Villa Grimaldi, had the same effect. Denials conveyed in the form of standardized responses that every person seeking information about a missing loved one received strongly suggest a state-devised plan, despite the lack of a memo instructing the various governmental entities to operate that way.

At any time and at any place, a person might vanish, be abducted, or be disappeared in the countries (primarily France) occupied by the Nazis. The same was the case in Chile. The cynical explanations from Chilean military and civilian personnel that represented the arrests as existing only in the family members' imagination by suggesting that the missing person had gone off with a lover or had left the country only augmented the feeling of terror. Plagued by piercing and persistent doubts, the family members' path, Rojas writes, "was associated with the sense of frustration, anguish, consternation, desperation, as well as horror arising from what they suspected or imagined."[39]

Unlike the Chilean repressive apparatus that rarely allowed the veil of secrecy to fall, the Germans quickly dispensed with any pretense of reserve. Very early on, they began massive arrests and deportations in operations that were no longer limited to the cover of night or fog but that were now carried out in full daylight.

Déjà vu

An interviewer with the Voces de la Shoah project, which collects testimonies of survivors who live in Chile, explains, "It was so shocking to me when I worked on the interviews. Many referred to the Chilean dictatorship. What happened in Chile, no matter what some say about it not being comparable and regardless of whether it was caused by the right or the left, produced a retraumatization in Holocaust survivors. Just knowing that these situations were occurring here made them relive their own experiences over there."[40]

In the subjective imagination of a few Chilean Jews on the left, the massive arrests and arbitrary violence after the military coup were associated with the Shoah. For the psychologist Edith Benado, who grew up listening to stories about her family's flight from Nazi-occupied Bulgaria, "it was like going back to the same thing."[41] She says, "The generals' first speeches seared my soul. I kept telling myself, 'here it won't be Jews, or blacks, or homosexuals, but all of us who think differently.'" Edith fled Chile with her two small children, just like her aunt had fled the Nazis in Bulgaria. "For us, as Jews, who always have to move from one country to another, it is not difficult to adapt to a new place. Having to leave is normal, not frightful. We Jews are wanderers."

Leila Pérez, who was a prisoner during the early years of the dictatorship, has reflected on these issues ever since she arrived in exile in Germany, even though she is not Jewish.

I believe I made the mistake of thinking that it was same as the Nazis. When I was held in Chile Stadium, not only me but many other people held there said, "These guys are today's Nazis." The aesthetics of the Chilean military is based on German military aesthetics; many military officers have German last names and are blue-eyed blonds. The physical traits are quickly associated with the Nazi concept. Afterward, I made the connection when soldiers burned books outside the San Borja Towers. And two years later, when I was a prisoner at Tres Alamos and Puchuncaví, I saw these places were more like camps than jails. Then I connected the DINA with the SS. Just like the SS was directly under the führer, the DINA answered directly to Pinochet. There is a recycling of social repression techniques. . . . However, I now understand it is not the same thing. Auschwitz, as Hanna Arendt said, never should have existed. The same goes for Villa Grimaldi and the Roman circus. But the Shoah transformed quantitative into qualitative. It was dialectical: the massive international scale, the formalization of the state, and the industrialization of death. It's not that Villa Grimaldi is nothing; for me, it is everything.[42]

Frida Sharim thought about this question as well: "After the coup took place, the entire time I thought I was about to be taken. This time around, there would be no escape, I thought. I had saved myself from Europe, but no one is saved just like that, gratuitously. I felt it like karma. You cannot erase what you are."[43]

Frida was never imprisoned, but her sister Sara, University of Chile professor of philology, was arrested on August 5, 1975, in a roundup of professors from that university. The year before, Sara's oldest son had been jailed at the place she was later held, and several of her students had also disappeared. When the doorbell rang that night, she was watching television with her husband. When she was taken away, Sara was fully aware of what might happen to her. Each one of the eight nights she was imprisoned and kept incommunicado at Cuatro Alamos, "I thought to myself, look how history repeats itself," says Sara. "Little wonder people were made to disappear. People were made to disappear here because other people were disappeared in Europe! Those patterns are repeated. I was tremendously shocked, when I was seventeen years old and saw news reports about the Nazi concentration camps."[44] A photograph of a boy carrying his baby brother in the line for the crematorium remained etched in her memory. "I never forgot that image," she says. "I retained it in my retina. It stunned me. I said to myself, 'God! May this never come to pass in Chile!' And it did come to Chile! I immediately made the connection."

During her detention at Cuatro Alamos, "There were eight of us, eight women, shut in a room measuring two by two meters. We had to sleep two on each wooden bunk bed. There were four bunk beds and eight women. There were blankets. But the entire place was filthy. I don't think I ate more than a piece of bread. I couldn't stand the smell of rancid food. They served food that you couldn't eat." Her cellmates at Cuatro Alamos were all University of Chile professors, and all of them were leftists. Sara Sharim had been the left's candidate for dean of the School of Philosophy and Humanities. She shared the same cell with another Jewish professor, Eliana Dobry, Socialist Party member, and professor of logic and knowledge theory. Before her arrest, Dobry had helped people enter embassies to obtain political asylum and sheltered persecuted people in her home.

Although Cuatro Alamos bore exterior similarities to Nazi concentration camps, Sara regained her freedom. Her brother, the acclaimed actor and theater director Nissim Sharim, was fundamental in obtaining her release. Rosario Guzmán, a journalist with the *El Mercurio* newspaper, was interviewing him when Sharim told her, "I don't want to continue with this interview. My sister was just imprisoned." The journalist promised to ask her brother to exercise his influence to secure her freedom as soon as possible. Her brother was Jaime Guzmán, a close advisor of Pinochet's. At the same time, Sara's husband, Fernando Cuevas, spoke to Rabbi Angel Kreiman. It is likely that Sara's release was achieved thanks to the sum of these and other efforts. But another key factor was that for the first time, *El Mercurio* published the names of the forty university professors arrested in the roundup, effectively protecting them from disappearance.

One night I tell the girls, "You know what, I'm going to take off this skirt." I was using it day and night. I slept in the skirt. I got up in the skirt. I called it my depression skirt because it was an ugly blue knit. As I'm taking off the skirt, I hear my name called: "Sara Sharim, to the office!" "It's my turn, girl," I said to myself. But it wasn't! "Take your things and get out of here!" they tell me. "But it's almost midnight; how am I going to leave at this hour of the night?" They threw us out the door, just like that. Of the eight women in that cell, four of us got out. And that was the night I was about to take off that skirt!

Curfew was about to begin in twenty minutes. "We left and discovered that we were in the middle of a street. We had no idea where to go. Suddenly, one of the women said, 'Look, here comes a car.' All right, let's get it to stop. And the guy did stop. We told him, 'Take us wherever you want.' All of us professors were dismissed from the University of Chile on political grounds," she says.

For Edmundo Lebrecht, son of Walter Lebrecht, the refugee from Ulm who settled in Contulmo, his prison experience was a sort of déjà vu.

In your imagination, seeing the guard towers and barbed wire of Ritoque made you feel like you were in a Nazi concentration camp, but in a deserted place among the sand dunes. And all of a sudden they would conduct combat razzias. At two in the morning they would burst into the cabin where we were sleeping and attack us. They would order us outside in formation, half asleep, and they would fire. Pa-pap-pa. They wanted to keep us constantly terrorized.[45]

Even so, he noted, "There were vast differences. . . . The Ritoque and Puchuncaví prison camps had the appearance of concentration camps, but it would not be correct to call them extermination centers. They gave you food." However, he did find similarities between Nazi concentration camps and the torture centers of the Chilean dictatorship.

The Villa Grimaldi, José Domingo Cañas, and 38 Londres torture centers were similar to Nazi extermination centers. There they really did exterminate people. They destroyed people psychologically and physically. At José Domingo Cañas they didn't give us food. They would throw us the leftovers from what they ate. We got into the habit of chewing small pieces of orange peel.

When I was there, I immediately made the association because it is indescribable, impossible to talk about. I had read so much about the Nazi concentration camps and had seen so many documentary films. Whether you died or did not die might depend on whether or not your torturer had gotten some nighttime pleasure.[46]

In the Magellan Straits, facing the southernmost city of Punta Arenas, Dawson Island was the place of detention for approximately three hundred prisoners. Thirty of them had been leaders or cabinet ministers of the Popular Unity government who were kept isolated from the rest. Miguel Lawner, grandson of that couple who crossed the Dniester River one night in 1921, was one of them.

Exhausted from hard labor but wanting to ensure that the wood-burning heater in their barracks did not extinguish during the frigid nights on Dawson Island, the prisoners would talk into the night. They always talked in a low tone of voice because they suspected the place was bugged with a microphone concealed somewhere. On more than one occasion, the prisoners, including Luis Vega, Enrique Kirberg, and Benjamin Teplizky, all Jews like Miguel, discussed the parallels between the Nazi extermination system and the Chilean-style model they were experiencing firsthand. The similarities began with the characteristics of the physical place where they were enclosed at night. The new barracks they built, Miguel says, "without a doubt were based on the Nazi model."[47] When he is asked if he truly has no doubt, he replies, "I have no doubt. It doesn't necessarily mean they planned it that way, however. But the type of repetitive barracks, each one isolated from the other, corresponds to the German concentration camp model."

Architects have a special eye for detail, and architect Miguel agilely evokes his visual memory of the places where he was imprisoned.[48] "Dawson is the only camp that was expressly constructed to hold prisoners. All the other places were adapted to hold prisoners. Tres Alamos was an old Catholic Church complex, and other detention centers had been private houses expropriated by the military. Ritoque was a coastal vacation place that they armored, but it was not specifically built to serve as a prison camp. Dawson Island, however, was built with that purpose in mind."

Miguel and economist Carlos Matus, who had been minister of the economy and director of the Economic Development Agency (CORFO) for the Popular Unity government, fellow prisoners at Dawson, set themselves to the task of refurbishing the place where they were held from September to December 1973. The improved quarters were nearly ready when the prisoners were transferred to a new camp. Upon first laying eyes on the new barracks, some prisoners could not help crying.

The architect and former political prisoner Miguel Lawner resumes his story.

When we got there, Carlos Matus was the first to point it out to me. He said to me [*Miguel lowers his voice*], "Miguelito, we can't be in this place without going

Miguel Lawner's drawings, sketched from memory, chronicle the Dawson Island prison camp (Miguel Lawner)

crazy, so let's get to work. We're going to request permission to build us a better place." So that's what we did. We made ourselves a decent place with materials we stole from here and there, with help from some of the prison guards. The first place had been a former military base. It had a certain degree of humanity, despite being very overcrowded. But this one was quite depressing. Starting with the double barbed wire, the machine-gun guard booths above, the sentry towers, the lights; in short, it was a true concentration camp.

Luis Vega, an attorney from Valparaíso who was transferred to Dawson Island from the Esmeralda naval cadet ship that had been turned into a prison, contends in his book published from exile in Tel Aviv that Walter Rauf, the Nazi architect who settled in Chile, designed the new facilities.[49] Rauf was one of the designers of the Nazi concentration camps as well as of the trucks into which lethal gas was piped, in 1939, prior to the installment of gas chambers in extermination camps. According to Vega, Rauf, who had lived in Chile since 1958, not only provided architectural consultation but also instructed the Chilean military on the art of interrogation and treatment of prisoners. Despite the Dawson Island prison's decided Nazi characteristics, Miguel cautions that Rauf's authorship of the Dawson camp design has never been proven.

Miguel recalled an incident that illustrates that for Dawson prisoners, or at least the Jewish prisoners, the similarity with the German concentration camps was very present.

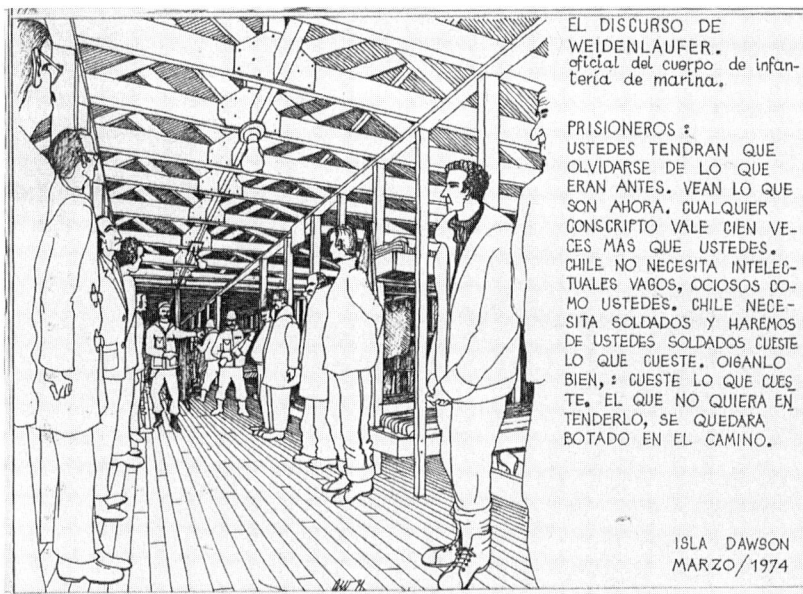

Military commander's speech to Dawson Island prisoners regarding the institution of a harsher regime (Miguel Lawner)

Near the end of our imprisonment at Dawson, we decided to build a roof to protect the castles of firewood that we ourselves brought every day that winter. Without firewood for the stove to heat up the barracks, we could die from the cold. So it was vital, a matter of life or death, to ensure that the firewood did not get wet. I was above hammering the boards while most of the others were forced to carry sacks of gravel from the seashore to the barrack yard to prevent it from becoming a mud sty. Groups of eight fellows, watched by the guards, were coming up from the beach with sacks on their shoulders. When they came up to where we were, I would come down to help spread the gravel evenly with a rake. I was still above on the roof when a group of fellow prisoners came up, and I was whistling some old song. I remember that Benjamin Teplizky, a Jewish friend, stared at me and said, "How can you whistle like that? Don't you realize that this is the 'final solution'?"

In their nightly conversations, Miguel debated his prison companions' contention that what the military coup had installed was the Chilean equivalent of the "final solution." His theory proved correct, he notes, when they got out of Dawson Island prison alive and were dispatched into exile. On both continents and in both generations, there was "ferocious persecution with unimaginable methods. The hatred the dictatorship was capable of generating was similar to what Hitler generated," Miguel says. Yet, he acknowledges, the magnitude was different.

Pinochet may have wanted to do something similar but he was not able to because the world had changed. The level of information was not comparable with what existed in the 1940s. We had the United Nations that did not exist before. Consequently, international pressure constituted a fundamental element that restrained the dictatorship's hands. We clearly felt it. They did not have free rein like Hitler to do whatever he wanted. That is the enormous, great difference. The world had changed, and the conditions were not in place for what Pinochet frankly wanted to do.

8

Paths to Healing through Memory and Justice

THE REUNION OF THE REMNANTS

They believed themselves to be the last Jews of Europe. Just freed from the concentration camps and slowly coming back to life, some survivors returned to the city or town from which they had been forced to leave. They found their homes occupied by others and their families lost or decimated. Nothing was the same as before. Now they were displaced people without a place on earth to call their own. Much of the world had observed with indifference—making sure to keep their doors shut—as Jews clamored in the anteroom of death. Now, their refusal to succor the survivors amounted to another turn of the screw.

In some places, victims continued to be pariahs. In postwar Austria, Nazis and their collaborators had become respectable citizens of society, and the few surviving Jews were marginalized.

> We refer to the social reality of postwar Austria, in which survivors of the Shoah led a marginal existence, stigmatized and rootless. They were refugees and displaced persons; their families had been murdered and they found themselves in an alien environment. Their tormentors enjoyed social acceptance from everyone else and led absolutely normal lives in the circle of their loved ones.[1]

The survivors had no choice but to depart once again. Upon reaching Israel, United States, Brazil, Uruguay, Argentina, and also Chile, they looked for their peers.

Jaime Karszenbaum, originally from the Polish town of Sarnak, arrived in Buenos Aires, by way of Siberia.[2] To that place of tundra, forests, and coal mines at the outer fringes of the world, two hundred thousand Polish Jews were deported. Some were residents of towns from eastern Poland, the zone that fell under the control of the Soviet Union after Germany and the Soviet Union signed a nonaggression pact. Thousands of other Jews fled to the Soviet zone after the German invasion of Poland on September 1, 1939. But Stalin did not trust them, and beginning in 1940, one year before the Nazis began deporting Jews to extermination camps, he sent Jews to forced labor camps in Siberia, where they remained throughout the war period.

Karszenbaum, who was twenty-three years old when the war broke out, worked cutting trees in the Siberian forests. Only when the temperature fell under forty degrees below zero Celsius were they permitted to refrain from working. But sometimes the Soviet commanding officers hid the public thermometer and they were forced to work just the same. No coat was capable of blunting the penetrating cold of the endless Siberian winters. In the brief summers, when during a single month, the temperature rose above freezing, clouds of mosquitos descended.

The Jews who lived the harsh experience of Siberia did not know they were the fortunate ones. At the end of the war when they were allowed to leave, Karszenbaum set out for Poland, convinced that he had much to tell his family. As he neared home, he began to hear other stories and learned about the catastrophe from which he had been saved. Of the 3.3 million Jews who lived in Poland before the war, three hundred thousand had survived.[3] Karszenbaum had escaped the Shoah thanks to deportation to Stalin's labor camps in Siberia.

In Buenos Aires, Karszenbaum was one of the founders of the *she'erit hapleita*.[4] Translated literally from Hebrew as "surviving remnant," the *she'erit hapleita* were mutual support organizations formed by survivors in many parts of the world. The She'erit HaPleita of Metropolitan Chicago explains the origins of these mutual societies this way: "The groups fostered an environment which allowed people with similar histories to get together. . . . The groups became extended families which allowed members to celebrate their lives and accomplishments while at the same time lament and talk about the tragedy that they endured."[5]

In the Jewish tradition, rites to remember a deceased person lead mourners, and the family in particular, along a road that enables them to come to terms with what had been the presence of the deceased and from now on will be his or her absence. The process of coming to grips with the loss begins with the tearing or keriah of the shirt that the mourner will wear during the first week after the loved one passes away. After the burial, which must take place within forty-eight hours, the family, seated on the floor, enters shiva, the initial six days of mourning, during which they do not work. During religious services over the course of the following eleven months, kaddish, the prayer for the dead, is recited with a quorum of ten adults. On the first anniversary of the death, known as the yahrzeit, the family and people closest to the deceased return to the cemetery to place the tombstone.

But how does one mourn when the date of death is unknown? Without a date of death, how does one mark the yahrzeit year after year?[6] And how to leave stones at the grave when the deceased person's body has not been recovered and there is no tomb? Every Shoah survivor faced such religious dilemmas. The most absolute majority of victims did not leave a body for burial. Each survivor sought a way to mark the annual yahrzeit anniversary, frequently for an entire extended family.

When Karszenbaum arrived in Buenos Aires, he looked for people from his hometown of Sarnak. With them, he formed a *fahrein*, a small organization of people from the same town or geographic region, a form of communal organization that existed before the Shoah. Each year, Karszenbaum's *fahrein* held a commemorative ceremony, often in a Jewish cemetery. In the late 1950s, they formed the *she'erit hapleita*, whose members were not necessarily connected by geographic area. There they spoke about what had happened to them. Like the *fahrein*, the *she'erit hapleita* held private ceremonies to remember their families and destroyed towns. A long time passed before the symbols of the Shoah and the survivors' testimonies became public. "Other Jews and society as a whole were not prepared for processing survivors' extreme experiences," notes Jonathan Karszenbaum, grandson of Jaime and executive director of the organization Generations of the Shoah of Buenos Aires.[7]

With the founding of the state of Israel, Yom Hashoah was established to remember Jewish victims of Shoah on the twenty-seventh of the month of Nissan according to the Hebrew calendar, which coincides with the date of the Warsaw ghetto uprising, April 19, 1943. Others have reclaimed the ancient tradition of Yom Hakadosh Haklalí, a day of general mourning that commemorates an event that occurred in the year 587 BCE, when King Nebuchadnezzar of Babylonia breached the walls of Jerusalem and began a military siege that lasted thirty months. The date the siege began, Tammuz 9, which corresponds to late December or early January, was designated to remember all people whose date and place of death or both is unknown. In 2005, the UN General Assembly established January 27 as Holocaust Commemoration Day, anniversary of the liberation of Auschwitz prisoners to remember all Jewish, Romani, homosexual, and other victims.

The Generations of the Shoah organization not only observes Yom Hashoah, which is most widely commemorated in the Jewish world, but also March 8 and 9, the end of the war, the moment when, in the words of Jonathan, "the survivors definitely become survivors and their lives are no longer in danger."

In the postdictatorship years of Chile and throughout Latin America, family members of forcibly disappeared persons faced similar dilemmas. Without a body, a date, or even the certainty the person was killed, "the mourning process is suspended in time."[8] As of 2010, August 30 has been commemorated as the International Day of Forcibly Disappeared Persons, promoted by the Federación Latinoamericana de Asociaciones de Familiares de Detenidos-Desaparecidos (FEDEFAM, Latin American Federation of Associations for Relatives of the Detained-Disappeared) and approved by the United Nations.

At the commemoration "Remembering Anne Frank and Diana Aron" held in Peace Park in December 2006, Anamaria Aron indicated that for many years her family had lacked a minyan—that is, a quorum of ten Jews—to say kaddish for her sister Diana. This made Rabbi Daniel Zang's recitation of it at the ceremony as small stones were placed along the "wall of names" for Diana and other victims all the more moving.

Carmen Hertz, human rights attorney and widow of Carlos Berger, situates the practice of remembrance in a social context.

> The Jewish people will never ever forget the Shoah. The Shoah is installed in its collective imagination to such a degree that one generation transmits it to the next. In Chile, unfortunately, that does not happen. We are always told that our remembering is recalcitrant. The recovery of collective memory in Chile has been the effort of groups of people, but the establishment and the political system, until very recently, did not help at all. We have to strive for that memory Jews recovered, embodied by Yad Vashem, which symbolizes the respect for remembrance.[9]

Survivors of the Shoah felt marginalized in postwar Austria; today survivors of detention centers operated by the Chilean military dictatorship sense that they are an uncomfortable presence for the government and any number of fellow Chileans. It was only as result of pressure exerted by former political prisoners and human rights activists of the organization Ethical Committee against Torture that moral condemnation against torture was achieved through the governmental National Commission on Political Imprisonment and Torture. No longer did surviving victims feel they had to keep their experiences private; the commission's mandate gave them permission to make their experiences known in the public sphere.

Ernesto Lejderman is both survivor and a family member of victims. His parents, Bernardo Lejderman, an Argentine, and María del Rosario Avalos Castañeda, a Mexican, were gunned down in the early hours of December 8, 1973, outside an abandoned mine in Quebrada de Angostura, located in northcentral Vicuña. There the couple hid with their two-year-old son Ernesto, waiting for someone to help them flee Chile by crossing the Andes border on foot. Before she was shot, María del Rosario managed to hide Ernesto behind a boulder, saving his life. Army lieutenant Juan Emilio Cheyre left the child at a convent in La Serena. His grandparents recovered him and raised him in Buenos Aires.

Ernesto has been an active member of Hijos e Hijas por la Identidad y la Justicia contra el Olvido y el Silencio (HIJOS, Sons and Daughters for Identity and Justice against Forgetting and Silence), an organization founded in Argentina by children of forcibly disappeared persons. Just as Shoah survivors were only able to speak among themselves about the horrors they had experienced, Ernesto could not find someone willing to listen to him until he joined the organization. When he began participating in HIJOS, he was "surprised to discover that there I was able to talk, whereas I couldn't with other friends. It was incredible. I tried to talk about it, but I didn't find listeners on the other end. People were not prepared to hear, not even my closest friends. Among my relatives, no one, except for an uncle, would talk about my father."[10]

In July 2013, Ernesto went to the offices of Generations of the Shoah in Buenos Aires to converse with the organization's director, Jonathan Karszenbaum. Jonathan, the grandson of a Polish survivor of the Siberian work camps, told Ernesto, "Maybe your friends did not understand, or maybe they didn't dare ask the questions that you were waiting for." Many stories related both to the Shoah and the systematic violation of human rights in Latin America were taboo and could not be broached in Latin America.[11]

In Hebrew, "zikaron" means "memory," but "yizkor" means "one will remember," suggesting an active memory that projects into the future. Yizkor is associated with a series of prayers recited on four occasions during the year. In the Yizkor memorial service, one makes a commitment to carry out acts of solidarity and good deeds in the name of the person remembered. The very act of naming a person is an act of remembrance. Yizkor includes a special prayer in memory of Jewish martyrs that is fully relevant for victims of all human malevolence: "May their heroism and the devotion of their sacrifice echo in our hearts, and the purity of their souls be reflected in our lives."

Spanning several generations, Jewish remnants of four continents have paved a road for all regions of the world emerging from extremely repressive authoritarian situations.

ACTOR-WITNESSES

Why did I survive and he did not? Was my body more resistant to the blows, electric current, hunger? Was my mind more resilient, allowing me to buffer humiliation and to find the precise words to reply to my torturer? Maybe it was just a matter of luck. But how can I give meaning to my life now without them?

Every person emerging from the darkness of Auschwitz, Belsen, Buchenwald, Treblinka, Birkenau, Sobibor, and all other Nazi death factories in 1945 asked themselves these questions. Similar questions are still asked by many survivors of Pisagua, Londres 38, Villa Grimaldi, and other torture centers of Augusto Pinochet's Chile.

Some survivors never say a word to anyone, not even their parents, spouse, or children. At some given moment, their voice cracks or a shadow crosses their face, and their children think but don't dare ask out loud, what happened to him or her? Or maybe they never suspect that their father, mother, grandparents are survivors.

What happened to her mother was what Marcela Godoy always wanted to know and what she still wants to know. But in her family, it was and continues to be prohibited from conversation. Her mother was born to a well-to-do Jewish family of Berlin. She was forced to leave public school to attend a Jewish school, when laws were decreed prohibiting Jews from going to school alongside non-Jewish Germans. The family arrived in Chile in 1936, when her mother was thirteen years old. This is practically all Marcela knows about her mother's life prior to Chile. What did she see? What compelled her maternal grandparents to leave at that precise moment? Who bid the family farewell as they crossed the ship's ramp? What happened to those who stayed behind? Whenever Marcela brought up the subject and asked these questions, her mother simply became mute. Once, her mother's young nephew, who lived in France, was given a school assignment to ask his elder relatives about their lives before World War II. His aunt in Chile simply replied that she had been a member of an anti-Nazi party. She had opened the door just a bit, only to tightly shut it once again. "It is very hard not knowing your own history," said Marcela. "My mother is ninety years old, and probably I will never know it."[12]

Like Marcela's mother, Jorge Hirsch never told his children what he went through in Germany; not even about the death of his parents in Treblinka, when he was nineteen years old. He did not tell them how he escaped from a forced labor camp near the German-Dutch border. Until the day he died, fairly young, in 1974, "he never told us a thing," said Tomás Hirsch, the youngest of Jorge Hirsch's three sons.[13]

> In 1995 we discovered letters between him, already in Chile, and his parents. The exchange of letters is quite dramatic because they narrate how the situation evolved. The first letter from his parents said: "It is good that you left because things here are very bad." Three more months passed, and another letter said,

"Well, the neighbor and another person were taken away. No one knows where they are." Another three months later, the next letter said, "Your father lost his job and we have to wear a Magen David on our arm." The next letter said, "They kicked us out of the city, and now we have to live somewhere else." Another four months, a letter said, "Your dear aunt has disappeared." It was the last letter he received.

Surveying the records of Yad Vashem, Tomás learned that his grandparents died in the Treblinka extermination camp.

Elisa Goldschmidt, mother of the three Hirsch brothers, on the other hand, talked about it, and "from the time we were very little, she taught us to learn and understand, but not hate," explains Tomás. He describes the lessons he and his brothers learned from their mother. She was "a very special person," he says, who taught them the value of committing oneself

to life, to human rights, justice, solidarity and to giving meaning to one's life. She deeply despised, almost viscerally, Germans, the Nazis, but she always transmitted to us the importance of not letting hatred frame our lives but instead drawing strength from that history as a commitment to life. The lives of each of us three brothers center on a social commitment to changing the world. I believe my mother was the source of that spirit, as well as seeing my father's pain and deciding that we wanted our lives to be different.

For Matzuni and Pamela Berger, their uncle Carlos was a distant figure. They were born after his death, and their father told them practically nothing about the circumstances in which his older brother died. Eduardo Berger, a physician who died on June 17, 2009, was with his sister-in-law Carmen Hertz when an official, without bothering to get out of his military jeep, informed them that all the political prisoners held in Calama had been shot dead because they had attempted to escape. Shortly thereafter, Eduardo left Chile for Canada; there he married, and he and his wife had their two daughters. In 2008, at the Berger home in Ottawa, Germán Berger, the son of Carlos and Carmen, filmed a scene for his documentary *Mi vida con Carlos*. In the scene, his cousins Matzuni and Pamela remark that this is the first time they are learning about the brutal killing of their uncle by the Caravan of Death. To protect himself and them from a painful subject, Eduardo had chosen not to talk about it. Germán's film enabled them to talk: "This movie broke the silence that reigned in my family more than thirty years. I made the film for one single reason: the tremendous sadness that prevented everyone from talking about my father."[14]

Elie Wiesel, deported with his family to Auschwitz and then to Buchenwald, where his parents and younger sister died, addresses the same painful difficulty.

> The survivors . . . remained silent. At first out of reserve; there are wounds and sorrows one prefers to conceal. And out of fear as well. Fear above all. Fear of arousing disbelief, of being told: Your imagination is sick, what you describe could not possibly have happened. Or: You are counting on our pity, you are exploiting your suffering. Worse: they feared being inadequate to the task. . . . They were afraid of saying what must not be said, of attempting to communicate with language that eludes language, of falling into the trap of easy half-truths. Sooner or later, every one of them was tempted to seal his lips and maintain absolute silence.[15]

Wiesel overcame those fears to speak in name of those who did not survive. He embraced as a mission of his renewed life not only giving testimony about what happened in the concentration camps but, above all, denouncing the violation of human rights wherever it occurred. His labor of love was recognized when he was awarded the Nobel Peace Prize in 1986.

The reluctance to talk about the experience in the detention and torture centers of Chile was due to a society unwilling to listen. As an attorney with the Vicariate of Solidarity throughout all those years and until the institution closed in 1992, Carmen Hertz heard testimony from many people shortly after they had gotten out of the dictatorship's prisons.

> In the transition period, society did not give them space to talk, not because they did not want to talk about it, but because the subject was uncomfortable for everyone else. If you began talking about the dictatorship period, you were an uncomfortable person. In Germany, due to the Allied military triumph, due to the Nuremberg trials, all Holocaust and Nazi crimes became engraved in the collective European imagination as the most brutal crimes of the twentieth century. Yet, here in Chile, what happened during the dictatorship has never been publicly acknowledged.[16]

At first, former Chilean political prisoners limited their testimonies to depositions in judicial proceedings. However, they rarely testified about their own experiences; instead, they served as witnesses for another prisoner with whom they had shared a cell or whose voice or shout they heard. Given that the agents who carried out these human rights violations never confessed to their crime, survivors' testimonies are the most decisive element of proof in such cases. Despite having endured similar abuse, however, they tended to downplay and minimize the importance of the physical or psychological mis-treatment they personally had experienced. In addition, because many people detained by the Chilean dictatorship regard their imprisonment through the lens of politics, they tended at first to refer to themselves as "former political prisoners," not "victims." Only in recent years have former political prisoners accepted their condition as "survivors," a concept that gained force after the first criminal complaints were filed in the mid-1990s and after the creation in 2004 of the National Commission on Political Imprisonment and Torture, which for the first time in Chilean history recognized torture as a serious human rights violation.

Julio Laks

The negative connotation of the word "victim" is described by Julio Laks, arrested on September 22, 1974, with his wife, Rosalía Martínez, and friend María Cristina López Stewart, who remains forcibly disappeared to this day.[17]

> The term "victim" has always bothered me. It contains a measure of truth, but the problem is that it does not differentiate between victims of German racial genocide—Jews and gypsies—and Communist victims of Nazism. The difference between the countless "innocent victims" and us precisely is that we were members of political organizations and social activists. The word "victim" does not describe political activists. After Pinochet's arrest, the word "survivor" was used for the first time. We had involuntarily obscured our own experience, which we considered more akin to that of witness than victim.

After arriving in Israel as a refugee in January 1975 and later settling in Paris, where he lives today, Julio Laks testified in many international arenas, de-nouncing what was occurring in Chile. He also gave depositions in court pro-ceedings, such as in the case of the priest Antonio Llidó, with whom he shared a cell in the torture house on José Domingo Cañas Street. His sworn state-ment describes the priest's blood-stained shirt and how he suffered from inter-nal hemorrhages and torn muscles. Yet when it came to talking about what he himself had experienced in the same place, Julio kept the tone and subject matter light.

> People were surprised that I spoke with such ease about what had happened to me. When I talked about my experience, often I would do so from a distance that some people found shocking. They were astonished that I spoke as if I were talking about someone else. Much later, I realized that I tended to talk about light things, such as prison humor. I am a person who enjoys telling jokes, so

that was my manner of talking about that period of my life, but actually it was a way to protect myself.

Julio gives an example of something "funny" that happened during his imprisonment at José Domingo Cañas.

Maybe it's more tragicomical than funny. At first I was placed in a room where men and women were sitting on the floor. Then I was taken to a small room outside the house that was actually a windowless cupboard measuring six square feet. I think it was a Sunday because the commanders were rarely around on Sundays. The place was left in charge of young guys, the guards and lower-ranking personnel. They opened the door to the closet where we were sitting and asked if we were hungry. One of the forms of torture was sleep and food deprivation. But they did not seem aggressive, so we replied a bit provocatively, "How could we not be hungry!" So the guys asked us if we wanted some clam soup. We answered, "It's one thing that you mistreat us, hit us, torture us, but please don't make fun of us. Don't make fools of us." They replied, "We're only asking if you want some." Five minutes later they brought an enormous pot filled with clam soup. We hadn't eaten in a week, and now they gave us clam soup.

Julio tells the story as an example of the absurdity of prison existence. "For me, it was a way to exemplify the crazy world we were in, where there no rules of any kind, and a different reality."

The first time he testified in a court case was concerning Antonio Llidó. In 1999, Spanish judge Baltazar Garzón asked him to testify in the trial in Madrid on behalf of Spaniards murdered and disappeared in Chile. Talking about Llidó triggered memories of close friends in Chile as well as his own imprisonment, which he had suppressed.

Everyone who testified appeared so shaken. I even proposed that psychological support be provided. But I thought it wasn't my problem, and I calmly went to testify before Garzón.

I calmly began talking about my imprisonment and about our disappeared friends. It was going well until, suddenly, I became mute with a knot in my throat, and I could not talk any more. I felt desperate. I couldn't even say that I was unable to speak. At that moment I saw a pitcher and a glass on the desk. I told myself, "That's my salvation. I'll serve myself a glass of water." But when I reached out for it, I realized the pitcher was empty. Garzón reacted at once. In a flash he leaped up, took the pitcher, and went to fill it with water. I then realized that some things were still stuck inside me and I had not overcome them, if they ever can be overcome.

Sensing that "for the first time I was speaking to someone who was on our side and could take action" helped him surmount the impasse and resume his deposition. In the context of a court investigation, "testifying acquired value in relation to memory and justice. Although not much was done by way of justice, at least I put it on the record," adds Julio. In the case of Antonio Llidó, Julio contributed much more than court record. His testimony and that of Rosalía Martínez were fundamental in the indictment issued on May 13, 2003, of the DINA leaders and another six agents for the abduction of the Spanish priest.

Shoah survivors frequently evoke the concept of "never again" to explain what motivates them to share their testimony. In Chile, many commemorative events also evoke the idea of "never again" to narrate what happened during the military dictatorship in the hope that awareness of that history will galvanize civil society to prevent its reoccurrence.

Julio, however, finds the slogan "never again" politically naïve: "I think there can't be a 'never again' as long as exploitation and capitalism persist. It is repeated every day, today and tomorrow, throughout the world and in Chile too, with the Mapuche people." His own family history reflects the repetition of exile and displacement. His father and mother, born in Poland, met in Belgium, where his maternal grandparents moved after the surge of Nazi antisemitism in Warsaw. In 1939, the young couple went to Chile, where they had relatives. Afterward, the dictatorship caused them suffering when it imprisoned their son and exiled their daughter. They remained alone in Chile for years but eventually reunited with Julio in Paris. "There will always be horrors, and there will always be violence," says Julio. "You simply must denounce it."

Gladys Díaz

When in 1976, journalist Gladys Díaz, imprisoned at Cuatro Alamos, was allowed contact with the outside world again after six months of confinement at Villa Grimaldi, she testified to a judge that her boyfriend, Juan Carlos Perelman, was being held at Villa Grimaldi and was in danger. "I have the honor," stated Gladys, "of being the first prisoner to testify in a case involving a disappeared person."[18]

She was released in 1977 and ever since then has testified before courts and international human rights entities in Algiers, Rome, Paris, and many other places. After participating in a press conference in Paris, she recalled, "I just walked and walked, crying. But talking so much, helps you heal." For many years Gladys was a volunteer guide at Peace Park. She would frequently tell and retell her own story and that of other prisoners to groups of Chilean and foreign visitors.

> It gives you the feeling of having fulfilled a duty. Of not letting those events be forgotten. That you are one of many who are conveyors of that memory. That gives you a deep inner peace. I often go to Villa Grimaldi to speak to classes and groups. I did not plan to become a witness to history, but life placed me in that role because I am a witness to many disappeared people who came through there. I feel like I am a human rights activist. Whenever it's necessary to defend the memory of those comrades, I will be there. And I am there to oppose nuclear energy. You stand up for a better world in every way.

Lelia Pérez

Arrested at sixteen years of age the day after the military coup and a second time in October 1975, Lelia Pérez participated in the process to reclaim Villa Grimaldi, the place where she was detained and tortured. For a long time, she too was a guide there, conducting visits to reconstruct the memory of that place, and she has participated in historic memory seminars in Germany, where she lives six months of each year.

Both Lelia and Gladys Díaz were plaintiffs in the Villa Grimaldi case, a voluminous trial that unified hundreds of cases and culminated October 27, 2006, with the indictment of Augusto Pinochet as "author behind the author" of thirty-six counts of abduction, one count of homicide, and twenty-three cases of torture.

In exile, testimony became an instrument of the fight for truth, a tool for securing international condemnation of Chile. "It had vital significance, after having been so violently defeated, at such a high personal price, at the physical, psychological, and family level. It was as if I had discovered a road on which I gradually began to stand, a road of resilience," says Lelia.[19] "The deep pain I feel from having lost all these disappeared and executed people who I saw makes my testimony an act of personal justice and reparation."

From the Germans she learned how to guide others who transmit historic memory to the younger generations.

> At a place where crimes were committed there is a golden rule: do not terrify. Horror produces two reactions. One is a distancing from the issue, as a result of the horror. The second is the morbid factor. Neither produces learning.

In addition, if you are talking about a discriminatory situation, the teaching method cannot discriminate. If you talk about authoritarianism, you cannot be authoritarian. If you talk about negative pressure against people, you cannot pressure people. You have to generate the conditions that encourage people to participate.

In 2005, Lelia attended a conference that culminated with a visit to Auschwitz. Standing on the platform where the trains once brought people to their deaths, she remembered a conversation with her mother many years earlier.

My mother had gone to the movies, and before the movie there was a news brief called *El mundo al instante* [The world in an instant]. She told me and my sister about the news she had heard of a very mean doctor who had experimented on children at Auschwitz and then killed them. I must have been eight or nine years old. I remember that night thinking to myself, 'How lucky that I'm far away from that bad man who experimented on children.' That sense formed part of my understanding about the world. I remembered that at the exact place where Mengele selected the children. I had traversed time and geography, thousands of kilometers and many years, yet that story told to me by my mother connected me to that place. It provided me an emotional tool for understanding that Auschwitz is my commemoration place.

Gunter Seelmann

A refugee from Nazism, a prisoner of the Chilean dictatorship, and an exile in the country where he was born and from which he had fled, Gunter Seelmann has given his testimony on both experiences countless times in schools, universities, synagogues, and at the Doctors' Professional Society, where he founded its Human Rights Committee.

In September 2003, with his friend and prison companion Octavio Ehijo, he coauthored the testimonial book *Te recordamos, Quiriquina* (We remember you, Quiriquina). In the book's introduction, the authors express their hope to contribute to historic memory and their desire to pay tribute to others who shared the harsh experience as a way to "help heal the deep wounds in Chilean society" and reclaim "the essential values of democracy and human rights."[20]

"I was very young during the time of Nazism, but during the Chilean dictatorship I was a mature adult. At least I thought I was mature, and it appears that in most aspects that was the case. It is understandable that transcendence is an aspiration we all share. In my case, and in the case of Primo Levi and of every person who went through even worse things in life, the transcendence we aspire to," he says in a hushed voice, "is to leave a record for posterity that we were here."[21]

Gunter agrees with Julio Laks regarding the concept of "never again": "Our hope is that the experience may never be repeated. Yet the entire history of the human species on this planet tells us that it has been repeated many times. I just hope people have knowledge about what happened, because half of today's Chileans did not experience the dictatorship."

In 2000, he was in Buenos Aires for a roundtable discussion about human rights in the context of the Shoah. The last participant was an Auschwitz survivor who was meant to narrate his experience to the audience. He got up, paused, and said, "My friends, please forgive me, but I don't know what to tell you. I have talked about it so many times in so many different auditoriums and different places that I have no memory left. I no longer know what to say. Forgive me." Gunter was moved by the man's words. He acknowledges that he doesn't always have the spirit to tell his experience one more time, but so far words have not failed him.

Häftlinge 49.543

Late at night, when silence reigned at Auschwitz II-Birkenau, the Rapport-fuhrer Joachim Wolff would visit the musicians of the concentration camp orchestra who were appointed to play military marches when the columns of prisoners left for another hard day of forced labor.[22] After playing, the orchestra members put away their instruments, formed a column, and went out to work just like the any other *Häftlinge* ("prisoner" in German). Only no one played music for them as they set off for work.

Both the repressor and the Jewish prisoner Heiner Lewin, a virtuoso musician, luthier, and master watchmaker, had been born in the same town. Perhaps for that reason, the Nazi official confided in the *Häftlinge*. The German army had retreated from the front to the east and at any moment the Allied forces would arrive along the French coast. At a moment when rumors spread throughout the concentration camp of the imminent defeat of the Germans, Lewin dared ask a question that troubled the prisoners:

"*Herr Untersharführer*, do you believe the Germans can still win the war?"

"Not necessarily," Wolff answered after reflecting briefly, "the chance is less and less."

"If that's the case, then after all . . . everything that is going on here . . . here and in other camps . . . the world will find out. Don't you think the Germans will have to pay the piper?"

"Not at all. There will be no account to settle. No one will find out about anything."

". . . According to the instructions of the Führer himself, not even one *Häftling* should come out alive from any concentration camp. In other words, there will be no one who can tell the world what has happened here in the last few years. But even if such witnesses should be found—and this is the essence of the brilliant plan of our Führer—NOBODY WILL BELIEVE THEM. It was he who began and put into practice something exceptionally simple, but which surpasses the power of comprehension of the non-German civilized person. . . . Even if we lose the war, which is not yet certain, no one will present us with the reckoning. At most a few bigwigs will have to bear the consequences. Your 'judgment,' if it ever comes to that, will have to take place in a court, which will base itself on antiquated legal formulas that have no application to our 'crimes.' . . . The Germans will come out of this unscathed and will live forever."[23]

When Auschwitz was evacuated in mid-1944, the prisoners, including the orchestra members, were transferred to different concentration camps. Lewin was taken to Mauthausen, where he died. But we have knowledge of the conversation because a witness, *Häftlinge* number 49.543, did survive. That *Häftlinge* was the Auschwitz orchestra director. He recovered his life, his dignity, and his name: Szymon Laks. He recorded his testimony and the conversation he heard in his book *Music of Another World*.

Three decades after his liberation, another man with the same last name was arrested in Chile by the DINA secret police and submerged into a world as surreal and subhuman as Auschwitz. The Chilean survivor was Julio Laks, also a musician, abducted and held in the clandestine extermination center at 1367 José Domingo Cañas Street in October 1974.

Throughout his life as an exile in Paris, Julio embraced the mission of making known the work of Szymon. He gave a piano concert at the Polish Institute of Sciences in Paris, playing works by Szymon accompanied by a Polish singer. He played two other concerts at the Institute and one at the Polish Library with other singers as well as a major work for piano, *Ballad in Tribute to Chopin*. Szymon is becoming increasingly known as an accomplished musician, and whenever Julio performs his work, he sustains the memory of two continents and two generations.

Simón's Box

A nightmarish road awaited each family after the arrest of a family member in Chile. When an arrest was unrecognized or denied by military officials, families entered a labyrinth, with dead-end alleys ending at a wall, a maze through which they endlessly walked in their efforts to determine the loved one's whereabouts and fate.

Family members "did not find them," notes psychologist Paz Rojas. "They did not return home and were nowhere to be found." When they could not immediately track them down,

> they initiated a tireless search for their disappeared family members, without information or with false information, incessantly walking and walking, asking and asking in order to find them. They went to places of detention, stadiums, jails, military bases, always with their photographs, inquiring about them with other prisoners, other families, the prison guards, or people who like them were also tirelessly searching.[24]

Following a route that required personal effort and that entailed numerous judicial procedures, shared with countless other people, family members experienced an emotional seesaw, as their hopes for obtaining justice rose only to fall flat again in the face of repeated denials from the courts and cynical official replies: he or she went off with a lover or left the country.

The situation was all the more anguishing for families outside Chile, such as in the case of Luis Alberto Guendelman. From inside his house in California, where he had lived for several years, Simón Guendelman answered the telephone. It was a call from Santiago, Chile, to inform him that his younger brother Luis, who was known as Lucho, had been arrested. Around 10:30 p.m. on September 2, 1974, seven men invaded his house and, in the presence of his wife, Francisca Hurtado, took him away in a Chevy pickup. Over the next thirty years, Simón and other family members made hundreds of phone calls and visits and sent dozens of letters.

Alejandro Guendelman, a cousin who was close to Luis, was the only blood relative remaining in Chile. Alejandro took it upon himself to clean up Luis's house in the Bellavista neighborhood behind Santa María Hospital. After Luis was arrested and the house raided, the house was left in disarray and unoccupied for several months. It was Alejandro, too, who accompanied the attorney from the Vicariate of Solidarity to file the first writs of habeas corpus. He also spoke to Rabbi Angel Kreiman, who asked him to return in a couple of days. When the rabbi failed to answer his calls, Alejandro went to the synagogue to wait for him. The rabbi informed Alejandro that he had inquired in various places but could not come up with anything and then asked him not to come back there again. Alejandro insisted that an uncle passing through Santiago contact General Eduardo Cano, appointed Central Bank president in September

1973, whom the uncle had known for many years. "He who does nothing has nothing to fear" was the military official's reply.

In the office of his advanced engineering firm Sim/Tech in Emeryville, California, Simón Guendelman opened a file cabinet drawer and took out a cardboard box.[25] Many family members of disappeared persons and people extrajudicially executed possess a similar box, file folder, or maybe a large envelope containing the compilation of decades of efforts to locate the loved one. Simón opens his box for the first time in many years. Like a Pandora's box sealed for centuries, on lifting up the lid, it conjures the memories of sincere and insincere promises, hopes dashed, and a few genuine clues in the quest to learn the truth regarding Lucho's fate and to achieve justice.

> This box contains all the files related to my brother's case. I want to show them to you. It is a very large file. It's been some years since I last looked through these files. We mailed hundreds of letters and there are many, many letters in reply.
>
> Here we have a letter from the State Department, dated November 1974, two months after my brother's disappearance: "A Chilean government source has formally informed our embassy in Santiago that Mr. Guendelman is being held in the Tres Alamos detention center in Santiago. That source describes him as in a good health."
>
> We filed several writs of habeas corpus during the course of the years. Here I have the responses: "Your brother is not in police custody. We have no record of your brother."

The writ of habeas corpus numbered 1052-54-1974 was the first filed for Luis. In March 1975, it was denied. The five thousand writs filed for other people between 1973 and 1987 likewise were denied. In all those years, the courts accepted only ten. The systematic denial of writs of habeas corpus was a clear indication of the judicial branch's complicity with the repressive policies. If the courts had granted the writs, "death, disappearance, and torture could have been prevented in a great many cases," state the drafters of the Rettig Report in 1991.[26]

Simón resumes his story.

> I spent a lot of time on the telephone, which was very expensive in those days, in addition to writing letters and sending telegrams. I was in regular contact with various departments of the United Nations, the Inter-American Commission on Human Rights, and government agencies of the United States and Europe. Amnesty International helped us a lot, and I came to know people who

Compendium of files attests to efforts to locate and seek justice for Luis Guendelman (Simon Guendelman) held important positions with Amnesty. The only ones who really helped were the Propeace Committee, a few members of the United States Congress and Amnesty International.

In addition to people who stated having been held with my brother in different detention places, the United States Department of State was another important source of information, and I spoke several times to the person in charge of Chile.

My mother traveled to Chile and ended up living there a few years. As a consequence of our efforts, the DINA began looking for her, so she always stayed at different places. They changed my police file to something like "extremist living abroad." I didn't dare go to Chile. If I recall, the first time I returned to Chile was in 1981. We hired a lawyer to expunge my police file.

You have to understand what I was doing. Here are letters signed by Edward M. Kennedy, Bill Clinton, Tom Harkins, and Jesse Helms. My conversations with Helms, the archconservative senator from North Carolina for thirty years, lasted until 1998. The last letter I received from him states: "I have always believed that gentlemen must have the capacity to disagree without being disagreeable. Therefore, I value your right to disagree with me about the current situation of former president Pinochet."

Here's one from 1976. There were different campaigns that I ran for different reasons. And here is another letter from 1975, from Senator Edward Kennedy . . . and one more letter from Mr. Kennedy. I was invited to testify at the United States Congress hearings, held in 1975, regarding human rights violations in Chile.

Testimonies from victims' family members such as Simón and statements from freed prisoners who told what they had lived through were decisive in the ratification of the Kennedy Amendment, which prohibited the sale of arms to Chile. The influence of Senator Edward Kennedy of Massachusetts resulted in the US Congress approving the amendment in 1974 and extending it in 1976 after the assassination of Orlando Letelier.

"Here is a letter from Mr. Miguel Schweitzer," Simón continues.

During fifteen years, every year, I sent my brother a birthday card. I sent many to Pinochet and the Justice Ministry. Here is Justice Minister Schweitzer's reply to the card I sent in 1974. I did not send them by mail; instead, I would ask someone to personally deliver them. Schweitzer wrote back: "I confirm receipt of your letter of September 22 with which you included a birthday card to be delivered to your brother Mr. Luis Alberto Guendelman. It would have been a pleasure for me to help mitigate your brotherly pain, and I would have had it delivered to Luis Guendelman but unfortunately, after making all pertinent inquiries of corresponding officials, it has not been possible to ascertain the whereabouts of your brother Luis Alberto who, according to the Interior Minister, does not appear on its list of detainees, and there is no information about his arrest. Under these circumstances, as I am unable to fulfill your request, I am obligated to return the birthday card." And here is the card he returned me.

Taking more papers from the box, Simón adds, "Here is a letter sent from Germany, which I can't read because I don't know German." Another letter evokes anger, as he remarks, "The Organization of American States . . . they sure were mother fuckers. And I believed them! They never did a thing, but they wrote the most beautiful letters. All their letters ended with such marvelous words such as "of my most distinguished consideration." They made me feel so good!"

His file box seems bottomless.

I got a call from Chile and later received a copy of an article published by *El Mercurio* stating that after the International Red Cross visited detention camps in Chile in September 1975, the organization's highest official declared in a press conference that human rights are not being violated in Chile. So then I wrote the guy a letter asking if he would help me clarify my brother's case if in fact there are no human rights violations in Chile. This guy from the International Red Cross answered me in a letter: "I have never been in Chile. I never held a press conference." Essentially, he was telling me, "*El Mercurio* lies! But please don't publicize this letter."

In April 1975, the first criminal complaint was filed on behalf of Luis Guendelman, based on facts gathered for the writ of habeas corpus. Later, the military court applied the amnesty decree law to close the case. Simón's narrative does not pause.

I was able to contact Henry Kissinger. It is as a result of Kissinger's inquiry about my brother's case when he visited Chile that my police file was expunged.

Here we've got a letter from the Guild of Architects, a document from the Truth and Reconciliation Commission, another letter from Amnesty International, and one from the Center for Justice and Accountability . . . plus one from socialist Michael Harrington, New York congressperson Shirley Chisolm, John Sparkman, Henry Gonzalez, and Joseph Montoya.

His letter campaign did not slow down with the transition to democracy during the first decade of the 1990s.

I wrote Senator Barbara Boxer, Secretary of State Madeleine Albright, Senator Alfonso D'Amato of New York, the US National Security Council, and Barbara McCloskey. They were all so very friendly, but no one did a thing. . . . Here we've got a letter from Rabbi Hearst of the San Francisco Bay Area Ecumenical Committee of Concern for Chile. All of them had good will for helping but were ineffectual. I also spoke to the Catholic Church of Chile and the United States.

He did not limit himself to writing letters to just progressive politicians. He sent letters to conservative politicians such as New York senator Jim Buckley of the Republican Party and, as noted, Jesse Helms, who was elected senator for North Carolina in January 1973. During his next thirty years as senator, Helms remained an unconditional ally of Pinochet, with whom he shared a visceral anticommunism. During his first visit to Chile, in July 1976, Senator Helms stated that "Chile's enemies exaggerate with malicious criticism that does not reflect reality."[27]

Augusto Pinochet was arrested in London on October 16 of the year Simón received his last letter from Senator Helms. The Spanish legal action fired up hope that justice might finally be achieved in Chile. Since 1999, just two months after Pinochet's arrest, more than five hundred criminal complaints were filed in Santiago and in the provinces. In the context of this climate of renewed judicial optimism, on July 11, 2000, the Guild of Architects filed a criminal complaint against Pinochet for the crimes of abduction and first-degree murder committed against seven architects, including Luis Guendelman. The complaint was grounded to a great extent on depositions by a dozen people who saw Luis in DINA detention centers.

"I divide people this way: those who wanted to help and those who didn't even bother to reply to our letters," notes Simón. "Undoubtedly you have felt this. I was a pretty naive person. I now feel that in this important chapter of my life, people took advantage of me. It was a terrible process. I turned into a very agnostic, cynical person; I no longer believe what governments say."

Family members of forcibly disappeared persons like Simón Guendelman, an active member of the Committee of Solidarity with Chile that helped refugees arriving in California, paved the way for truth and justice through their criminal complaints and writs of habeas corpus. Those were the initial steps people took on a long road, frequently failing to reach their desired destination.

In the case of Luis Guendelman, however, the persistent efforts by his siblings, his mother, his cousin, and other relatives and friends paid off. On August 31, 2009, Victor Montiglio, a special investigative judge for the Santiago Court of Appeals, issued an indictment of and prison sentences with parole for twenty former DINA agents "as coauthors of the crime of aggravated abduction of

Luis Alberto Guendelman, perpetrated in the city of Santiago on September 02 of 1974."[28]

Simón closes the box of letters and returns it to the file cabinet. The letters will remain there for who knows how long until he adds the next document to the file.

ON TRIAL IN AACHEN AND IN SANTIAGO

Aachen, the westernmost city of Germany located on the border with Belgium and the Netherlands, was the birthplace of Otto Frank. Known since Roman times for its hot springs, it was the summer vacation spot where his daughters, Anne and Margot, visited their grandmother. Gunter Seelmann was also born in Aachen. In 1925, Otto and Edith Frank married in the Aachen synagogue; Frederick and Ana Seelmann, Gunter's parents, were married there as well.

The flames that engulfed the Aachen synagogue, during the night of November 9, 1938, heralded a radical alteration in the lives of these families and thousands more. With his wife and small son, Frederick Seelmann traveled to a continent far away, while his friend Otto would become the sole witness of a decimated family. In 2010, Aachen was the venue of an act of reparation by Germany, recognition of its historic responsibility for crimes against humanity.

In 2000, German prosecutor Ulrich Maas, director of the governmental agency Central Office of the State Justice Administrations for the Investigation of National Socialist Crimes, initiated legal proceedings against Heinrich Boere after determining that neither his cardiac condition nor his advanced age were impediment against his standing trial. The trial culminated in March 2010 when an Aachen judge sentenced Boere to life imprisonment for the murder of three persons in 1944. The aggravated homicides of three members of the Dutch resistance, the court ruled, were crimes against humanity, committed by Boere as a member of the Waffen Brigade, composed of fanatic National Socialist Party volunteers.

The Waffen Brigade was found guilty of the deaths of fifty-four people. Its modus operandi consisted in looking for victims at their homes and then shooting them on the spot once the Waffen Brigade had identified them. Shortly after the Nazis took over his town of Maastricht and all the Netherlands in 1940, Boere joined the National Socialist Party, spurred by a recruitment poster.

The trial against Heinrich Boere, number six on the Simon Wiesenthal Center's list of most-sought Nazis, may very well be one of the last on crimes against humanity committed by the Third Reich. In 2002, the Simon Wiesenthal Center launched its Operation Last Chance to bring remaining war criminals to trial. By late 2011, according to Efraim Zuroff, its director, the center had identified more than six hundred suspects residing in thirty-two countries. Previously secret files declassified in March 2012 revealed that "approximately 9,000 war criminals escaped to South America, with an estimated 5,000 in Argentina, between 1,500 and 2,000 in Brazil, between 500 and 1000 in Chile, and the rest in Paraguay and Uruguay."[29]

Boere's conviction, sixty-six years after the events, originated in the historic trial at Nuremberg that began on November 20, 1945, six months after Germany's defeat. Discredited by some critics as an act of revenge by the victorious Allied forces, the trials of the twenty-four Nazi leaders led to the Statutes of Nuremberg, which define three crimes: war crimes, crimes against peace, and crimes against humanity. Nuremberg had been the scene for massive National Socialist rallies, and it was there that antisemitic laws were enacted in 1935, creating the conditions for the genocide that followed. The trial vindicated the city of Nuremberg, as it gave birth to the system of universal protection of human rights.

In 1948, the Nuremberg Code led to the creation of the Universal Declaration of Human Rights, and, in 1949, to the Geneva Conventions that defined the word "genocide," which had been coined five years earlier by the Polish Jewish refugee Raphael Lemkin. A standard was established for respect of fundamental human rights.

For Roberto Garreton, the positive legal effects arising from the horror of the Shoah are nothing short of "sensational." Garreton was director of the Vicariate of Solidarity legal department during the dictatorship and then UN High Commissioner for the Congo in 1997. Garreton explains the significance of international human rights protection: "Shoah led to the Universal Declaration of Human Rights. In the history of humankind, it's the first text that says everyone is equal. That too makes the declaration fantastic."[30] He adds,

What used to happen in Latin America before this culture developed? Military coups. The coups would end, and the dictator would be back. No one called for trial and punishment for the perpetrators. No one ever said "Let's create truth and reconciliation commissions." No one ever spoke of crimes against humanity. Absolutely nothing. All this was born from the Shoah. That reaction factor is what we as human rights defenders in Chile, in Bosnia, in Zimbabwe, uphold. We in Chile need a post-Shoah reaction too.

At the time of the military coup, the series of international human rights conventions we have today did not exist. Only the Geneva Convention of 1949, the Convention for the Prevention on the Prevention and Punishment of the Crime of Genocide, and the UN Charter were in effect in Chile. The International Covenant on Civil and Political Rights was ratified in 1972 by

President Salvador Allende but only came into force during the dictatorship on March 23, 1976. The Convention against Torture and Other Cruel, Inhumane or Degrading Treatment and Punishment also came into effect during the dictatorship, in 1988.

The first International Conference on Human Rights, held in Tehran in 1968, declared the Universal Declaration of Human Rights mandatory for all states, even though it was not a treaty. The institutions that arose in Chile to defend lives trampled on by the dictatorship based many legal actions on the Universal Declaration. In the late 1990s, the treaty ratified by Pinochet was cited as grounds for every complaint filed against him, particularly Article 2 of the International Covenant on Civil and Political Rights that establishes the obligation to try to bring authors of human rights violations to justice.

Even in the earliest years of the Vicariate of Solidarity, its legal staff customarily founded their writs on the Universal Declaration. Staff especially relied on the Universal Declaration when it came to war councils, summary military trials without the semblance of objective justice, during which defense lawyers were often only allowed to meet with their clients half an hour before the trial. Article 9, which prohibits arbitrary arrest or expulsion from a country, and Article 10, which enshrines the defendant's rights to an impartial trial, were particularly relevant to the situation thousands of persecuted people faced. Roberto Garreton recalls,

> We often invoked the Universal Declaration of Human Rights, but not always. Why not always? You have to understand those times. Sometimes we received messages from the courts that said, "Please don't invoke the Universal Declaration because it irritates the judges!" Every so often we would invoke it as a matter of principle and whenever a new issue arose for discussion.
>
> Then, without warning, we would organize a campaign: from now on, we will invoke it on every writ of habeas corpus we file. The judges were furious. Obviously, our overriding concern was with the prisoners, so why continue to provoke the judges? But internationally, whenever we sent denunciations outside the country, we always invoked the Universal Declaration.
>
> Later a few judges gradually became aware of their error, but they did not convey this in their rulings. "Don't plead the Universal Declaration so much!" they would tell us. "You have to understand that we have a conscience, but we are under pressure."

By repetition, in the practice of the best teachers, human rights lawyers increasingly educated judges on international law through their briefs. More than two decades passed before Chilean magistrates began showing signs of assimilating the lessons. Not until 1998 with the ruling in the Enrique Poblete Córdoba case and subsequently with greater force in January 2004 with the ruling in the Miguel Angel Sandoval Rodríguez case did the courts demonstrate a certain evolution in judicial thought. Citing the Geneva Convention and the Universal Declaration of Human Rights, the Fifth Chamber of the Santiago Court of Appeals, in January 2004, issued the first sentences in the case of a disappeared person. The abduction from a public street of the twenty-six-year-old tailor Miguel Angel Sandoval, on January 7, 1975, by DINA agents and his subsequent internment and torture at Villa Grimaldi, resulting in his death, constituted crimes against humanity, the ruling affirmed. Under these treaties, crimes against humanity and genocide, committed in Europe by the Nazis or in Chile by military, are not subject to statutes of limitation, amnesties, or any condition that might otherwise prevent conviction.

Carmen Hertz was a member of the team of lawyers who developed the case known as Caravan of Death. This case involved a series of aggravated homicides committed against political prisoners in October 1973, carried out by General Sergio Arellano Stark as a direct representative of military junta president Augusto Pinochet, who ordered the scheme. The mission resulted in the extrajudicial executions of fifty-six people and twenty forced disappearances in the northern cities of La Serena, Copiapo, Antofagasta, and Calama. Hertz's husband, the journalist Carlos Berger, was murdered in Calama.

On April 27, 2000, Hertz appeared before the Santiago Court of Appeals to argue for the removal of lifetime senator Augusto Pinochet's immunity so that he would be able to stand trial in the Caravan of Death case. She described what happened after the Puma helicopter landed in Calama.

On October 19, around 3:00 p.m., I ran to the public jail to inform Carlos Berger of the results of my efforts. At that hour, thirteen political detainees had already been removed from the prison, in a particularly violent manner—handcuffed and heads hooded—by military personnel unknown to Carlos. Within minutes after I left the jail, around 4:00 p.m., Carlos Berger and another thirteen detainees were removed from prison premises and taken to an unknown location, and minutes later the massacre now known to all of us occurred. . . .

Military officers Sergio Arredondo González and Marcelo Moren Brito arrived at Calama prison and proceeded to illegally remove the attorney Carlos Berger and the other twenty-five political prisoners. Furthermore, evidence substantiated the fact that . . . they were transported in military vehicles to the zone known as Topater, on the outskirts of Calama, where personnel of that posse willfully proceeded to torture the detainees, stabbing them with a curved sickle, and then shooting them in different parts of their bodies.

Moreover, it has been proven that thirteen of the detainees died in that place and that the remaining fourteen, including attorney Carlos Berger, were taken to an as yet unknown location.

The hearings took place in a prodigious moment. Pinochet had logged more than five hundred days under house arrest in London, while the House of Lords debated whether to accept the extradition request from Madrid to enable him to stand trial for the murders of seven Spaniards during the dictatorship. Persuaded by Chilean government claims of humanitarian consideration for the aging former dictator, the House of Lords chose a second option, returning him to Santiago. A week after Hertz and fellow attorneys argued before the Santiago Appellate Court, on May 3, 2000, Pinochet once again walked on Chilean soil.

The Chile that witnessed him raise up his cane in greeting and lift himself up from the wheelchair had changed since his arrest. No longer paralyzed by fear, Pinochet's victims had filed more than four hundred criminal complaints against him. Chile's governing officials and the former dictator's unconditional allies who rescued him had argued that under principles of national sovereignty only Chilean courts should try him. The eyes of the world were focused on Chile.

In this climate of expectation, on June 8, 2000, the Court of Appeals agreed to deprive the lifetime senator of his congressional immunity, thus confirming probable cause of his participation in the aggravated abduction of Carlos Berger and twelve other people in the city of Calama. Defying all predictions, the Supreme Court upheld the removal of immunity, clearing the way for Judge Juan Guzmán Tapia, on December 1, 2000, to indict Pinochet and order him to be put under house arrest. During the two years the case remained active, Pinochet's legal team never addressed the charges against its client. Their sole defense consisted of pleading for humanitarian consideration of their client's alleged state of incurable dementia. The defense strategy proved successful on July 1, 2002, when the five members of the penal chamber of the Supreme Court dismissed Pinochet from the Caravan of Death case.

The same year Pinochet was indicted, the German prosecutor in Aachen indicted Heinrich Boere. Despite the defendant's advanced age, humanitarian considerations were deemed inadmissible grounds for dismissing charges. In December 2011, when Boere was ninety years old, he was taken out of the geriatric residence where he lived and moved by ambulance to the prison where he began serving time.

Boere's indictment and conviction were a historic precedent with implications for the legal proceedings against the former Chilean dictator, which was the focus of the media the world over. The conviction of the Dutch Nazi—who never expressed regret for the crimes he committed—resulted from the first indictment of a foreign Nazi collaborator by a German court. Before the Boere trial, Germany had become a haven for Nazi war criminals of other nationalities who became naturalized German citizens in order to benefit from a law prohibiting the extradition of German citizens. In 1952, another Dutchman, Klaas Carel Faber, like Boere, a member of the Waffen Brigade, escaped to Germany from a prison in the Netherlands, where he was serving time for the murders of eleven people. Germany repeatedly denied the Dutch court's extradition request. In May 2012, Faber died in Germany, where he lived as a fugitive for sixty years.

It is likely that these two cases—one concerning the man who was the embodiment of the cruel dictators of Latin America and the other concerning a German mid-level officer—created transatlantic bonds. Pinochet's indictment was possible owing to the web of human rights treaties that originated after the genocide of 6,000,000 Jews and at least 250,000 Romani. Quite possibly, the concept of universal justice that was strengthened by the Spanish case against Pinochet contributed to Boere's conviction.

Hertz places the trials in their historical context.

> When cases involve systematic and massive crimes against humanity originating in a state, they cease to be merely a domestic matter of the country where the crimes were committed. World peace is at stake. . . . These crimes concern everyone. That's why we had the Nuremberg court, the court on the former Yugoslavia, that's why we had the court on the crimes of Rwanda and that's why the International Criminal Court was created.
>
> In Chile, attempts have been made to supplant justice on religious grounds. The idea of forgiveness is completely colonial and religious. Societies establish justice and constitutional states, among other reasons, to prevent personal vengeance. Forgiveness is a perverse concept that they tried to institute here.[31]

No one would have dreamed of suggesting to Otto Frank that he forgive the men who caused the deaths of his beloved Edith, Margot, and Anne. Likewise, no surviving children of Heinrich Boere's victims have been asked to reconcile with him. A legacy arising from the Shoah is recognition that only justice can ensure that crimes against humanity are not repeated. Nothing more but nothing less, demand Carmen Hertz and family members of all forcibly disappeared, extrajudicially executed people and survivors of political imprisonment in Chile.

In January 2014, the Legal Medical Service, a government forensic agency, confirmed the identities of skeletal remains discovered in 1990 in a pit sixteen

kilometers north of the highway to San Pedro de Atacama. The bone fragments were identified as belonging to six people murdered by the Caravan of
Death in Calama; one of the six was Carlos Berger. At the funeral held on
April 13, 2014, Germán Berger addressed his family, his mother, and the mul-
titude who joined them at the ceremony.

> My dear old man: it's strange to be here today, burying the remains of your
> body that the desert returned to us. It is so hard because the horror of the crime
> committed against you and the anguish of knowing you are disappeared have
> become indelible wounds in our soul. But here we are just the same, and we will
> always be here, again and again. Here is your family, here are your friends, here
> are the other families who continue searching. Here too are the souls of your
> murdered comrades. Here is a part of this country that you once dreamed of
> changing. . . . This funeral is a celebration of memory. It celebrates my father, all
> murdered men and women comrades, and it is a celebration of my homeland
> and my people, of a country that rises up and is capable of dreaming.[32]

Jorge Klein, Son of Partisans

Walter Rosenfeld dozes in a reclining armchair in his room in a Jewish nursing
home. The stories of his adventure-filled life that he delighted in telling again
and again now remain inside him. Only when he is shown a small photograph
of a smiling Jorge Klein does a spark of recognition light up his eyes as they
focus on the image, only to close once more. Perhaps the face of the person he
loved like the son he never had triggered the memory of absence and experiences that traced a long route from Europe.

Every generation needs a guardian of family memories who will transmit
those memoirs to the next generation. In this family, Walter gladly took on
that role. Now Corina Rosenfeld, Walter's niece and Jorge Klein's cousin, has
assumed the role of transmitting the family history to the next generation.[33]

It was Egon Rosenfeld, Corina's father and Walter's brother, who, as head of
the Rosenfeld tribe in Chile, brought the extended family together year after
year for the Jewish festivities of Passover, Chanukah, and Rosh Hashanah. Yet
he never told them what he endured in a concentration camp.

In Vienna, Rudy Klein and Lotte Piper, Jorge's parents, lived in the same
neighborhood as Walter. Lotte's sister married Walter in 1935, the same year
she and Rudy wed.

Few Jews grasped what was coming. However, Walter had an intuition. The
day after the German annexation of Austria, known as the Anschluss, in
March 1938, Jews of Vienna who had actively participated in Austrian society
for eight hundred years were harassed and humiliated and their houses and

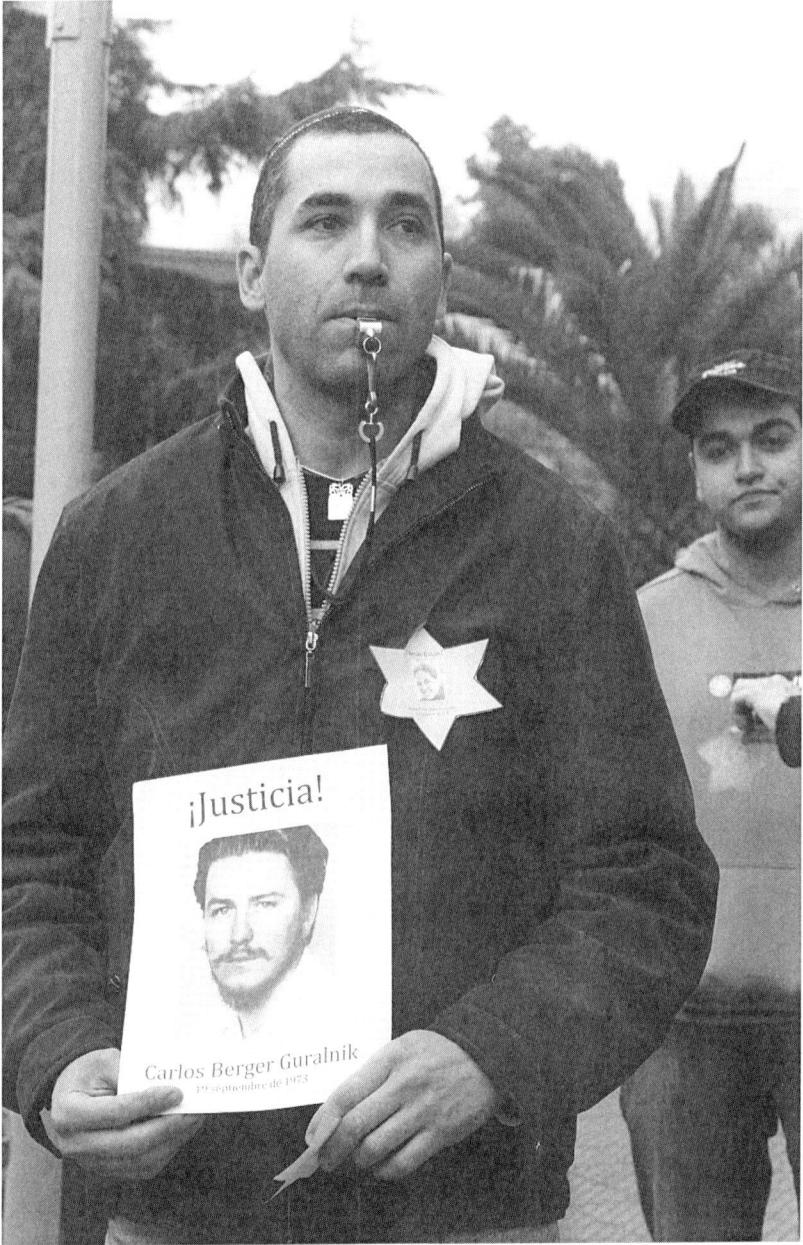

Jewish protestor carries image of Carlos Berger, 2012 (Claudio Mandler)

businesses were robbed. Walter immediately departed for Romania and then accepted a job in Cairo, where he lived with his wife for the duration of the war.

On November 9, 1938, during the pogrom popularly remembered as the night of broken glass, Corina's father was one of six thousand Jews who were rounded up and deported to Dachau. His arrest awoke the family to an intuition that terrible days lay ahead, and they began thinking about leaving Vienna.

Rudy and Lotte left for France, believing they would be safe there. When Germany invaded France, on May 10, 1940, both joined the Resistance. From the few accounts Rudy and Lotte shared about that period of their lives, Corina deduced that they served as messengers and sentries. She thinks their participation in the Resistance was nonviolent, because "they would not have been capable of carrying arms and killing people." Constantly moving from one place to another in southern France, they camped in the woods, following the movement of the German troops.

When the Germans retreated from Soviet territory and German troops strategically concentrated along that eastern front, the partisans began to feel more secure. Rudy and Lotte settled in Moulins in central France. Their son Georges was born in that city, on December 29, 1944. As soon as the war ended, the family traveled to the French region of Canada, but four years later, family ties pulled them to Chile. Walter and his wife, Lotte's sister, had arrived the year before, in 1948, and other members of the family had been in Chile since 1939.

Rudy Klein opened a shoe repair shop downtown on the corner of Merced and San Antonio streets, where people sat down to read the newspaper and sip a cup of coffee while waiting for their shoes to be repaired. It was a novel idea at the time. Moreover, special machines enabled a speedy shoe repair.

Georges was five years old when the family arrived in Chile. He learned Spanish at the Alianza Francesa school and soon became known as Jorge. His performance as a student was excellent, and on finishing primary school, he entered the Instituto Nacional, a prestigious school in Santiago. He was an outstanding student and graduated with honors.

He entered the University of Chile Medical School, and, despite the demanding and stressful academic burden first-year med students encounter, Jorge found time to take a philosophy course at the School of Education. Sometimes he would join a friend at the Jewish University Center to attend talks or take part in other cultural activities.

Jorge shared many afternoon teas and lunch at the home of his high school friend Carlos Lorca, a fellow medical school student. Jorge's parents considered him "like another son," says Raul Lorca, the youngest brother of Carlos. Both shared a passion for chess as well as the conviction that it was absolutely necessary to build a more just society. For young people like Jorge and Carlos, their decision to study medicine in the mid-1960s, when social change movements were shaking Chile and the world, was a political choice. At this time, Jorge met his future wife, Alice Vera Fausto, a Brazilian, and after graduating from medical school, he worked at the University of Chile Psychiatric Hospital.

Practically the entire family, with the exception of his cousin Corina, opposed Salvador Allende. Corina explains that "they thought Allende would install a system that would bring suffering. They associated socialism with Nazism and feared they would have to leave the country again. The fear was just in their heads; the reality did not bear it out."

Walter's small metallurgical factory, where he manufactured auto chassis parts, was expropriated. Since he had been a good boss, the workers treated him with great respect and permitted him to go to the factory every day, which was now under the union's management. Even so, the factory's expropriation sowed fear among the rest of the family.

The night after the military coup, with curfew imposed, the family was alarmed: where was Jorge? When he failed to appear the next day, they were further confounded, and they became even more apprehensive. Three days later, when curfew was lifted in daytime hours, they learned that many people were being held in Chile Stadium. Alice went there every day, asking for him, and carrying a small package of food and clothing in the hope of delivering it to Jorge. At the point when Chile Stadium ran out of space to hold any more people, detainees were transferred to the National Stadium. Alice then went there every day to inquire about her husband. She was told that Jorge was inside that stadium, so she passed food and clothing through the fence in the hope that it would reach him. Three months later, when the stadium was closed as a prison camp, she realized Jorge was not there.

Alice then decided to speak with the defense minister. General Patricio Carvajal received her very rudely and stated that her husband had never existed. To prove that he indeed existed, Alice went to the Instituto Nacional. In the school's register of graduates, Jorge Klein's name had been blotted out with a thick line of black ink.

So where was Jorge? None of his relatives knew that Jorge had been a member of the Socialist Party or that in the latter months of the Popular Unity government he had become a Communist Party member. And they did not have an inkling that he was a trusted assistant to President Salvador Allende. Many years would pass before they learned that Jorge had been inside La Moneda when it was bombed.

Military personnel stormed La Moneda to arrest those who remained inside. A group of forty people, including Jorge Klein, left the building in single file through the Morandé Street door. They were forced to lie face down on the street with their hands on the back of their neck. This procedure, accompanied by blows, was repeated the next day at the Tacna military base in north Santiago.

We now know that on September 13, perhaps as Alice was on her way to Chile Stadium with a package in the hope of finding him there, Jorge and twenty other people had been removed from the military base. His fate remained unknown to his family during two decades, until key witnesses provided initial clues in their testimony to the National Truth and Reconciliation Commission. Today we know they were machine-gunned at Fort Arteaga, in the Andes foothill zone of Peldehue, and buried under several feet of soil to conceal the crime.

Born among French partisans, Jorge, at twenty-seven years of age, died infused with the spirit for justice that spurred his parents, Rudy and Lotte, to fight against the Nazis.

In the summer of 2001, Chile's coroner office at the Legal Medical Service received the bone fragments discovered by Judge Amanda Valdovinos in a pit on the premises of Fort Arteaga. Circumstantial information from surviving witnesses, a highly trained interdisciplinary team of forensic specialists, and a blood bank that provided the genetic profile of more than thirty-three hundred family members of disappeared persons are the three elements that enabled the definitive identification. When, as in Jorge Klein's case, only fragments of bone remained—in 1978, Pinochet ordered mass graves be dynamited or dumped into the sea after the first bodies of forcibly disappeared persons were discovered—DNA forensic testing was required from one of five laboratories in the world accredited for that purpose.

Patricio Bustos, Legal Medical Service director from 2007 to 2016, described the intrinsic significance of the forensic work carried out by his institution in cases involving human rights violations: "In identifying Jorge Klein or any other victim, we are cutting off the hand that conceals the crimes. We are placing truth, science, technology, humanitarianism, and professional and institutional ethics at the service of truth as it always should have been."[34] Himself a survivor of Villa Grimaldi, Bustos drew from his own experience to offer the following reflection.

Remembering a disappeared person is different from remembering an executed prisoner who has been identified. I was with people who were later murdered and with people later disappeared. The memory is different. With those who were murdered, there was a body, we know who the assassins are, whereas with the disappeared we only know that they were lifted onto a truck that drove off in an unknown direction. You are aware that both are dead, but a funeral initiates mourning from a social perspective and for the family.

In mid-October 2011, Vanessa Klein Fausto, who lives in Rio de Janeiro, received a telephone call from Chile's Ministry of Justice. She had planned to travel to Chile to celebrate Uncle Walter's 103rd birthday on October 17, 2011, but the call prompted her to travel sooner. Her father's remains had been identified. The blood sample she donated years earlier enabled the reunion she had yearned for.

At the same time, a delegation of the International Federation for Human Rights arrived in Santiago. In court proceedings coordinated by the federation, in December 2010, the Criminal Court of Paris sentenced thirteen Chilean defendants, in absentia, to prison sentences ranging from fifteen years to life imprisonment for the abduction, forced disappearance, and torture of four people of French origin: Alfonso Chanfreau, Jean-Yves Claudet, Etienne Pesle, and Jorge Klein. Now the French attorneys were requesting that Chilean judicial officials comply with the arrest warrants for the men responsible for the crimes.

It was a coincidence that the French attorneys happened to be in Chile when the forensic identification of Jorge Klein was confirmed. "The Legal Medical Service always communicates the information to the judges, who then communicate and schedule families when an identification is confirmed. We could never have planned such a marvelous synchronicity," notes Bustos.

That the Legal Medical Service had positively identified her beloved cousin initially horrified Corina. To learn that "my cousin had been executed in the same manner as Jews forced by the Nazis to dig their own mass graves gives me a sinking feeling in my stomach." Still, "it gives me a sense of peace because the uncertainty is over. Even though three finger bones are all we have, it's enough to know that he was there."

The dictatorship blotted out Jorge Klein's name with ink and then used a machine gun and bulldozer to eliminate traces of his physical existence. But a drop of blood lovingly donated by his daughter sufficed to restore his identify. His phalange pointed directly at those guilty of his crime and revealed the truth of what occurred during the dictatorship.

In an unusually intense heat for early spring in the southern hemisphere, at noon on October 28, 2011, some sixty people gathered at Santiago's General Cemetery. Corina Rosenfeld observed the scene from her wheelchair in the shade of a spiny acacia that was in bloom. The small coffer of luminous mahogany that was placed in a crypt of the Memorial to Disappeared Detainees looked like a jewelry box, but its contents were more precious than any jewel. Vanessa spoke of the *saudade*, the nostalgia, the long-awaited reunion evoked for her. She spoke, too, about her father's legacy that she would transmit to her own children, both of whom were older at the time of the funeral than she was when her father was snatched from her life.

Uncle Walter passed away three days after Jorge's funeral. During his last weeks, in moments of slight lucidity, he would exclaim, "War is coming! Something must be done! I see people going about their lives, and they have no idea what's coming."

"The other day, I went to the coast," Corina said. "Because of my illness I had not gone in a very long time. I sat looking at the sea, and thought to myself, 'There's Jorge.'"

TO HONOR THEIR NAMES

"Today your name returns to remain with your people where you belong!" During more than thirty-six years, the names Jacobo Stoulman and Matilde Pessa, the parents of Sara Stoulman, who spoke these words on December 8, 2013, in the Jewish cemetery in Santiago, were barely mentioned in Chile's Jewish community.

As of May 29, 1977, when they began waiting for their parents to return from a trip to Buenos Aires, the three Stoulman sisters felt the cold winds of isolation. Even though many members of the Jewish community knew their parents, few came forth to support them. "If the Instituto Hebreo director or leaders of any other institution approached our family, I never heard about it," affirmed Jenny Stoulman, who was a high school junior at that school when her parents disappeared.[35] A similar experience was endured by family members of the other seventeen people of Jewish origin, whose names were etched on the glossy black surface of a monument in the Jewish cemetery. At the time the arrests occurred, Jewish institutional leaders remained passive. Four decades later, they had not acknowledged the Jewish names on the government roster of disappeared and summarily executed persons.

On July 12, 1997, the Jewish Progressive Center organized the first tribute to the memory of fifteen Chileans Jews murdered by the military regime. Hortensia Bussi, widow of Salvador Allende, presented a red carnation to the mother of Recaredo Ignacio Valenzuela; Volodia Teitelboim gave a flower to Jorge Müller's father; Alejandro Hales did the same to the family of Raúl Pellegrin. Thus, all family members received red carnations in honor of their loved ones. "We believe it our duty and a right to rescue them from oblivion, to destigmatize their figures, and make known their real human dimension," stated program coordinators Isidro Neves, Miguel Saidel, and Gunter Seelmann.[36] No representative of any Jewish institution or any rabbi attended the ceremony, however.

In August 1998, in the context of the observance of Tisha b'Av commemorating the destruction of the Temple in Jerusalem with mourning rituals, Rabbi Roberto Feldmann's Kol HaNeshama synagogue remembered Jewish victims of the military dictatorship. With several family members in attendance, the ceremony was the first held by a Jewish religious community in Chile. For the 2006 "Remembering Anne Frank and Diana Aron" ceremony coordinated by the Jewish Progressive Center, the Israeli Ambassador, the Jewish Representative Committee president, and the Women's International Zionist Organization attended, but only a single rabbi, Daniel Zang of the Sephardic religious community of Santiago, attended and participated in it.

In light of the Jewish institutions' past omissions, it was significant that in 2013 Chile's largest synagogue, Círculo Israelita de Santiago, donated a plot of the Jewish cemetery, which it administers, to build a monument. Moreover, an architect member of the Chilean branch of B'nai B'rith designed the memorial. Notwithstanding the project's positive symbolic value, when family members were invited to the B'nai B'rith to learn details about the forthcoming memorial inauguration ceremony, they were taken aback by the conditions the Círculo Israelita had laid down for the ceremony. No organizations or political parties would be permitted to attend, no flags or political symbols, shouting of slogans, singing, or flowers would be allowed at the ceremony; any future visit to the memorial after the unveiling would have to be approved by the institution; no subsequent modifications could be made to the memorial; there could be no publicity about the event, and the names of all who wished to attend the event had to be submitted beforehand.

Family members of Carlos Berger, David Silberman, Jorge Klein, Diana Aron, Jorge Müller, Ernesto Traubmann, Elías Jana, Recaredo Ignacio Valenzuela, Jacobo Stoulman, and Matilde Pessa listened attentively to the reading of the conditions. Carlos Arriagada, nephew of Jorge Müller, was the first to speak: "You seem to think we family members have four eyes and six arms. But we have never been disrespectful." Denni Traubmann, son of Ernesto Traubmann, expressed astonishment at the apprehension reflected in the conditions; nevertheless, he emphasized the memorial's importance: "A dream is about to come true. It is something I have needed so very much."

A year earlier, on September 4, 2012, Denni and his sister, Lily, accompanied by members of the Association of Families of Disappeared Detainees, the Communist Party Central Committee, and the Jewish Progressive Center, bid farewell to their father at Santiago's General Cemetery, as former Inti Illimani group member Max Berrú played music. A practically intact skeleton, recovered in patio 29 of the cemetery, had been identified as corresponding to their father, last seen alive in the Defense Ministry, after his arrest on September 12, 1973.

In her elegy, Lily described her father's refusal to "remain indifferent to poverty and abuse." He was an individual who "always chose the road of struggle against evil . . . , not out of obligation but because his conscience and ethical values so dictated," she said. Mireya Garcia, leader of the Association of Families of Disappeared Detainees, portrayed Ernesto as "a person who gave his all to his ideals."

But although this moving funeral afforded his father a dignified burial in a niche of the Memorial to the Forcibly Disappeared Detainees, Denni attached great importance to the memorial in the Jewish cemetery. The black granite memorial represents "our society's darkest hours," and "the fissures represent . . . the rupture that tore society apart," states its designer, the architect Andrés Zeldis.

As cemetery administrator, the Círculo Israelita donated the plot for the memorial, but the Interior Ministry's Human Rights Program funded its

Lily and Denni Traubmann at the funeral of their father, Ernesto Traubmann, September 2012 (Claudio Mandler)

construction. Forty memorials have been funded by the Human Rights Program as "expressions of symbolic reparation to prevent repetition and to evoke public reflection." The Jewish cemetery memorial is only the fifth to be installed in a cemetery; most of the rest have been erected in public places to stir public conscience.

The memorial was placed in a prominent location of the Jewish cemetery. Facing it are monuments to people who fell in Israel and to victims of the Shoah that were erected by Hungarian refugees as well as the monument to deceased members of the Fifth Firefighters Company of Ñuñoa (Israel Pump Brigade). Behind it lie the graves of Shoah survivors who arrived as refugees to Chile and died there.

While international bodies such as the Inter-American Court of Human Rights address human rights violations by insisting that states compensate for the damage they have caused, the cemetery memorial speaks not only to the state's responsibility but also to negligence on the part of the Jewish community. In her words before the people gathered that December afternoon, Sara Stoulman underscored the moral reparation represented by the memorial.

> It is an inscription that everyone who passes this place will recognize. Reading each name, they may wonder about the person behind the name, how he or she lived, and his or her legacy. It is a way to rise above history without being erased from it. To erase and deny is to omit the past, and this memorial reincorporates as part of a chain a series of links that had been part of it but were missing.

Denni Traubmann remarks, "I am happy that it was achieved. But other steps must take place before I can feel fully repaired. The main step is that the Instituto Hebreo should teach the true history about these people. With that gesture, I would be inclined to say that the Jews of Chile have begun to change their way of thinking."[37]

Despite the prohibition against publicizing the inauguration, more than three hundred people arrived at the Jewish cemetery on Pedro Donoso Street, exceeding the number of chairs that had been set up under an awning. Representatives of every Jewish institution, including the Israeli Embassy, the Jewish Representative Committee, the Zionist Council, the Women's International Zionist Organization, as well as seven rabbis from five different synagogues, attended. Also in attendance were human rights attorneys, staff of the governmental Human Rights Program, and representatives from the Museum of Memory and Human Rights, Villa Grimaldi Peace Park, and the Association of Families of Disappeared Detainees.

Rabbi Eduardo Waingortin, Jewish chaplain at La Moneda since 2012, recounted the millennial history of Jewish persecution.

> All dictatorships are terrible, and we can tell stories about dictatorships beginning with the Egyptian Pharaoh when the newborn baby boys were killed and thrown into the Nile. We hear the echo of mothers and fathers from throughout history: Jews of Spain with their terrible expulsion and later the pogroms and the Shoah. In this chain of pain, the dictatorship that occurred in Chile and the murders and disappearances form a direct link that prompts us to remember that we are one people and we must remember. . . . These people whose bodies never reappeared need a dignified place in the most cherished and sacred site of our community.

Before concluding the ceremony by intoning the funeral prayer *male rajamim* and reciting the kaddish mourning prayer, Rabbi Waingortin noted that truth, justice, and peace constitute the three pillars that hold up the world according to ancient Jewish scholars.

> Not all the truth has been uncovered. . . . We cannot contribute to the issue of truth. If that were possible, each of us would do so. Nor is there anything we can do in regard to justice. If there were, we would do so, as the murderers should face the consequences of their acts, but some of them are dead by now. The only thing we can do as a community is to embrace the victims and try to achieve peace.

The rabbi's words echoed deep in Anamaria Aron, seated among the public. At the military hospital, a Jewish doctor recognized her sister Diana, who had been seriously wounded by DINA agents at the moment they arrested her. The doctor never said a word to the Aron family. Nor did he ever testify in court that he had seen Diana wounded in the hospital. He confessed to an aunt, demanding that she never divulge what he told her as long as he was alive. The aunt kept silent and kept her word. Only after the doctor's death did the aunt tell Anamaria.

Thinking of his cousin Luis, Alejandro Guendelman insisted,

> I think that as long as people are still alive—the guy who brought him to Cuatro Alamos, the guy who took him to Villa Grimaldi, the one who took him from there to the next place of torture, and then to the military hospital, the helicopter pilot, and the guy who threw him over the edge into the sea—it's not too late. It's been only forty years. As long as people are alive and no effort is made to get them to testify and acknowledge the facts, they are washing their hands of

the matter. I believe you if you say we can't find out what happened in Masada hundreds of years ago. But here there are still many doors to knock on and many people to ask. Here we have complicity and silence.[38]

Ilán Sandberg, who as a teenager belonged to Hashomer Hatzair, is an attorney with the governmental Human Rights Program. He was at the Jewish cemetery for the inaugural ceremony and believes the memorial should encourage a transition from passivity to concrete action. "At the institutional and community level," he remarks, "there is much that can be done." B'nai B'rith or other institutions, he explains, could sign on as parties to a lawsuit to forge a unified front and above all to show that for the community the symbolic value of the memorial is not enough and that it is willing to take concrete action to fight for truth."[39]

"It's possible that Rabbi Waingortin is right regarding peace," says Jenny Stoulman,

> but in my case, having experienced it from the inside, I believe one can strive for peace without knowing all the truth, but it is easier when you can close an entire chapter. They could call people who know something to contribute to justice. If someone could tell me what happened [to my parents], I would be grateful. At least they have recognized that these people were Jews and now honor their names. It is a first step, but it does not erase the tremendous silence [of all these years]. Yet I don't believe they'll do anything else.[40]

The memorial, as described by the architect, was made from "a material that, like a mirror, reflects our own image, as anyone of us could have been represented there. The base is surrounded by black gravel, symbolizing segregation. Finally, a strip of grass surrounding the entire monument represents hope." "I hope the memorial will foster memory and actions in support of justice," repeats Alejandro Guendelman. "Until the breach between nonaction and action is closed, it will remain a beautiful monument but one lacking in deep and honest reflection about its meaning," he adds.

Ten days after inauguration of the memorial monument in the Jewish cemetery, on December 19, 2013, the Jewish Progressive Center convened approximately four hundred people at Peace Park, constructed on the site of the former Villa Grimaldi torture center.[41] With blessings from rabbis Alejandro Bloch and Chaim Koritzinsky, a black marble plaque, with the names of twenty people of Jewish descent carved onto its surface, was placed on a wall.

Anamaria Aron spoke on behalf of the families of the twenty people whose lives were honored by the event:

It's true that other friends have accompanied us, but the community's isolation was a much harder pain to endure, it's been a sharp pain. . . . When a group or a community forgets its past, it is because the previous generation did not tell them what happened. That is our responsibility. I think that today we are doing just that. We are giving testimony and leaving a trace to tell young people and future generations what happened. That's what survival means.

Jewish Cemetery Memorial to seventeen Jews summarily executed or forcibly disappeared, December 2013 (Claudio Mandler)

9

In Every Generation

By way of conclusion, the six stories that follow exemplify a dimension of Jewish identity that is seared by trauma but that transcends personal tragedy, channeled as a powerful ethical legacy. The first set speaks to the mysterious, if not mystic, closing of a circle of Jewish identity, reclaimed and resignified, while the second set attests to the compelling memory of beloved relatives that fosters a staunch commitment to social justice in their descendants.

CIRCULAR STORIES

Inevitable Return

As Walter Lebrecht crossed the doorway into the visitors' room in Tres Alamos, his son Edmundo observed him from the long table where the prisoners waited for their weekly visitors.[1]

Edmundo had spent a month in the catacombs of the DINA. He had spent six days—actually, "six days and six nights, because they worked day and night," he explained—at José Domingo Cañas. From there he had been taken to Cuatro Alamos, "a purgatory" within Tres Alamos, where "they decided whether or not to kill you." It was also, he adds, "a place for you to recover from the wounds inflicted during torture in order to return you to the torture center, an isolation center, where you were held incommunicado."

Four men shared the same cell. Two cellmates subsequently were forcibly disappeared and remain so to the present day. Edmundo was transferred to Tres Alamos, which meant his condition as prisoner had been recognized—a key to survival—and, therefore, that he was free to communicate with anyone from the outside world.

"I had been there a week and a half when the DINA came for me again. It was traumatic for the other prisoners with free communication status because

I was the first to be returned to a torture center. We all thought the worst was past us, but then we realized that it still could go on," he recalled. "They took me out again, and that was the worst part, at José Domingo Cañas. It was very, very hard. That time they arrested my wife, who was seven months pregnant. My son Manuel was born in prison. She had no political involvement; they arrested her to pressure me to talk."

At the time he was waiting in the visitors' area for his father, he had been held twenty days. When he saw his father enter the visitors' hall, Edmundo wanted to tell him what he had been through. Revolutionary Left Movement members shared an ethical code that included not talking to others about what had happened to them in prison, But Edmundo desperately wanted to break that unwritten rule to let his father know how the dictatorship he supported had treated his son.

And so he did. From the other side of the long table, where the prisoners and their visitors gazed at each other surrounded by soldiers carrying machine guns, Edmundo began telling his father what he had gone through. "My father literally said to me, 'I don't want to hear any of that.' It was something that just didn't fit with my cultured father, with the man who had been persecuted in Germany," Edmundo says. "Not even the repression exercised against two of his sons made him change."

In the city of Ulm from which Walter had fled, Nazis set up a concentration camp in an ancient fort, locking up political and union leaders in underground prison cells. Perhaps, in an attempt to repress his memories of those times, Walter never told his children about how the Nazis had done that. Now the figure of his son held prisoner by the dictatorship confronted Walter with the nightmares that had tormented him so many years.

His father's untold story, however, was in fact a key element in Edmundo's recovery of his freedom. Jews who had returned to Ulm heard about Edmundo's imprisonment and launched a campaign demanding that he be set free. At the time that Edmundo was still in Tres Alamos, they persuaded the city of Ulm to grant him German citizenship. An official from the German Embassy handed him a German passport, and he boarded a plane for Europe. On April 30, 1975, for the first time in his life, Edmundo stepped foot on his father's homeland, where his wife and his infant son, Manuel, born in prison, were waiting for him. Walter Lebrecht left Ulm in desperation at twenty-five years of age. At twenty-three, Edmundo arrived in Ulm to a hero's welcome.

The driving force behind the efforts to free this Chilean was Alfred Moess, a schoolmate of his father and a Jew who returned to Ulm after having lived in England and Palestine during World War II. He wrote letters to the editors of the local newspapers and convinced the Amnesty International chapter of

Ulm to sponsor Edmundo. The campaign organized by Moess, who was a retired accountant, took off and put pressure on Chile's Interior Ministry. Of Moess, Edmundo says, "Simply, he was my German father and my savior."

> When they have tried to annihilate you physically, psychologically, and intellectually, it is a triumph to return. In Alfred's case, the Nazis did not want him to live there. For him, returning to Ulm was a triumph over the Nazis. In my case, I was defeated politically, I and all my comrades, but the fact that I am alive today and have returned to Chile is a personal triumph over the dictatorship. This goes for Alfred as well. He belonged to Germany. Returning was a personal triumph. Even though so many Jews were slaughtered, the fact that Alfred survived and returned was a triumph over Nazism.

Edmundo notes not only his firm belief that he had to return to Chile but also the deep emotions that living in his father's city evoke in him. "The same city that expelled my family took me in." Laughing, he repeats what he has

Edmundo Lebrecht, 2012 (Adriana Goñi)

said in many interviews with German newspapers: "Ulm is the only city in the world where I feel Jewish. That's not rhetoric. It's a logical projection of my father's life."

In 2011, during a September 11 event at Hashomer Hatzair commemorating victims of human rights violations in Chile, Edmundo elaborated on that sense of an inheritance: "As a psychologist once told me, my father sent me to continue his life that had been truncated in Germany."

Edmundo returned to Chile in 1988 and subsequently began dividing his time each year between the two countries. In Ulm, he directed theater and taught acting classes; in Chile, he divided his time between Santiago and Contulmo, where he was elected city councilperson.

Family Heirlooms

On July 25, 1985, a girl with light-brown hair and blue eyes came into the world. Had it been a different time, she would have been born in a clinic in Concepción or Santiago. But this baby, named Gabriela by her Chilean parents, was born in Dusseldorf, Germany, as the consequence of a series of events that unfolded twelve years before she was born, on September 11. Her story is linked to her father's story and also to that of her maternal grandfather, both of whom were former political prisoners in exile.

In early April 1974, after eight months of having been held as prisoner of war by the navy on Quiriquina Island, Gunter Seelmann was sleeping soundly in his bunk when he was awakened by a light shining in his face. The sentry, flashlight in hand, ordered him to pack his meager belongings because in a few more hours he would leave the island.

What was going on? Where were they taking him? What did the intelligence services have in store for him? Many questions circulated in his head in the darkness. The same questions troubled his prison mates when he told them of his imminent and unexpected transfer.

When marines delivered him to the Talcahuano investigative police headquarters, the director of that office showed him a memorandum signed by the head of the Second Naval Zone. The memo stated: "Dr. Gunter Seelmann is a dangerous element due to the influence he has over civilians and the Quiriquina Island garrison. Therefore, the Interior Ministry has ordered him transferred to the jail of the Santiago investigative police."[2] He understood that in reality the transfer was the first step toward commuting his imprisonment to expulsion from the country.

As a refugee in England with her family, Hanni Grunpeter was separated from her father when he was imprisoned on the Isle of Man. She had experienced that separation as a young girl, barely aware of her mother's anguish or her mother's efforts to sustain both of them. From the window of the Naval Hospital, she observed the ferry carrying Gunter and the first group of twelve detainees to Quiriquina Island. Immediately she ran to naval officers to leave him a pair of sweaters—it was September and quite chilly in the last weeks of the southern hemisphere winter. There was no certainty that Gunter would receive the sweaters, but with that act, Hanni began a mission to alleviate her husband's suffering on the island prison and obtain his release.

That Gunter was born in Germany and had left that country as a refugee proved fundamental to the success of the efforts on his behalf. Heinz Ehrenbach, a cousin whom Gunter had first met while taking a course in Germany some years earlier, was also key. Otto Ehrenbach, Heinz's father, had thrown himself off a train that was headed to Auschwitz, choosing to kill himself rather than suffer in the concentration camp. Now Heinz helped save a cousin threatened by the Chilean military. He arranged for a delegation of German congressmen traveling to Chile to denounce the way the dictatorship had trampled on human dignity and to include Gunter's name among others whose immediate release they would demand.

Germany was still reluctant to receive Chilean refugees. Lutheran bishop and German citizen Helmut Frenz was fundamental in achieving a change in German policy in this regard. Frenz was very important in Gunter Seelmann's destiny and that of thousands of other Chileans who were eventually admitted as refugees to the German Federal Republic. Frenz confronted the German ambassador, saying, "This man fled Germany as a boy to save himself from the Nazis. If you don't allow him to return to Germany, the Chilean military is likely to kill him. That will weigh on your conscience, Mr. Ambassador."[3]

Gunter was destined to return to Germany. After spending a week in the Santiago jail, he climbed the boarding stairs into a Lufthansa jet, expelled from Chile under Decree Law 504. Hanni managed to hand the stewardess a suitcase with Gunter's notarized documents, including his university diplomas, which enabled him to find work at the university in Düsseldorf, the city where his cousin Heinz lived. In May, Hanni and the children joined him in Düsseldorf.

They quickly became part of the community of Chilean exiles and began to help new arrivals. In 1978, in a Lutheran church in Düsseldorf, they participated in a hunger strike in support of family members of the disappeared who were conducting their first hunger strike in Chile.

The three Seelmann-Grunpeter children grew up in Germany speaking German. In a Jewish community of Düsseldorf, David celebrated his bar mitzvah. Both daughters married exiles in Germany, and their first three grandchildren were born there. One day, David's teacher came to the house. Hanni asked whether her son had misbehaved. But the teacher had something else on her mind. She needed to talk to Hanni. Recalling the teacher's words fifty years later deeply moves her. The teacher had this to say:

> I know you are Chilean exiles and that you are Jews. I would have liked to tell you that my father was a hero. But he was not. I don't think his hands were stained in blood, but I do remember our village cobbler. Practically overnight, I was forbidden from going to the cobbler shop because he might hurt me. I didn't understand it. No one would explain what was going on. I grew up absolutely ignorant. Today I feel the need to tell you everything. Many people of my generation had similar experiences.

"Then we began talking about Chile," recalls Hanni. "She made the connection with the Jewish cobbler who repaired everyone's shoes, whom she was forbidden from visiting." Nearly in a whisper, Hanni describes her response to the teacher's confession: "Perhaps I subconsciously connected things. But I did not say that history repeats itself. In the first situation, a man was persecuted simply because he was a Jew; in the other, a man was persecuted because of his beliefs. The cobbler was a good German. Gunter was a Chilean. Both were rejected and punished."

Gabriela, the first grandchild born in Germany, grew up speaking both Spanish and German, the language her grandfather Gunter spoke at her age:

Gunter Seelmann, January 2020 (Círculo Israelita de Santiago)

"In my mind, I have never separated the Jewish exile from the Chilean political exile. They may be quite different historically, but I have always associated one with the other. I believe all my family's history is basically one of a permanent exile. History is cyclical. Maybe it won't happen to me, but it could be that my children or grandchildren will go through the same thing simply because history has marked them."[4]

A few years ago, Gabriela discovered a small golden Maguen David (star of David) in her mother's jewelry box that her mother had stopped wearing

Hanni Grunpeter, 2012 (EPES Foundation)

when the family left for exile in 1974. Gabriela caresses the Maguen David that she has worn on a chain around her neck ever since and wonders about the still unknown stories it will unveil in the course of her own lifetime.

On December 15, 2012, at Ruaj Ami, a religious community in Santiago, Gabriela celebrated her bat mitzvah, attributing to her grandparents' influence the process now culminating with full incorporation as a member of the Jewish people. She told the people attending the ceremony the following: "There is a mistaken notion that when you form your identity or pass from childhood to adulthood—which is the original sense of the bat mitzvah ritual—you break with your family and with all you have learned up to that point. For me, developing this facet of my identity has not meant a rupture. On the contrary, it has confirmed and reaffirmed all the principles I learned from childhood."

Cohanim

José Cohen Abramovich, born in a town near Odessa, was forced to fight on behalf of the czar in the Russian-Japanese war.[5] A Jew played a fundamental role in the humiliation Russia encountered in that conflict. His name was Jacob Schiff, and he was a German immigrant who used his fortune earned as a banker in New York to aid Jews affected by abuse throughout the world.[6] To punish the Russians for the massacre of Jews in the pogroms of Kishinev (1903), Schiff lent the Japanese empire an estimated two hundred million dollars. The Russians were defeated in 1905. When the Russians unleashed their wrath against the Jews, José Cohen boarded a ship for Buenos Aires. From there he continued on to Santiago. To his children and grandchildren born in Chile, he would recite the serial number engraved on the rifle he used in the war where he learned to be a soldier.

In Chile, José Cohen married Berta Steingel Broder, who like him was an immigrant from Ukraine. He supported his wife and their two sons with a grocery store he opened in Santiago, near the corner of Vicuña Mackenna and Portugal avenues. Those were the years of the Great Depression, and Don José allowed people to pay him for their groceries at the end of the month. When the time came for customers to pay what they owed him, he would send his eleven-year-old son León to collect the debts. When León knocked on the debtors' doors, not infrequently they would yell, "Get out of here you filthy Jew" or "So now you've come to charge us, you shitty Jew."

This was one of the first family stories featuring the word "Jew" that Gregory Cohen, León's son and José's grandson, remembers hearing as a child. Many years later, his father came home and told him about an incident in which he had been treated in a similar fashion, which emblazoned in Gregory's mind the idea that to be a Jew sometimes meant people despised you.

Yet he knew that mutual respect and even affection were possible between Jews and non-Jews. The friendship between a Jewish girl and a Catholic boy, portrayed in the film *Hand in Hand* (a 1960 film by Philip Leacock), impressed him when he saw it at ten years of age. Moreover, he had an example in his own home: the love between his father and his mother, Rosa Elena Muñoz, who was not Jewish. Even though she was not Jewish, his mother "always had praised Jews" and she wanted both her sons circumcised.

His father "repeated a thousand times" to his sons the stories about the Nazi persecution of Jews as well as the story of Uncle Santiago Kohen (who spelled his surname with a "k"), who Gregory visited in his tailor shop on Matucana Street. Uncle Santiago had escaped from Berlin the very night of Kristallnacht.

Family history intertwined with his own experiences as a target of antisemites, experiences that were made worse by the terrible events of those times, to transform León Cohen into a fervent fighter against Chilean Nazis. In the late 1930s, León and his cousins participated in brigades that confronted homegrown Nazis in Plaza Bogotá and other places around Santiago, such as the University of Chile. Three months of military service qualified León, who was a Radical Party member, to serve as martial defense instructor of the Communist Youth Organization. He was also a leader of the League of the Rights of Men, an organization formed to pressure President Juan Antonio Ríos to break ties with the Axis nations. These chronicles that his father would relay to him transfigured his father into an iconic personality and forged in Gregory another facet of Jewish identity: nonpassivity when facing injustice.

As a young man, León actively supported Pedro Aguirre Cerda's presidential campaign and all the other Radical Party candidates. Years later, disenchanted with the Radical Party, he supported Salvador Allende for president, working on his campaigns in southern Chile.

When Allende won the presidency, Gregory was in his third year at the prestigious Instituto Nacional secondary school. In 1972, Gregory entered the University of Chile School of Engineering, and shortly thereafter, he joined the Communist Youth Organization. "There I found that part of the left merged with the secular Jewish part," says Gregory. "I associated all my father's political activity with being Jewish. My father told me about it in terms of his particular interests: Nazis, Hitler, and his Jewish friends. Therefore, I associate his political activism with being Jewish," he adds.

On the morning of September 11, 1973, Gregory told his parents not to expect him home that night. He planned to remain at the university to defend the government from there. His brother did the same at the University of Chile Medical School. "Our parents were very afraid, but my father had to understand us because in his youth he had done the same thing. I waited to receive instructions from the party. Luckily, the weapons never arrived—otherwise they would have reduced us to dust," he recalls.

As of that first day of what would turn into more than sixteen years of dictatorship, Gregory followed his father's example, but from his own cultural resistance path, as he describes it.

> Something made me a communist. The influence of what happened with the Jews was very important. The first stories about Jews I ever heard were always about mistreatment, persecution, or death. Those were the stories my father told us about the Second World War. There were victims of Nazism, victims of fascism, victims of whomever, of persecution in Ukraine, Russia, Rome. Continuing farther back there was always persecution. Then it came to Chile, this time with persecution against everyone. Somehow or another, there is continuity.

Gregory participated in the creation of the Agrupación Cultural Universitaria (ACU). Founded in 1976 at the Engineering School on Beaucheff Avenue where he studied, the ACU was the first university organization created in opposition to the dictatorship. During an era when meetings and gatherings of any kind were forbidden—more than three people together constituted a meeting—theater, film, and music festivals organized by the association were cultural activities that became the first massive political acts. Thousands of people filled the Caupolican and Cariola theaters, eager, in those days of cultural blackout, to experience different artistic expressions and clearly eager as well to participate in dissident events.

In 1980, at ACU's third festival, Gregory debuted what may very well be his most emblematic play of those years, *Lily, yo te quiero*. Jointly written with Roberto Brodsky and with Gregory himself in the cast, the play "served as very important survival therapy in those years, both for us as well as the audiences that came to see us," he notes in a January 12, 2011, interview with Radio Cooperativa.

During a public demonstration in 1981, when the Communist Party made a strategic shift to throw the first *miguelitos*, Gregory was arrested. Many people were arrested, but he was one of few who was jailed for an extensive period of time. His arrest was widely reported and denounced. Actors stationed themselves on a corner facing the police station where Gregory was initially held, on guard to prevent the CNI from taking him, which subjected detainees to more than the blows that were standard fare from police. Nicanor Parra, Enrique Lihn, Jorge Edwards, Carlos Matamala, Felipe Alliende, and other well-known Chilean intellectuals were gathering signatures demanding his release, when he was transferred to Santiago's penitentiary.

He was in prison for three months. Arguing that the arrest was an abuse of power since no charges had been pressed against him, his lawyers persuaded the court to release him upon payment of bail. The Supreme Court absolved him in a landmark ruling that recognized the lack of merit for the arrest. Gregory resumed his political opposition from within the cultural sphere. In 1982, with Igor Rosenmann, another Jewish dissident, he restaged *Lily, yo te quiero*.

In early November 1987, a blood-stained letter threatening seventy-seven actors, including Gregory, was left outside the actors' union office. Signed by a previously unknown Comando Trizano, it warned: "If you don't leave the country by November 30, we will kill you." All the actors named in the letter were assigned police protection. But the actors themselves mocked the threat by wearing white T-shirts with a red circle in the middle with the words "shoot me first." Hundreds turned out for a rally on November 30, including Christopher Reeves, on behalf of the Screen Actors Guild, in support of the Chilean actors. "Superman saved us," Gregory states.

Ten months later, Gregory was given a sublime opportunity to express his opposition. "Sir, what do you have to say to a dictator?" asked a serene off-camera voice to a man immersed in reading a book. It was the "No" campaign,

Gregory Cohen and Igor Rosenmann in *Lily, yo te quiero* (Gregory Cohen)

the first fifteen minutes of televised free expression in fifteen years, allowed as of September 5, 1988, a month before the national referendum. The "sir" lowered his book, glanced to either side, and with a roar stuck out his tongue, on which could be seen a "No" campaign sticker.

Gregory's participation in the "No" campaign publicity spot—a concept he himself proposed—was quite significant, he notes today. It was twelve powerful seconds in the career of this cultural dissident. "Ah! It felt so good to be able to do that!" he says. "It was wonderful to vent everything contained inside me and stick my tongue out at the dictatorship with a message of dissidence. It stemmed from desperation as well as hope at a singular point in time. It was a synthesis; it said everything." Later came more plays, four novels, and films. In 2011 would also come Oscar, the memorable character of the *Los 80* television series, who harbors a persecuted woman and ends up being tortured on account of his solidarity. The script he learned to give life to Oscar "was more than a text," he says. "I simply put into action what I carried in my body, what I remembered, without trying to generate or build something. It was a situation I had personally experienced," he adds.

In dictatorial Chile, as in Europe under Nazi dominion, the goal of repressive policies was not only to kill people but to destroy an entire culture, dehumanize, and break the spirit of everyone associated with that culture. Many Jews in Europe who were walled in inside ghettos engaged in large and small acts of resistance every day. The Warsaw ghetto uprising on April 19, 1942—the first major Jewish rebellion against the powerful German military forces—has become a universal symbol of the unflinching human spirit. Yet it is less known that the uprising owed to an extraordinary network of daily expressions of resistance, in schools and libraries, through talks, music, and also theater. Emanuel Ringelblum resisted by preserving historic vestiges; Jaim Kaplan by creating schools in the ghetto; Wladyslaw Szpilman through music; Jonas Turkov through theater; and Mordejai Anielewicz and some hundred or so young people by fighting with a rifle in their hands.[7]

Gregory Cohen, as well as his great friend Igor Rosenmann, are heirs to that tradition of resistance.

Gregory, moreover, is a descendant of the genealogical line of Aaron, who served as his brother Moses's spokesman before Pharaoh. Despite having consented to the manufacturing of the golden calf, Aaron and his children were designated *cohanim* (plural of the Hebrew word "cohen," meaning "priest"), enabling them to officiate in the sanctuary and transmit blessings to the people. All people whose surname is Cohen are heirs of the priestly class that initiated with Aaron. "This is a powerful surname; it weighs on you. It takes you to the heart of Jewish identity," says this descendant of José, Santiago, and León

Cohen and of *cohanim*. "Inevitably," he concludes, "Jewishness strongly influences my social conscience. It restores in me a bit more of a sense of being Jewish."

Snapshots of New Generations
Catherina's Heirs

The girl with long wavy auburn hair in an old-fashioned dress appeared to observe Patricia with light-blue eyes from the black-and-white photo. Who was she? When she asked, her mother would invariably reply "a cousin from Europe." Many years later, as a teenager, while visiting the home of an uncle who lived in the United States, Patricia was surprised to find a photograph of the same girl. "Who is that girl?" she asked. "Are you kidding? Don't you know that was your sister Catherina?" he answered.[8]

That response and the subsequent story of Catherina had a lasting effect on Patricia's life.

Patricia's father, Kalman Politzer, was a Czech immigrant, and her mother, Catalina Kerekes, was a Hungarian refugee; both were Jewish, and they met and married in Chile. Her father concealed the fact that he had left a wife and child behind in Czechoslovakia. After the Nazi invasion, both were deported and transported in cattle cars to a concentration camp. Catherina died there. Her father never completely got over the death of his first daughter, and he died when his second daughter was about the same age as Catherina was when she died in the concentration camp.

Patricia is today a noted journalist whose gift with words has helped shed light on the era of military obscurantism. The discovery that she had a sister who died in a concentration camp marked her forever, reinforcing the humanitarian values she had acquired in her family circle. "My family inculcated in me the concept of freedom as an irrevocable value with such force that it has marked my entire life," Patricia says. "In my university years during the Popular Unity government, I made a commitment and worked to make the dream of a better Chile proposed by President Salvador Allende a reality. During the Pinochet dictatorship, I never doubted what I had to do: fight so that Chileans could be free again."[9]

Patricia's first daughter, Susana, with wavy auburn hair and clear eyes, bears a surprising resemblance to Catherina, the girl in the photograph. In 1981, the same year her husband, Arturo Navarro, was threatened by the CNI, successor to the DINA, and forced to leave the editorial staff of the opposition magazine he had founded, her second daughter, Catalina, was born.

Catalina Navarro, also a journalist, worked for several years in communications at the National Human Rights Institute. She no longer works at that institution but she never left human rights far behind. In the late 1990s, she participated in the Funa movement. Organized by children of disappeared persons, during the movement's height (1999–2004), the group held street demonstrations to publicly ostracize individuals who had collaborated with the military dictatorship's repression but had never faced trial. Nearly one hundred former repressors were targeted.

Catalina explained what motivated her to take part in these events. "Funa said that it is unacceptable for these people who had tortured and killed people on account of their beliefs to sit quietly at home and evade responsibility for the crimes they committed." Singing one of the movement's emblematic songs— "Olé olé, olé olá, just like the Nazis, it will happen to them, wherever they go we will Funa them"—groups of young people would go to a building where a former repressor lived or worked. Then they would unfurl a banner that read "If there's no justice, there is Funa!"[10]

"The Nazis went to other countries, assumed different identities and hid. Here the dictatorship's criminals do the same." When they left the army or the CNI, she notes, they went to work for private firms as well as government agencies, "attempting to conceal their past criminal involvement so no one would find out."

> I believe that my participation in Funa owes to the fact that I am Jewish and from my awareness of Shoah. Ever since I can remember, I have heard that we must keep the memory of it alive so it will never happen again. My family history in Europe and what happened here under dictatorship go hand in hand. For me the idea of "never again" inevitably brings me closer to Judaism. Somehow, my personal history intersects with Jewish history, Chilean national history and European history.

Patricia, her mother, has said, "Personally, I believe that fighting for freedom and social justice is the essence of my Jewish identity. That's what I learned from my parents and that is what I have tried to transmit to my daughters."[11]

The words and life routes chosen by this mother and her daughter preserve Catherina's memory.

Following an Uncle's Path

Another photo: a baby dressed in white held in his grandmother's arms.[12] His smiling parents can be seen standing nearby. Other people are seated near them. The baby is Carlos Arriagada, the first grandchild, on the day of his baptism. The maternal grandmother is Irma Silva. Seated behind them are his Jewish grandfather Rodolfo and his uncle Jorge. It's the only photo of the nephew with his uncle.

"Jorge has always been a photograph for me," says Carlos. "These days we all have videos and things recorded with our cell phones. But I have never heard Jorge's voice. Whenever I have been with filmmakers, and especially Patricio Guzman, who filmed *La memoria obstinada*, I have asked them about old films Jorge might appear in. It remains a challenge for me to get to know him, to know how he spoke. My entire life I have tried to know him."

Carlos was born in April 1973, a year and a half before his uncle Jorge was detained; his brother Felipe was born six years later. Despite never having met him, Carlos and Felipe feel connected to Jorge. "He is a constant presence," affirms Felipe. However, that is not because their family made Jorge present. "In my recollection," Carlos says, "my family never spoke to me about Jorge; they never told me what happened to him." He adds, "To protect us, no one—neither my parents nor my grandparents—told us Jorge's story when we were little, in those difficult years. All my life, I have wanted to know more about him."

Over time, the brothers have gradually learned about their uncle. When he was eleven, Carlos discovered the book *¿Dónde están?* in the house. When everyone had gone to bed, he began leafing through the book, published by the Vicariate of Solidarity. The stories of disappeared people shocked him. In the middle of the book, with the narratives in alphabetical order, all of a sudden, a very familiar picture leaped from the page. It was his uncle Jorge.

He was also stunned to read in the same book the accounts of many women social workers. "After I read these stories, I wanted to become a social worker," he says. Carlos graduated with a degree in social work and wrote his thesis on the role of social workers in human rights defense agencies during the dictatorship. Relying on "what I learned with my grandparents, what I experienced with them, since I understood the injustice," he explains, "I have sought a way to work for justice, in my own way. Back then I identified my vocation. My decision to become a social worker has to do with following the same path."

Over time, Felipe has sketched in his mind an image of his uncle as filmmaker and rock and roller. "He had long hair. He had a gift for music and art. My uncle was ahead of his time. Once my mother told me, 'He would have been a super cool uncle for you today.' He had the same tastes I have; he liked bossanova." Raised in a family and school environment inclined to the political right, Felipe said, "It makes you see life differently."

In 2000, when he was in college, Felipe traveled to Europe for the first time. He looked for Northeim, the German town where his grandfather was born.

No member of the Müller family had ever returned to Northeim. It became somewhat of an odyssey when he discovered there were several towns with the same name. Accompanied by two friends, he at last arrived in the correct Northeim. "I didn't know if the house still existed. I was obsessed with the house the family had abandoned in Germany," explains Felipe. Walking along, guided only by a photograph of the Müller house, all of a sudden he recognized the three-story building. "It was a very lovely moment. It connected me to my grandfather's history, as I had imagined it. Facing the house was a place for making long-distance telephone calls, so I called my grandfather, and I told him, 'At this very moment, I am in front of your house.' It made him happy."

The next day, he went to the Jewish cemetery. The place was in disarray, but Felipe managed to find the tomb of his great-great-grandfather Hermann Rodolph, whose death clinched the family's decision to leave Northeim. He cleaned the gravestone and left a small stone in remembrance. The ritual drew to a close over a day and a half in Northeim and the pilgrimage of a grandson, fifty years after his great-grandparents and grandfather fled to an unknown place called Chile.

His brother Carlos notes,

> One day, when my grandma Irma was very ill and hospitalized in Clínica Alemana hospital, she handed me a chain with a medallion she always wore. The medallion is round, with "Chile" written in the shape of prison bars with a person holding onto the bars. On the back, it says, "For all you have done for Jorge." Political prisoners made it for her and sent it to her through the Vicariate of Solidarity. She handed it to me and asked me never to leave Opi, my grandfather Rodolfo, alone. She died at dawn the next day. I have never forgotten my promise to her.

Ever since, Carlos has lived in his grandfather's house, taking care of him and intending to keep him company "until he goes off to reunite with Jorge and my grandmother."

A large patchwork *arpillera* tapestry, hanging in the house, was made by Irma. In the final months of 1983 and during much of 1984, Irma lovingly embroidered stitch after stitch, sewing patch after patch, with needle, thread, and cloth, narrating the story of Jorge and Carmen's disappearance ten years earlier on November 29. In seven of the *arpillera*'s eight scenes, Irma appears in yellow in front of the gates to Cuatro Alamos, in front of the courthouse doors, and in the street with the Association of Families of Disappeared Detainees. In the last scene, an orange-clad figure of Jorge lies up in a flowering tree. Down below at the foot of the tree, Irma takes a flower and sets out on a new road that lies ahead to continue the legacy her son left her and her husband. Through Irma's *arpilleras*, the couple's participation in the folk group they started, and their refusal to abandon their efforts to seek justice for Jorge, his parents followed the road paved by their son, embracing his commitment. In their own way, the nephews also follow that road, forged by their uncle and traveled by their grandparents, giving life to memory.

Looking to the Past for Meaning

Mounds of dirt appeared with increasing frequency, but few would ever gleam with headstones that Jews typically erect on the first anniversary of a person's death.[13] Small stones, signs that others remembered the deceased, would never accumulate on the graves.

Now the Konujowska sisters would leave Charcow for good. In this corner of Ukraine, no families would remain to place stones on the tombs of their parents or grandparents. The tailor Konujowska had died of typhoid after being forced by the czar to work for the army during the war. If his five sisters and mother had survived the last pogrom unharmed, it was because villagers hid them. But the next time, they might not win the game of Russian roulette they were playing. Instead of counting on their luck to continue, they decided it was time to leave.

Encouraged by letters from their uncle Benjeroff, who had become rich in Buenos Aires, the sisters and their mother left aboard a ship. They had barely arrived in 1927 when Elisa, thirteen, and her sister, twelve, began working in their uncle's haute couture tailor shop. It employed a hundred people and operated day and night. In time, the Konujowska sisters would marry and their social and economic conditions would improve.

On day in 1939, a Jew from Warsaw showed up at the shop. Elisa noticed him. His name was Hersz León Lejderman, a serious, quiet young man, who had golden fingers for tailoring. They got married and promptly opened their own shop they called Modas Enrique (Enrique Fashions), the name he went by in Argentina.

Much later, Elisa learned the reason for her husband's somberness. He had arrived in Argentina with his father, but his mother and a sister were in Canada. Another sister and brother in Warsaw were murdered by Nazis. Enrique held that separation and that loss deep inside him. However, their firstborn son soon arrived; he would scatter the sad memories and fill the house with light.

Bernardo Mario, born March 24, 1943, was an inquisitive child. He learned to play the accordion and guitar and then began painting watercolors. He also took a typewriting course. A passionate student of Jewish history, Bernardo learned Hebrew and studied for his bar mitzvah at Temple Libertad, a prestigious synagogue located around the corner from the Lejderman family's spacious apartment. At sixteen he earned a teaching certificate and at eighteen he entered law school in Buenos Aires. A young man of boundless energy, Bernardo was a university student body leader and organized summer youth camps. With the same enthusiasm, he embraced political idealism and joined leftist political parties. He traveled to Mexico and fell in love with María del Rosario Avalos. In 1971, they arrived in Salvador Allende's Chile, intending to pursue their idealistic vision.

Attorney Arturo Barrios, who knew the couple in Santiago, describes Bernardo as "a man who read, who studied extensively, and who was a revolutionary, in the correct sense of the word. He was a revolutionary of knowledge; he firmly believed that the Latin American countries had to make their own Latin American revolutions."[14] Moreover, "we always knew he was Jewish and that his parents had been persecuted in Europe as Jews."

It was Barrios and his law partner who in 1972 arranged for Bernardo to work with the Socialist Party governor of Vicuña, in north-central Chile. "It was a mistake on our part," says Barrios, because in the small town of Vicuña, the couple and their year-old baby stood out as strangers. Fully aware that their status as foreigners would lead the residents of the town to regard them with even more suspicion, as soon as the coup occurred, they left their house and hid in abandoned coal mines in the hills above Vicuña, hoping that muleteers would cross them over to Argentina. But no muleteer wanted to get involved. During three months, they went from one site to another, in the hostile mountainous climate of extreme heat by day and cold at night. Once in a while, Bernardo would go down to the village of Gualliguaica or to Vicuña to get food, and one time a man gave them clothing to help with the cold nights. That person was arrested and forced to show the military where the foreign couple was hiding.

The compassion of Charcow villagers who saved the Konujowska sisters was absent in Vicuña that dawn of December 8, 1973. With the same cold calculation of the czar's men who terrorized Jews, the platoon of soldiers advanced upon a defenseless family. For thirty-three years, there was no tomb for Bernardo, where visitors could leave stones in his memory; to this day, the whereabouts of María del Rosario's remains are still unknown. Before his second birthday, then, Ernesto had lost his parents. But he became like a son to his grandparents Elisa and Enrique, who raised him.

Jewish history has given Ernesto elements that help work through his personal history. Until he was twenty, his closest circle was almost entirely Jewish. He lived in the traditional Jewish neighborhood of Villa Crespo, in Buenos

Aires, and went to the ORT school.[15] Yet his father was "more closely connected to Judaism than me," he says. "I think that my identity as a Jew has to do with my history, my family's history, and the history of a people. For me, Jewish identity is not just a religion and it is not related to a particular country. It's about a history and cultural roots. I respect that sense of belonging to a history and a people."

He has observed and experienced firsthand the repetition of that history in his family. His grandparents lost what was most precious to their lives. His grandfather Enrique, at sixty, fell into depression and didn't want to work anymore. At only fourteen years of age, the son-grandson began to work, manufacturing bags, backpacks, and fanny packs. In four years, Ernesto had established a small factory that sustained his grandmother when she was widowed.

That some community leaders in Argentina and Chile have questioned whether women and men of Jewish descent who were kidnapped and murdered in secret places or simply summarily shot, as was the case with his parents, were real Jews gives him pause. "Some say they were second, third-, or fourth-class Jews, that they were not first-class Jews," Ernesto notes. "I say you have to save the lives of fourth-, fifth-, and tenth-class Jews—and non-Jews too. A distinctive Jewish value calls for protecting the life of any person at any place. That is a value I learned."

On December 8, 2012, the Mothers of Plaza de Mayo organized a massive commemorative event in Buenos Aires to remember the three mothers who were kidnapped and forcibly disappeared in 1977. The date coincided with the thirty-ninth anniversary of the murders of Bernardo Lejderman and María del Rosario Avalos. The three hundred people attending the event gave voice to the names of their loved ones. With all his strength, Ernesto shouted, "Bernardo! María del Rosario!" "Sometimes it hurts to remember. But after analyzing this a very long time, I now understand that remembering is necessary because it's not just a personal or individual thing. It affects a community, a country, a nation, and a city," says Ernesto.

Because of the pain they felt and their belief that the boy had to be protected from that pain, his grandparents never told Ernesto the truth about how his parents died. Until he was fifteen, he believed they had died in a traffic accident. But he had nagging doubts. Whenever he was alone at home, Ernesto would rummage through furniture drawers. One day, at last, he found a notebook filled with newspaper clippings about the murder of his parents in Chile. When he mustered the courage, he asked his grandmother about it, and she admitted it was true.

"I believe the process of remembrance and memory is very important because it is not only an individual exercise: it's collective," says Ernesto. "What happened in the dictatorships of Latin America was genocide, planned and carried out just like it was during the Shoah. You are a victim of genocide, not merely one single person who is killed. It is much larger in scope and much more significant; it's also much, much more dangerous because the side effects are felt for generations afterward, as in the case of my grandparents and great-grandparents."

Two photos speak to this story. The first shows a young attractive couple. He has a moustache; she has thick, dark brown hair cascading over her shoulders. In her arms she carries an infant. Both look directly at the photographer, both smiling broadly. Embracing, they are a single unit, a nucleus. The photo evokes many connections, permitting a stranger who might see it to identify with this marriage, this child, this family, and the happiness exuded by the young couple looking forward to the future.[16] In the second photo, an elderly couple observes with evident affection a young boy standing between them. He, however, rigidly holds his grandfather's and grandmother's hands. There is a corporal distance between them and the boy at the center of the photo and their lives. It is the photo of the new situation; the boy is a token of love. He is implicitly burdened as the enduring vestige from that love. He has inherited a vestment. That vestment is expressed in the child who has grown up to be the bearer of the memory of both generations, and like his parents, he is a fighter for justice.

Ernesto's tenacity produced results; the men who killed his parents were eventually sentenced to ten years in prison, although in May 2009 the Supreme Court decreased that sentence to five years. On December 10, 2006, he was able to inter his father at the Memorial to the Disappeared in Santiago's General Cemetery. In August 2013, on a nationally broadcast television program, Ernesto exposed Juan Emilio Cheyre as the military officer who gave him to the nuns in La Serena and publicly called on the former army commander-in-chief to tell the truth about how Bernardo and María del Rosario were murdered. His denunciation forced Cheyre to resign his position as director of Chile's Electoral Service, to which he had been appointed by the government.

To his quest for truth and justice for his parents, Ernesto has added another mission. Ernesto learned his grandfather had a sister, Hanna Lejderman, who died in a Nazi concentration camp. "I want to find out about her life in Warsaw," he says. It's something that has long been on his mind, and his desire to know more has only grown more acute in recent years. He wants to "find out what lies there under the ground, what's back there. You search for meaning in the past."

YIZKOR—IN MEMORIAM

Persons of Jewish origin forcibly disappeared or summarily executed
during Chile's dictatorship:

Diana Frida Aron Svigilsky, 1950–74

Carlos Berger Guralnik, 1943–73

María de la Luz Frankovich Pérez, 1927–73

Luis Alberto Guendelman Wisniak, 1950–74

Manuel Elías Jana Santibáñez, 1929–75

Ronni Karpen Moffitt, 1951–76

Jorge Max Klein Pipper, 1945–73

Bernardo Lejderman Konujowska, 1943–73

Jorge Müller Silva, 1947–74

Abraham Muskatblit Edelstein, 1937–86

Raúl Pellegrin Friedmann, 1958–88

Juan Carlos Perelman Ide, 1944–75

Matilde Pessa Mois, 1935–77

Miguel Rivas Rachitoff, 1935–74

David Silberman Gurovich, 1941–76

Jacobo Stoulman Bortnik, 1934–77

Ernesto Traubmann Riegelhaupt, 1924–73

José Joaquín Valenzuela Levi, 1958–87

Recaredo Ignacio Valenzuela Pohorecky, 1956–87

Boris Weisfeiler Bernstein, 1941–85

NOTES

INTRODUCTION

1. When interviewed in 1958, the Reverend Martin Luther King Jr. remarked, "The national Jewish bodies have been most helpful, but the local Jewish leadership has been silent. Montgomery Jews want to bury their heads and repeat that it is not a Jewish problem. . . . I agree that it is not a Jewish problem, but it is a fight between the forces of justice and injustice. I want them to join with us on the side of justice." Quoted in Melissa Fay Greene, *The Temple Bombing* (London: Vintage, 1996), 180; and Marc Schneier, *Shared Dreams: Martin Luther King, Jr. and the Jewish Community* (Woodstock: Jewish Lights Publishing, 1999), 45.

2. On October 12, 1958, the Temple, the most prominent synagogue in Atlanta, was bombed in retaliation against the outspoken support of its rabbi, Jacob Rothschild, for civil rights. For further information on this incident and the response of southern Jews to the civil rights movement, see Green, *The Temple Bombing*.

3. Michael Lerner. *Jewish Renewal: A Path to Healing and Transformation* (New York: Harper Perennial, 1995), 180.

CHAPTER 1. EXODUS

1. Nathan Ausubel, *A Treasury of Jewish Folklore* (New York: Crown, 1989), 319.

2. Ausubel, *A Treasury of Jewish Folklore*, 315.

3. Interview with Leonardo Baticoff, September 2013. All translations from non-English sources, including interviews, are mine unless otherwise indicated.

4. The Pale of Settlement was where Jews of Russia were permitted to live between 1835 and 1917. Spanning 621,200 square kilometers from the Baltic to the Black Sea, in 1897 the territory became the mandatory residence for an estimated 4,900,000 Jews, who represented 94 percent of the total Jewish population of Russia and close to 12 percent of the area's total population, according to historian Irving Howe in *World of Our Fathers* (New York: Simon and Schuster, 1976).

5. Mark Zborowski and Elizabeth Herzog, *Life Is with People* (New York: International Universities Press, 1952), 152.

6. Abba Eban, *Heritage: Civilization and the Jews* (New York: Summit Books, 1984), 241.

7. Howe, *World of Our Fathers*, 5.

8. Interview with Perla Aron, May 20, 2009.

9. Howe, *World of Our Fathers*, 58.

10. Ricardo Feierstein, *Historia de los judíos argentinos* (Buenos Aires: Ameghino, 1999), 67.

11. Interview with Miguel Lawner, February 17, 2010.

12. "The Romanian Jewish Community," www.romanianjewish.org/en/cap4, and "The Holocaust in Romania," accessed August 17, 2021, www.yadvashem.org/yv.

13. Interview with Miguel Lawner, February 17, 2010.

14. Interview with Jorín Pilowsky, September 22, 2009.

15. Eban, *Heritage*, 169.

16. Eban, *Heritage*, 170.

17. Interview with Edmundo Lebrecht, February 2, 2010.

18. *Emil J. Gumbel Collection: Political Papers of an Anti-Nazi Scholar in Weimar and Exile* (New York: Leo Baeck Institute, 1990).

19. Comuna de Contulmo, Servicio Nacional de Tourismo, Ministerio de Economía, Fomento y Turismo, 2014, https://www.contulmo.cl/alcalde/.

20. The four Müller brothers were Ernesto, Rodolfo, Francisco, and Carlos. Rodolfo died on June 8, 2021, at ninety-nine years of age.

21. Daniel Lipson, "The Jewish Soldiers of the Kaiser's Army," Librarians, https://blog.nli.org.il/en/jewish_germany_army/; "12 of 12,000: Fallen German-Jewish Soldiers in the First World War," Judisches Museum Berlin, https://www.jmberlin.de/en/12-of-12000-introduction.

22. William Sheridan Allen, *The Nazi Seizure of Power: The Experience of a Single German Town, 1922–1945* (Danbury, CT: Franklin Watts, 1965), 160.

23. Interview with Rodolfo Müller, March 2, 2011.

24. Bar mitzvah is a Jewish celebration at thirteen years of age that marks spiritual maturity within the community.

25. Peter Gillman and Leni Gillman, *Collar the Lot: How Britain Interned and Expelled Its Wartime Refugees* (London: Quartet Books, 1980).

26. Herbert Bronstein, ed., *A Passover Haggadah: The New Union Haggadah* (New York: Penguin Books, 1982), 56.

Chapter 2. Strangers in a Strange Land

1. Interview with Gunter Seelmann, September 23, 2009.

2. Interview with Tomás Hirsch, August 24, 2011.

3. Interview with Hans Stein, October 27, 2010.

4. Interview with Rodolfo Müller, March 2, 2009.

5. Irmtrud Wojak, "Chile y la inmigración judeo-alemana," in *Entre la aceptación y el rechazo: América Latina y los refugiados judíos del Nazismo*, ed. Avraham Milgram (Jerusalem: Yad Vashem, 2003), 129–30.

6. Jorge Pinto Rodríguez, ed., *Modernización, inmigración y mundo indígena: Chile y la Araucanía en el siglo XIX* (Temuco: Ediciones Universidad de la Frontera, 1998), 50–51, 101, 104.

7. Brian Loveman, *The Legacy of Hispanic Capitalism* (New York: Oxford University Press, 2001), 41–42; Judith Elkin, *The Jews of Latin America* (New York: Holmes and Meier, 1998), 35.

8. Ricardo Feierstein, *Historia de los judíos argentinos* (Buenos Aires: Ameghino, 1999), 67.

9. Wojak, "Chile y la inmigración judeo-alemana," 140.

10. The 1,005 Nazi members registered in Chile in 1939 made its local National Socialist party one of the largest in the world, in proportion to the German population in Chile, estimated at thirty-five thousand, in the 1930s, according to Raffael Nocera, *Chile y la Guerra, 1938–1943* (Santiago: Lom, 2006), 44.

11. The Radical Party is a centrist political organization that challenged Roman Catholic Church hegemony when it was founded in the mid-nineteenth century.

12. Ramon Zañartu, ed., *Berman, hombre de acción* (Santiago: Talleres Gráficos de La Nación, 1940), 25–31.

13. Edmundo Lebrecht told the story about his uncle Heiner Lebrecht in an interview with me on February 2, 2010.

14. Interview with Raúl Sohr, May 2, 2012.

15. Archivo Nacional, vol. 4209, Ministerio de Relaciones Exteriores de Chile.

16. Moisés Senderey, *Historia de la Colectividad Israelita de Chile* (Santiago: Dos Ydische Wort, 1956), 113.

17. "Ship Bound Refugees Find Havens through Action by HIAS-ICA," Jewish Telegraphic Agency, April 2, 1939.

18. Zañartu, *Berman, hombre de acción*, 25–31.

19. Jacobo Pilowsky, *A yid af der velt* (Santiago: self-published, 1970).

20. Pilowsky, *A yid af der velt*.

21. Personal correspondence with Arye Pilowsky, November 24, 2011.

22. Israel Gutman, *Holocausto y memoria* (Jerusalem: Centro Zalman Shazar de Historia Judía, 2003), 291.

23. Gutman, *Holocausto y memoria*, 294.

24. Gutman, *Holocausto y memoria*, 296.

25. Gutman, *Holocausto y memoria*, 292–94.

26. Archivo Nacional, Ministerio de Relaciones Exteriores de Chile, carpeta E3-10-1-1.

27. Archivo Nacional, Ministerio de Relaciones Exteriores de Chile, carpeta E3-10-1-1.

28. Archivo Nacional, Ministerio de Relaciones Exteriores de Chile, carpeta E3-10-2-2.

29. Archivo Nacional, Ministerio de Relaciones Exteriores de Chile, carpeta E3-10-2-2.

30. Archivo Nacional, Ministerio de Relaciones Exteriores de Chile, carpeta E3-10-2-2.

31. Richard Breitman, "What Chilean Diplomats Learned about the Holocaust," Nazi War Crimes and Japanese Imperial Government Records, Interagency Working Group, July 2001.

32. Interview with Raúl Sohr, May 2, 2012.

33. Personal correspondence with Rona Fields, May 17, 2009.

34. Personal correspondence with Rona Fields, May 17, 2009.

35. "The Jews of the Sudetenland," Holocaust Education and Research Team, 2009, http://www.holocaustresearchproject.org/nazioccupation/sudetenland.html.

36. Irene Stoliar, *Los shomrim de Los Andes: Historia del Movimiento Kidma-Hashomer Hatzair en Chile* (Santiago: Gráfica LOM, 2008), 25.

37. Interview with Denni Traubmann, March 21, 2009.

38. Interview with Denni Traubmann, March 21, 2009.

CHAPTER 3. COMMUNITY DILEMMAS

1. For more information, see Henry Minczeles, *Histoire générale du Bund: Un mouvement révolutionnaire juif* (Paris: Denoël, 1999); Tony Michels, *A Fire in Their Hearts: Yiddish Socialists in New York* (Cambridge, MA: Harvard University Press, 2009); and Kenneth B. Moss, *Jewish Renaissance in the Russian Revolution* (Cambridge, MA: Harvard University Press, 2009).

2. Interview with Jorín Pilowsky, September 22, 2009.

3. "A 20 años del martirologio de los escritores judíos de la URSS," *La Palabra Israelita*, August 1972.

4. Gunter Seelmann pointed this out to me in a conversation we had in August 2014.

5. Mario Sznajder, "El judaísmo chileno y el gobierno de la Unidad Popular," in *Proceedings of the World Congress of Jewish Studies: The History of the Jewish People* (Jerusalem: Word Union of Jewish Studies, 1993), 5.

6. Interview with Raúl Sohr, June 27, 2014.

7. Interview with Perla Aron, May 20, 2009.

8. All quotes of Issac Ickson are from the author's interview with him on June 25, 2014.

9. Interview with Mauricio Guzmán, November 14, 2013.

10. Víctor Farias's *Salvador Allende: Antisemitismo y eutanasia* (n.p.: Maye, 2005) was controversial. This testimony corroborates that Allende's position changed.

11. Interview with Haim Hayet, November 9, 2010.

12. "Delegación representativa del ishuv de Chile visitó al Dr. Salvador Allende, presidente electo," *La Palabra Israelita*, October 30, 1970.

13. "Delegación representativa del ishuv de Chile visitó al Dr. Salvador Allende."

14. Valeria Navarro, "Comunidad judía en Chile y Argentina durante los regímenes militares, 1973–1990/1976–1983: Dirigencia y derechos humanos" (master's thesis, University of Santiago, 2008), 81.

15. A third brother, Ernst, one of the founders in Chile of the organization that was a precursor to Hashomer Hatzair, immigrated to Israel with his wife, Miriam, arriving in July 1947 at Negba Kibbutz. On December 6, 1947, Ernst died at the start of the War for Independence during an Arab attack.

16. *La batalla de Chile* is an epic three-part documentary film, directed by Patricio Guzmán, that documents the two and a half years of the Allende government as well as life under dictatorship in 1975 and 1979. There was a hiatus of several years in the filming process due to the arrest and expulsion of Guzmán and other members of the

film crew after the coup. Müller and his girlfriend, actress Carmen Bueno, were abducted by military agents on November 28, 1974, following the premiere of his film *A la sombra del sol*.

17. Interview with Rodolfo Müller, March 11, 2009.

18. Interview with Daisy Rosenberg, daughter of Walter Rosenberg, March 16, 2014.

19. Interview with Corina Rosenfeld, December 5, 2011.

20. Interview with Mauricio Guzmán, November 14, 2013.

21. Interview with Mauricio Guzmán, November 14, 2013.

22. "A la opinión pública," *La Palabra Israelita*, August 17, 1973.

23. Martín Ruíz, "El antisemitismo de *La Prensa*," *El Siglo*, August 29, 1973, 4.

24. Ruíz, "El antisemitismo de *La Prensa*," 4.

25. Status report on Chilean Jewish community, April 22, 1974, American Embassy, Santiago, to Secretary of State, Washington, DC, reference number: State 079784, document number: 1974Santia02144_b.

26. Valeria Navarro, interview with Angel Kreiman, April 29, 2008, quoted in Navarro, "Comunidad judía en Chile y Argentina durante los regímenes militares, 1973–1990/1976–1983."

27. "Noticias de la Federación WIZO," *La Palabra Israelita*, January 11, 1974.

28. "Sociedades israelitas completan su aporte," *La Palabra Israelita*, May 10, 1974. In reply (October 2018) to my query, Manuel Riesco (of the Centro de Estudios Nacionales de Desarrollo Alternativo) notes that this sum is the equivalent of $38,683,710 pesos today (US$54,285). He calculates this using the value of one escudo in May 1974 as the equivalent of 3,457 pesos today. For further information, see the Centro de Estudios Nacionales de Desarrollo Alternativo's "Chile: Corrección Índice de Precios al Consumidor (IPC) e Índice de Remuneraciones Reales, 1960–2000" (Escuela de Ingeniería Comercial, Universidad ARCIS, Santiago, December 2000)

29. Interview with Isaac Icekson, June 25, 2014.

30. B'nai Brith is an international Jewish humanitarian organization, founded in 1843, that seeks to "strengthen healthier, more just, pluralistic and non-discriminatory societies."

31. On September 21, 1976, Letelier was assassinated in Washington, DC, by a bomb planted on his car by agents of the DINA, Chile's secret police. Ronnie Karpen Moffit, a young Jewish woman, who, like Letelier, was on the staff at the Institute for Policy Studies, also died in the attack.

32. Interview with Isaac Frenkel, July 17, 2014.

33. Interview with Isaac Frenkel, July 17, 2014.

34. "Sonia Epstein, alumna del Instituto Hebreo, recordó a poetas judeo-soviéticos inmolados por los verdugos stalinistas por el único pecado de ser judíos," *La Palabra Israelita*, August 23, 1974.

35. Interview with Raúl Sohr, June 27, 2014.

36. He mentions Israel as a factor because as of December 1974, when the US Congress approved the Kennedy Amendment, Israel became Chile's main military supplier. Israel was also Chile's ally in the UN, abstaining from voting on or voting against fourteen out of sixteen UN General Assembly resolutions that condemned

Chile's disregard for human rights between 1974 and 1989. See Hugo Harvey Parada, *Las relaciones entre Chile e Israel, 1973–1990* (Santiago: RIL, 2011).

37. All quotes of Marita Feldmann are from the author's interview with her on November 22, 2013.

38. Soviet troops and the Romanian Army surrounded Budapest on December 26, 1944, retaining control until the city surrendered on February 13, 1945.

39. "El Pedagógico" is the popular name for the Metropolitan University of Educational Sciences, a traditional hub of student activism, which, at times, spills over into demonstrations in adjacent streets.

40. Interview with Andreas Feldmann, January 16, 2014.

41. Interview with Andreas Feldmann, January 16, 2014.

42. Christian base communities were small Catholic grassroots groups, usually associated with a parish, but led by lay people in homes and community centers, that explored creative ways of worship and biblical study that highlighted social justice issues of the dictatorship years, when they flourished.

43. Personal correspondence with Roberto Feldmann, April 30, 2014.

44. Gregorio Goldenberg, *Un rabino sui generis* (Santiago: Ediciones EGEGE, 1986), 52.

45. Navarro, "Comunidad judía de Chile y Argentina durante los regímenes militares, 1973–1990/1976–1983," 94.

46. Mijael Vera, interview with Angel Kreiman, March 2010, www.Anajnu.cl.

47. Goldenberg, *Un rabino sui generis*, 182.

48. Navarro, "Comunidad judía de Chile y Argentina durante los regímenes militares, 1973–1990/1976–1983," 121; Vera, interview with Kreiman. The Diego Portales building had originally been called the Gabriela Mistral Cultural Center; it had been constructed in a record 275 days and hosted its first event, the third UN World Conference on Commerce and Development conference, in April 1972. After the coup, the military junta converted it into its administrative headquarters, since it had bombed La Moneda, and renamed it. In 2010 the building's original name and purpose as a cultural center was restored. Miguel Lawner was the architect for the original construction as well as the subsequent restoration.

49. Navarro, "Comunidad judía de Chile y Argentina durante los regímenes militares, 1973–1990/1976–1983," 179.

50. Goldenberg, *Un rabino sui generis*, 135.

51. Interview with Sara Sharim, November 12, 2009.

52. Goldenberg, *Un rabino sui generis*, 137.

53. Navarro, "Comunidad judía de Chile y Argentina durante los regímenes militares, 1973–1990/1976–1983," 121.

54. Fernando Villagrán, *Disparen a la bandada* (Santiago: Planeta, 2002), 238–39.

55. Goldenberg, *Un rabino sui generis*, 99.

56. Goldenberg, *Un rabino sui generis*, 99.

57. Interview with Perla Aron, June 19, 2009.

58. Interview with Rodolfo Müller, March 11, 2009.

59. Goldenberg, *Un rabino sui generis*, 181.

60. Interview with Isaac Ickekson, June 25, 2014.

61. Navarro, "Comunidad judía en Chile y Argentina durante los regímenes militares, 1973–1990/1976–1983," 119.

62. Navarro, "Comunidad judía de Chile y Argentina durante los regímenes militares, 1973–1990/1976–1983," 119.

63. Interview with Denni Traubmann, March 21, 2009.

64. Interview with Carmen Hertz, May 13, 2010.

65. One cousin was Enrique Kirberg Baltiansky, chancellor of the State Technical University, who was imprisoned after the military coup.

66. Interview with Rolly Baltiansky, May 20, 2010.

67. Interview with Miguel Lawner, February 17, 2010.

68. Interview with Gunter Seelmann, September 23, 2009.

69. Interview with Hanni Grunpeter, August 13, 2012.

70. Interview with Sara Caro, August 19, 2011. What she describes is still a well-known children's game in Chile.

71. Interview with Tomás Hirsch, August 24, 2011.

72. Interview with Perla Aron, June 19, 2009.

73. Interview with Perla Aron, June 19, 2009.

74. Interview with Miguel Orellana Benado, August 26, 2013.

75. Aaron Rakeffet-Rothkoff, *The Rav: The World of Rabbi Joseph B. Soloveitchik*, vol. 2 (Hoboken, NJ: KTAV, 1999), 50.

76. Interview with Joel Oseran, August 3, 2012.

77. Interview with Rosita Schaulsohn, September 12, 2011.

78. Stoliar, *Los shomrim de los Andes*, 11.

79. Interview with Mauricio Guzmán, November 14, 2013.

80. Interview with Darío Teitelbaum, June 2, 2013.

81. Interview with Haim Hayet, November 9, 2010.

82. Personal correspondence with Haim Hayet.

83. Interview with Isaac Icekson, June 25, 2014.

84. Interview with Kathy Castro, November 15, 2011.

85. Hashomer Hatzair members are called shomrim.

86. Interview with Darío Teitelbaum, June 2, 2013.

87. Interview with Juan Flores, June 10, 2013.

88. Interview with Sandra Oksenberg, August 5, 2013.

CHAPTER 4. THESE WE SHALL REMEMBER

1. "These we shall remember" is the free translation of "Eile Ezkera," a liturgical poem that remembers Jewish martyrology through the centuries. The poem acquired new meaning in the context of the millions murdered during the Shoah. Although the detentions described here were not motivated by the fact that the victim was Jewish, the phrase calls to mind the Jewish obligation to remember them.

2. Interview with Yael Mandler, October 2, 2013.

3. According to official reports, three hundred foreigners, including eleven US citizens, were held in the National Stadium. Charles Horman and Frank Teruggi, US citizens who were murdered by the military in the days following the coup, are believed to have been brought there as well.

4. Interview with Dina Krauskopf, October 26, 2011.

5. In the first half of the twentieth century, rural Chile was dominated by large landowners who controlled the lives of tenant farmers. In the early 1950s, landowners further dispossessed small- and medium-sized farmers of their lands, which exacerbated already miserable living conditions. With backing from the Catholic Church, in 1962 the Chilean government undertook agrarian reform. During the Allende administration, Jacques Chonchol, agriculture minister, and David Baytelman, director of the Agrarian Reform Corporation, carried that process further.

6. Interview with Daniel Jana Calderón, August 11, 2014.

7. Personal correspondence with Daniel Jana Torres, February 10, 2015.

8. Personal correspondence with Daniel Jana Torres, February 10, 2015.

9. Interview with Sara Caro, August 10, 2011.

10. Personal correspondence with Ivonne Szasz Pianta, April 30, 2013.

11. Lumi Videla was a vibrant university student leader and active member of the MIR. On September 21, 1974, she was abducted by the DINA. Surviving political prisoners have testified to the dignity and strength she retained in captivity and to how she demanded decent treatment for fellow prisoners. After she was savagely tortured to death, her corpse was hurled over the wall onto the grounds of the Italian Embassy.

12. Personal correspondence with Ivonne Szasz Pianta, December 13, 2012. *Cohanim* is a Jewish priestly class that descends from Aron, brother of Moses, a status that is passed on paternally.

13. Personal correspondence with Ivonne Szasz Pianta, December 13, 2012.

14. Interviews with Julio Budnik, June 24 and July 1, 2014.

15. Interview with Raquel Lipovetzky, June 24, 2014.

16. Interview with Jenny Stoulman, January 13, 2014.

17. Interviews with David Canales, May 28, 2015, and Enrique Correa, June 3, 2015.

18. Another passenger on the same flight Jacobo Stoulman took to Paris was Major General Raúl Iturriaga Neuman, appointed the year before assistant director of the DINA, who was involved in the assassination of Orlando Letelier and, two years before that, in the assassination of Carlos Prats and his wife, Sofía Cuthbert. It appears the DINA already had Stoulman under surveillance nine months before his abduction.

19. Interview with David Canales, May 28, 2015.

20. Canales testified in the Condor case before Judge Víctor Montiglio in 2010 and before Judge Mario Carroza in July 2015, specifically on the episodes involving the arrests from May to June 1977 in Santiago and Buenos Aires.

21. Interview with Julio Budnik, July 1, 2014.

22. Contreras attributes this version of the facts to the retired Argentine general Otto Carlos Paladino, who visited him in Punta Peuco on October 16, 1996 (Santiago Appeals Court record, rol. n. 2.182–98, "Operación Cóndor," 23:7176).

23. Santiago Appeals Court record, rol. n. 2.182–98, "Operación Cóndor," 23:7181.

24. Interview with Carmen Hertz, May 26, 2015.

25. Enrique Correa, born in 1915, was a telegraph operator and leader of the Chile Postal Employees Union. From 1969 to 1970, he served as secretary to Enrique Kirberg, chancellor of the Technical State University. During the Popular Unity government, he was administrative director for the undersecretary of transportation.

26. The Democracy Defense Law, an initiative of President Gabriel Gonzales Videla, was enacted in 1948, banning the Communist Party, removing thousands from electoral rosters, and banishing people to isolated regions of Chile. The law was repealed in 1958.

27. Interview with Enrique Correa, June 3, 2015.

28. Interview with Sandra Oksenberg, August 5, 2013.

29. Klaus Meschkat, *Der Stern*, October 4, 1973.

30. Personal correspondence with José Del Castillo Pichardo, September 19, 2013.

31. Interview with Juan Guzmán Tapia, September 21, 2010.

32. Interview with Jorín Pilowsky, September 22, 2009.

33. Interview with Jorín Pilowsky, September 22, 2009.

34. Interview with Gunter Seelmann, September 23, 2009.

35. Interview with Hanni Grunpeter, August 13, 2012.

36. Interview with Jorge T., August 23, 2013.

37. Interview with Igor Rosenmann, November 6, 2013.

38. In late 1971, Roberto Matta, joined by the Ramona Parra Mural Brigade, painted a mural twenty-five meters long by four meters high along the wall of the La Granja municipal public swimming pool, in south Santiago. The mural, titled *El primer gol del pueblo chileno* (The Chilean People's First Goal), celebrated the Popular Unity government's first anniversary. After the military coup, the mural was covered with layers of paint and plaster, which was believed to effectively destroyed it. However, in 2005, University of Chile students began the process of recovering and restoring the mural, a process that was completed in 2008.

39. Tres Alamos was a detention center located in the southcentral Santiago municipality of San Joaquin that operated from 1974 to 1977. Cuatro Alamos, on the same premises as Tres Alamos, a secret torture center run by the DINA, consisted of twelve small cells and one large cell as well as offices. Prisoners commonly were kept several weeks or even months at Cuatro Alamos with no contact with the outside world or government acknowledgment of their imprisonment before being transferred to Tres Alamos.

40. The Central Nacional de Informaciones (CNI) was founded in August 1977, after the DINA was disbanded, following its September 21, 1976, assassination of Orlando Letelier in Washington, DC. Like its predecessor, the CNI was responsible for abductions, torture, murder, and other repression of opponents to the dictatorship.

41. Interview with Tomás Hirsch, August 24, 2011.

42. The National Commission on Political Imprisonment and Torture, presided over by Monsignor Sergio Valech, was first convened by the Chilean government in 2003 and then reconvened in 2010–11. The commission confirmed 38,254 cases of people who were jailed and tortured during the military dictatorship.

43. Interview with Katia Reszczynski, June 15, 1999, by journalist Nancy Guzmán in connection with her book *Romo: Confesiones de un torturador* (Santiago: Planeta, 2000).

44. Interview with Luis Muñoz, April 22, 2014.

45. Interview with Luis Muñoz, April 22, 2014.

46. Nancy Guzmán, *Romo: Confesiones de un torturador* (Santiago: Planeta), 149.

47. Interview with Gladys Díaz, March 28, 2012.

48. Interview with Olga Weisfeiler, April 21, 2010.

49. Personal correspondence from Olga Weisfeiler, January 30, 2009.

50. US Embassy memorandum, Boris Weisfeiler, declassified document SA011AH, March 22, 1990.

51. Interview with Roberto Garreton, May 28, 2014.

52. Interview with Julia Concha and Luis Concha, Buenos Aires, August 18, 2014.

53. Amilcar Santucho, a Communist Party member, was the brother of Roberto Santucho, head of the Ejército Revolucionario del Pueblo, who died in July 1976 during a confrontation with police. Amilcar Santucho, who survived captivity (d. 1995), testified that he was tortured by Paraguayan police, while interrogated by Argentine, Chilean, and Uruguayan military, offering proof of the existence of Operation Condor.

54. In December 2012, federal judge Daniel Bejas indicted Jorge Rafael Videla and another forty defendants for more than 269 acts of abduction, torture, forced disappearance, and homicide committed between February 8, 1975, and March 23, 1976. On October 2, 2020, the Federal Oral Court of Tucuman handed down three life sentences and thirteen prison sentences ranging from ten to nineteen years, in the Operativo Independencia II case, or Megacausa No. 14, for 335 cases, including that of my cousin Dr. Máximo Eduardo Jaroslavsky, abducted and forcibly disappeared as of November 19, 1975. See "Operativo Independencia II: El Tribunal impuso 16 condenas y dictó 9 absoluciones," Télam, October 3, 2020, https://memoria.telam.com.ar/lesa-humanidad/202010/operativo-independencia-ii--el-tribunal-impuso-16-condenas-y-dict--9-absoluciones_n8898.

55. Pierre Vidal-Naquet, *Los judíos, la memoria y el presente*, trans. Daniel Zadunaisky (Buenos Aires: Fondo de Cultura Económica, 1996), 199.

56. Federal judge Daniel Refaca, who investigated state terrorism crimes in Argentina, estimated that 10 percent of the thirty thousand disappeared Argentines were Jewish. The Comisión de Solidaridad con Familiares de Desaparecidos en Argentina, an organization of families of the victims in Barcelona, placed the figure at more than 12 percent. Regardless of which figure is correct, Jewish victims made up a disproportionate percentage, given that in 1976, Jews represented no more than 0.98 percent of the total population of Argentina.

57. Equipo de Denuncia, Investigación y Tratamiento del Torturado y su Núcleo Familiar, Paz Rojas Baeza, and María Inés Muñoz, *La gran mentira: El caso de las "Listas de los 119* (Santiago: Comité de Defensa de los Derechos del Pueblo, 1994), 111.

58. The "list of the 119" case refers to a hoax orchestrated by the Chilean military dictatorship between April and July 1975 to explain the whereabouts of people arrested and subsequently disappeared that is known as Operation Colombo. Intelligence operatives invented a list of 119 names of people that they claimed had died in internecine fighting in Argentina and Brazil when the truth was they had been arrested by agents of the state.

59. Interview with Stella Calloni, January 29, 2013. See also Stella Calloni, *Operación Cóndor: Pacto criminal* (Mexico City: Editorial La Jornada, 2001); and Stella Calloni, *Los años del lobo: Operación Cóndor* (Buenos Aires: Editorial Continente, 2002).

60. Interview with Laura Elgueta, February 25, 2014.

61. Several surviving political prisoners, such as Julio Laks and Rosalía Martínez, a couple arrested in early October 1974, have testified in court that David Silberman was held with them at the house on José Domingo Cañas Street that had been converted into a torture center known as Cuartel Ollague, run by the DINA, in Santiago. On October 5, a group of prisoners, including Martínez and Silberman, was transferred to the Cuatro Alamos detention center. In mid-October, Silberman was returned to the house on José Domingo Cañas Street, where Julio Laks saw him again (interview with Julio Laks, May 2012).

62. According to a list of witnesses compiled by Simón Guendelman and updated on December 6, 1999, Enrique Arce testified that he heard Luis Guendelman sing from an adjoining prison cell. Copy of list in author's possession.

63. Interview with Alejandro Guendelman, December 16, 2013.

64. Interview with Juan Guzmán Tapia, September 21, 2010.

Chapter 5. Rescuers and Bystanders

1. Guillermo Blanco, *Camisa limpia*, 3rd ed. (Santiago: Lom Ediciones, 2008). Another novelized story about Francisco Maldonado da Silva is *La Gesta del Marrano* (1991) by Argentine author Marcos Aguinis.

2. Interview with Hanni Grunpeter, August 8, 2012.

3. Interview with Sara Caro, August 19, 2011.

4. Interview with Perla Aron, June 19, 2009.

5. Interview with Sara Caro, August 19, 2011.

6. Interview with Gladys Díaz, March 28, 2012.

7. Interview with Héctor Shalom, January 27, 2011.

8. The following narrative is based on the Yad Vashem description of the rescue of Betty and Marcel Friedman organized by María Edwards.

9. In 2017, Yad Vashem posthumously recognized Samuel del Campo as a Righteous among the Nations. He is credited with saving at least one thousand Polish Jews in Romania in his capacity as Chilean consul in Bucharest from 1941 to 1943, where he issued Chilean visas.

10. Israel Gutman, *Holocausto y memoria* (Jerusalem: Centro Zalman Shazar de Historia Judía, 2003), 329.

11. Introduction to the program Righteous Among the Nations, Yad Vashem. Yad Vashem (in English, "Hand of God") takes its name from Isaiah 56:5: "I will give them in my house and within my walls a monument and a name" (English Standard Version).

12. Rabbinical Assembly, *Etz Hayim: Torah Commentary* (New York: Jewish Publication Society, 2004).

13. This is the translation offered by Rabbinical Assembly, *Etz Hayim*.

14. Elie Wiesel reiterated the importance of this verse in his memoir *And the Sea Is Never Full* (New York: Random House, 1999), 88.

15. Stanlee Stahl, "Christian Rescuers" (talk, April 18, 2001).

16. Primo Levi, *If This Is a Man* (London: Penguin, 1979), 127.

17. Interview with Kathy Castro, November 15, 2011.

18. Interview with Gladys Díaz, March 28, 2012.

19. Interview with Sonja Friedmann, August 9, 2012.

20. José Aron Friedmann was the great-grandfather of Raúl Pellegrin Friedmann, otherwise known as Commander José Miguel, who led the Manuel Rodríguez Patriotic Front armed resistance movement to the dictatorship and was murdered on October 26, 1988, at Los Queñes. Raúl Pellegrin Friedmann was the son of Judith Friedmann, a cousin of Sonja Friedmann.

21. Interview with Frida Sharim, November 23, 2009.

22. Interview with Carlos Arriagada, August 24, 2012.

23. Interview with Rodolfo Müller, March 11, 2009.

24. Interview with Rodolfo Müller, March 11, 2009.

25. Interview with Rodolfo Müller, March 11, 2009.

26. Interview with Carlos Arriagada, August 24, 2012.

27. Interview with María Pilquín, August 27, 2013.

28. Interview with Eliana Bronfman, November 23, 2010.

29. Eliana Bronfman and Luisa Johnson, *De enterezas y vulnerabilidades: 1973–2003: Hablan los mayores* (Santiago de Chile: LOM, 2003).

30. Interview with Mario Tapia, July 29, 2010.

31. Interview with Carmen Hertz, May 13, 2010.

32. Haydée López, quoted in *Homenaje de sus compañeros de Centro Integrales de Salud* (Santiago: n.p., 1988), 27.

33. Victoria Baeza, quoted in *Homenaje de sus compañeros*, 31.

34. Interview with Eva Mateluna, August 11, 2010.

Chapter 6. Echoes of Anne Frank

1. Gunter Seelmann Erlenbach, *Evocaciones de mi vida* (Santiago: self-published, 2001), 37–38.

2. Jaap Tanja of the Anne Frank House Education Department in Amsterdam provided this archival information. The archives show that the van Pels, the other family hidden in the annex house, also had connections to Chile. Ida van Pels, sister of Herman van Pels and aunt of Anne Frank's beloved Peter van Pels, immigrated to Chile in November 1939.

3. Gunter Seelmann, "Vigencia del *Diario de Ana Frank*," *La Nación* (Santiago), December 10, 1992, 14.

4. Héctor Precht Bañados, "Ana Frank . . . y Chile," *El Mercurio*, January 6, 1974.

5. Gil Sinay and Robert Levy, "Desviación de principios fundamentales de la Fundación Anne Frank," *La Palabra Israelita*, January 16, 1974, 10.

6. Conversation with Isaac Caro, April 15, 2010.

7. Héctor Shalom and Silvina Chemen, *Testimonios para nunca más: De Ana Frank a nuestros días* (Buenos Aires: Editorial Universitaria de Buenos Aires, 2008)

8. Interview with Héctor Shalom, January 27, 2011.

9. Héctor Shalom, introduction to Ana Frank, *El diario de Ana Frank* (Santiago: Centro Gráfico, 2003), 40.

10. Anne Frank, *The Diary of a Young Girl*, trans. Susan Massotty (New York: Bantam Books, 1997), 79–80.

11. Frank, *The Diary of a Young Girl*, 251.

12. Seelmann, "Vigencia del *Diario de Ana Frank*," 14.

13. Corporación Nacional de Reparación y Reconciliación, *Informe de la Comisión Nacional de Verdad y Reconciliación*, vol. 2 (Santiago: Andros Impresores, 1996), 946.

14. Maxine Lowy, "Develando el crimen de tortura," interview with Hiram Villagra, Memoria y Justicia, April 2003, https://www.memoriayjusticia.cl.

15. Lowy, "Develando el crimen de tortura."

16. Lowy, "Develando el crimen de tortura."

17. Loreto Alamos, Gloria Duarte, Eugenio Escorza Chetty Espinoza, Myriam George, Gloria Maureira, Juan Manuel Pérez, and Aminta Traverso, *Infancia y represión: Historias para no olvidar, experiencias con niños y familias que han vivido la represión política* (Santiago: ARGE, 1992), 55.

18. Alamos et al., *Infancia y represión*, 61.

19. Alamos et al., *Infancia y represión*, 69.

20. Alamos et al., *Infancia y represión*, 186.

21. Alamos et al., *Infancia y represión*, 141, 143.

22. Alamos et al., *Infancia y represión*, 41.

23. Interview with Joop Kaldenhoven, January 22, 2013.

24. Interview with Els Nicolas, March 11, 2014.

25. Interview with Joop Kaldenhopen, January 22, 2013.

26. Interview with Els Nicolas, March 11, 2014.

27. Fernando Quilodrán and Boris Vildósola, eds., *Alberto Bolk: Vivencias de un preso holandés de la dictadura en el Estadio Nacional* (Santiago: self-published, 2013), 30–32.

28. *Koers*, Anne Frank House staff newsletter, 1994, 18.

29. Interview with Peter Gelauff, March 4, 2014.

30. Interview with Hernán Leemryse, March 23, 2012.

31. Interview with Peter Gelauff, March 5, 2014.

32. Interview with Els Nicolas, March 13, 2014.

33. Interview with Boris Vildósola, March 17, 2014.

34. Interview with Boris Vildósola, March 13, 2012.

35. Interview with Boris Vildósola, March 19, 2014.

36. Guest book, *Ana Frank, una historia vigente*, 2007.

37. Interview with Margarita Romero, January 23, 2012.

38. Interview with Anahi Moya, January 31, 2012.

CHAPTER 7. SELECTIVE MEMORY AND ITS LESSONS

1. Ellen Kennedy, "Pope Must Retract Rehabilitation of Bishop Williamson," MinnPost, February 10, 2009.

2. Horacio Verbitsky, "Su ruta," *Página 12*, February 19, 2009.

3. "Final Report of the International Commission on the Holocaust in Romania," November 11, 2004, 2, https://www.ushmm.org/m/pdfs/20080226-romania-commis sion-postwar.pdf.

4. "Final Report of the International Commission on the Holocaust in Romania," 3.

5. "Final Report of the International Commission on the Holocaust in Romania," 3.

6. "Final Report of the International Commission on the Holocaust in Romania," 45–46.

7. Michael Whine, "Expanding Holocaust Denial and Legislation Against It," *Jewish Political Studies Review* 20, nos. 1–2 (Spring 2008): 63.

8. German Criminal Code, published on November 13, 1998 (Federal Law Gazette I, p. 3322), as last amended by Article 2 of the Act of June 19, 2019 (Federal Law Gazette I, p. 844), https://www.gesetze-im-internet.de/englisch_stgb/englisch_stgb.html.

9. Article 261a of the Constitution of the Czech Republic was amended on December 16, 1992. Whine, "Expanding Holocaust Denial and Legislation against It," 62.

10. Interview with Karl Bohmer, October 28, 2010.

11. Paragraph 175 of the German Penal Code that criminalizes homosexuality, in force until 1994, had been expanded in 1935 by the Nazi regime. An estimated fifty thousand homosexual men were arrested by Nazis, of whom between five thousand and fifteen thousand were held in concentration camps.

12. Interview with Alejandra Morales Stekel, January 5, 2012.

13. Miguel Otero was appointed Chile's ambassador to Argentina during the first term of President Sebastian Piñera, member of the right-wing Renovación Nacional, of which Otero was a founder. Otero was a member of the dictatorship's legislative commission, an entity that operated in place of Congress that had been shut down by the military junta and that drafted and issued de facto laws.

14. All quotes of Elizabeth Lira are from the author's interview with her on January 21, 2011. The National Truth and Reconciliation Commission (1990–91) and the National Commission on Political Imprisonment and Torture (2004 and 2010–11) are commonly known as the Rettig and Valech commissions, respectively, in reference to the individuals who presided over them, the attorney Raúl Rettig and Bishop Sergio Valech.

15. On July 7, 2016, Juan Emilio Cheyre was indicted as accomplice in fifteen murders committed by the Caravan of Death in La Serena. In February 2019, he and other army officers were indicted for the torture of twenty-four persons, surviving political prisoners. *El Mostrador*, February 7, 2019.

16. Maxine Lowy, "Poder judicial bajo dictadura," 1998, www.DerechosChile.com.

17. Associated Press, "Cambian 'dictadura' por 'régimen militar' en textos escolares en Chile," *La Nación*, January 4, 2011.

18. Agrupación de Familiares de Detenidos Desaparecidos, "No es lo mismo Juana que Chana" (press release, Santiago, January 5, 2012).

19. Interview with Elizabeth Lira, January 21, 2011.

20. "Final Report of the International Commission on the Holocaust in Romania," 16–17.

21. Nicolae Minei, preface to *Zile însîngerate la Iași (28–30 iunie 1941)*, by Aurel Karețki and Maria Covaci (Bucharest: Editura Politică, 1978), 25, quoted in "Final Report of the International Commission on the Holocaust in Romania," 14n48.

22. Gheorghe Zaharia and Ion Cupșa, *Participarea României la înfrângerea Germaniei naziste* (Bucharest: Editura Politică, 1985), 53, quoted in "Final Report of the International Commission on the Holocaust in Romania," 14.

23. "The Responsibility of Knowledge: Developing Holocaust Education for the Third Generation," *Humanity in Action*, 2005, https://www.humanityinaction.org/knowledge_detail/the-responsibility-of-knowledge-developing-holocaust-education-for-the-third-generation.

24. Interview with Marcela Tchimino, January 30, 2012.

25. Abraham Magendzo, "La enseñanza del Holocausto en la escuela," *Educar-Chile*, August 28, 2007.

26. Interview with Verónica Romo, August 2005; Maxine Lowy, "Educación en Derechos Humanos," *Noticias Aliadas* 19, no. 2 (2005).

27. Interview with Patricio Oyarzun, August 2005.

28. Interview with Jaime Prea, August 2005.

29. María Isabel Toledo and Abraham Magendzo, "Régimen militar y transición a la democracia," *Estudios Pedagógicos* 34, no.1 (2009): 152–53.

30. Interview with María Eva Bustos, July 31, 2013.

31. Interview with Miguel Orellana Benado, August 26, 2013.

32. Daniel Feierstein, *El genocidio como práctica social: Entre el nazismo y la experiencia argentina* (Buenos Aires: Fondo de Cultura Económica, 2011), 151.

33. Interview with Marcela Tchimino, January 30, 2012.

34. Interview with Paz Rojas, June 21, 2013.

35. Paz Rojas Baeza, *La interminable ausencia* (Santiago: LOM, 2009), 115.

36. Eric Domergue, "Noche y niebla," *Espacios para la verdad, la justicia y la memoria*, no. 2 (September 2009): 14–15.

37. Office of the United States, Chief Counsel for Prosecution of Axis Criminality, *Nazi Conspiracy and Aggression*, vol. 2 (Washington, DC: US Government Printing Office, 1946), 533–34.

38. "The Holocaust: A Learning Site for Students," United States Holocaust Memorial Museum, https://encyclopedia.ushmm.org/content/en/project/the-holocaust-a-learning-site-for-students.

39. Rojas, *La interminable ausencia*, 54.

40. Interview with Silvana Veto, November 2, 2010.

41. Interview with Edith Benado, September 2, 2009.

42. Interview with Lelia Pérez, October 28, 2009.

43. Interview with Frida Sharim, November 23, 2009.

44. Interview with Sara Sharim, November 12, 2009.

45. Interview with Edmundo Lebrecht, February 2, 2010.

46. Interview with Edmundo Lebrecht, February 4, 2010.

47. Interview with Miguel Lawner, February 17, 2010.

48. In 2018, Lawner published *La vida a pesar de todo* (Santiago de Chile: LOM Ediciones), a collection of his drawings, accompanied by texts, that chronicle life in the Isla Dawson, Ritoque, and Tres Alamos concentration camps during the two years he was imprisoned.

49. Luis Vega Contreras, *La caída de Allende: Anatomía de un golpe de estado* (Jerusalem: Semana Publicaciones, 1983).

Chapter 8. Paths to Healing through Memory and Justice

1. Alexander Litsauer and Barbara Litsauer, *Vecinos perdidos: Emigración judía desde el Danubio al Río de la Plata* (Buenos Aires: Ediciones Continente, 2011), 194.

2. Interview with Jonathan Karszenbaum, January 29, 2013.

3. Jewish population in Europe in 1933, population data by country, *Holocaust Encyclopedia*, United States Holocaust Museum, accessed August 18, 2021, www.ency clopedia.ushmm.org.

4. The expression comes from a biblical passage (Ezra 9:14–15).

5. She'erit HaPleitah of Metropolitan Chicago, "The History of She'erit HaPlei tah of Metropolitan Chicago," accessed August 18, 2021, https://sheerithapleitah.com/ sample-page/the-history-of-sheerit-hapleitah-of-metropolitan-chicago/.

6. The yahrzeit is the anniversary of a death, a date on which each Jew remembers close family members by lighting a twenty-four-hour candle and reciting kaddish, the mourning prayer, at the synagogue.

7. Interview with Jonathan Karszenbaum, January 29, 2013. In 2016, Karszen-baum was appointed executive director of the Holocaust Museum of Buenos Aires.

8. Paz Rojas, *La interminable ausencia* (Santiago: LOM, 2009), 102.

9. Interview with Carmen Hertz, April 20, 2010.

10. Conversation with Ernesto Lejderman and Jonathan Karszenbaum, July 8, 2013.

11. Conversation with Ernesto Lejderman and Jonathan Karszenbaum, July 8, 2013.

12. Conversation with Marcela Godoy, October 26, 2012.

13. Interview with Tomás Hirsch, August 24, 2011. In 2018, Hirsch was elected to Congress.

14. "Mi vida con Carlos, el exitoso documental chileno," January 15, 2012, www .urbanbox.cl.

15. Elie Wiesel, *One Generation After* (New York: Random House, 1972), 13.

16. Interview with Carmen Hertz, October 24, 2012.

17. Interview with Julio Laks, May 9, 2012.

18. Interview with Gladys Díaz, March 28, 2012.

19. Interview with Lelia Pérez, May 10, 2011.

20. Gustavo Ehijo M. and Gunter Seelmann E., *Te recordamos Quiriquina* (Santi-ago: CESOC, 2003), 18.

21. Interview with Gunter Seelmann, September 5, 2012.

22. Szymon Laks, *Music of Another World* (Evanston, IL: Northwestern University Press, 2000), 5.

23. Laks, Music of Another World, 78–79.

24. Rojas, *La interminable ausencia*, 26.

25. Interview with Simón Guendelman, August 13, 2011.

26. Raúl Rettig, *Informe de la Comisión Nacional de Verdad y Reconciliación*, 2nd ed., vol. 1 (Santiago: Comisión Nacional de Verdad y Reconciliación, 1996), 101.

27. *New York Times*, July 1976.

28. Indictment, Operación Colombo episode, victim Luis Alberto Guendelman Wisniak, Santiago Court of Appeals, August 31, 2009.

29. See Operation: Last Chance, www.operationlastchance.org.

30. Maxine Lowy, "Educando a los jueces en derecho internacional," July 8, 2004, www.memoriayjusticia.cl.

31. Interview with Carmen Hertz, April 20, 2010.

32. Extract of speech given by Germán Berger at the funeral of his father, Carlos Berger, on April 13, 2014, at Santiago Cemetery.

33. Interview with Corina Rosenfeld, December 5, 2011.

34. Interview with Patricio Bustos, December 21, 2011.

35. Interview with Jenny Stoulman, January 13, 2014.

36. "Homenaje a los Desaparecidos y Ejecutados durante el Régimen Militar" (brochure, Centro Progresista Judío, Santiago, 1996).

37. Interview with Denni Traubmann, December 10, 2013.

38. Interview with Alejandro Guendelman, December 16, 2013.

39. Interview with Ilán Sandberg, December 10, 2013.

40. Interview with Jenny Stoulman, January 13, 2014.

41. For further analysis, see Valeria Navarro-Rosenblatt, "Del silencio a la memoria dividida: Los memoriales para los detenidos judíos en Chile," *Cuadernos Judaicos* 35 (2018): 183–98.

CHAPTER 9. IN EVERY GENERATION

1. Interviews with Edmundo Lebrecht, February 2 and 4, 2010. Edmundo died on August 29, 2013.

2. Interview with Hanni Grunpeter, August 8, 2012.

3. Interview with Hanni Grunpeter, August 13, 2012.

4. Interview with Gabriela Villalobos, February 8, 2012.

5. Interviews with Gregory Cohen, October 29, 2013, and March 18, 2014.

6. "Jacob Henry Schiff," Jewish Virtual Library, American-Israeli Cooperative Enterprise, https://www.jewishvirtuallibrary.org/jacob-henry-schiff.

7. "Generaciones de la Shoá y Sherit Hapleita: Resistir y sobrevivir," *Cuadernos de la Shoá*, no. 3 (September 2012).

8. Interview with Catalina Navarro, November 29, 2012.

9. Patricia Politzer, Passover community celebration, Ruaj Ami synagogue, Santiago, April 15, 2014.

10. Funa, derived from the Mapuche people's language, means something "rotten," or about to go to waste. It has become a term more widely used in Chile that denotes an exposé of something or someone who is rejected.

11. Patricia Politzer, Passover community celebration, Ruaj Ami synagogue, Santiago, April 15, 2014.

12. Interviews with Felipe Arriagada, January 24, 2012, and Carlos Arriagada, August 24, 2012.

13. Interview with Ernesto Lejderman, January 30, 2013.

14. Interview with Arturo Barrios, September 30, 2014.

15. ORT is the acronym of the Russian name of a Jewish vocational institution, Obshchestvo Remeslenava Truda, founded in 1880 in Russia, that today has offices in sixty countries.

16. Photograph analysis by Argentinian visual artist and photographer Nora Aslan and Chilean historian Paulina Orrego.

INDEX

Note: Page numbers in *italics* refer to the illustrations.

collaboration: between Chilean and Argentine intelligence, 83, 126–32 (*see also* Operation Condor); with military dictatorship, Rabbi Kreiman and, 57–58
collective blame, 140
Colombia Embassy, 82
Colonia Dignidad (Nazi colony), 96, 120–24
Comando Conjunto (death squad), 113
Comisión de Solidaridad con Familiares de Desaparecidos en Argentina, 270n56
Comisión Mixta Colectiva Ampliada (Community-Wide Mixed Commission), 45
Comité de Cooperación para la Paz (Committee of Cooperation for Peace in Chile). *See* Propeace Committee
Comité de Protección a los Inmigrantes Israelitas (Israelite Immigrant Protection Committee), 24
Comité Representativo de Entidades Judías de Chile (Jewish Representative Committee). *See* CREJ
commemorative events, 174, 209, 232–38, 242. *See also* remembrance
Commission on the Holocaust in Romania, 183–84
Committee of Cooperation for Peace in Chile (Comité de Cooperación para la Paz). *See* Propeace Committee
Committee of Solidarity with Chile, 219
Communist Party, 34–35, 60–61, 85, 92–94, 99–104, 110–14, 229, 233, 270n53; banning of (1948), 269n26; party financing, 100–103
communists, 60–61; Jewish, 109–14
Communist Youth Organization, 247
comparative trivialization, 177–78
concentration camps. *See names of camps*
Concepción, Chile, 56, 62–63, 134, 159–60
Concepción regional stadium (prison), 86

Concha, Julia, 125
Concha, Luis, 125, 131
Constanzo, Sgt. Belarmino, 55
Contreras, Manuel, 52, 103, 112
Contulmo, Chile, 16, 25, 194
Convention against Torture and Other Cruel, Inhumane or Degrading Treatment and Punishment, 222
Copiapo, Chile, 223
CORFO (Corporación de Fomento de la Producción de Chile; Economic Development Agency), 92, 195
corpses, "discovery" of, as coverup, 128–32
Correa, Enrique, 100, 103–4, 268n25
Correa, Orlando, 86
Cossacks, Russian, 116
Costa Rica, 81
CPJ (Centro Progresista Judío; Jewish Progressive Center), 77, 232–33, 237; "Remembering Anne Frank and Diana Aron" (commemorative event), 174, 233
CREJ (Comité Representativo de Entidades Judías de Chile; Jewish Representative Committee), 36, 38–39, 59, 96, 161–62; neutral position of, 43–47
crimes against humanity, 223
Cuatro Alamos (detention/torture center), 54–55, 108, 111, 129, 148, 193, 209, 239, 269n39, 271n61
Cuevas, Fernando, 193
cultural resistance, 113, 248–51
Cupşa, Ion, 184
CUT (Central Unitaria de Trabajadores; Chilean Federation of Workers), 172
Cuthbert, Sofia, 82–83, 126–27, 268n18

Dachau (Nazi death camp), 228
Dawson Island (prison), 195–98, 275n48
death squad. *See* Caravan of Death
deflection, as tactic of negationism, 179
del Campo, Samuel, 271n9
del Castillo Pichardo, José, 106
democratic transition, 47

Lejderman, Elisa, 256
Lejderman, Enrique, 256–57
Lejderman, Ernesto, 202–3, 256–58
Lejderman, Hanna, 258
Lejderman, Hersz León, 255
Lemkin, Raphael, 221
lenient sentencing, for perpetrators of
human rights crimes, 5
Leonidas Díaz, Elizabeth (child victim),
167
Lerner, Michael, 4
Letelier, Orlando, 46, 217, 265n31, 268n18
*Let's Learn about the Value of Life, Non-
discrimination, and Peace from the
Holocaust* (CD-ROM), 185
letter-writing campaigns, on behalf of
victims, 217–19
Levi, Primo, 140, 164, 188–90
Levy, Enrique Assael, 40
Levy, Robert, 42–43, 161–62
Lewin, Heiner, 212–13
liberation theology, 10
Lihn, Enrique, 248
Lipovetzky, Raquel, 92–93, 98
Lipschutz, Alejandro, 67
Lira, Elizabeth, 180, 183
lists: of disappeared and summarily
executed people, 78, 127; "list of 119,"
127, 130–32, 148, 270n58; of survivors,
89
Llidó, Antonio, 207–9
Loew (a Jew of Ulm), 15
López, Haydée, 154
López Stewart, María Cristina, 55, 207
Lorca, Carlos, 228
Lorca, Raul, 228
Los 80 (TV series), 250
l passports, 152
Luft, David, 40

Maas, Ulrich, 220
Macedonian Israelite Center of Temuco,
23
Magendzo, Abraham, 185
Maldavsky, David, 70

Maldavsky, Miguel, 37
Malik, G. J., 150
Man, Isle of, 19–20
Mandler, Yael, 77–78
Manuel de Salas (high school), 151
Manuel Rodríguez Patriotic Front,
272n20
MAPAM (Mifleget HaPoalim
HaMeuhedet; United Workers Party),
36–37
Mapuche (indigenous people), 25–26,
40, 83–86, 209
marginalization, feelings of, 133–37
Marmicoc (kitchenware factory), 41
Martínez, Rosalía, 207, 209, 271n61
Martínez de Perón, Maria Estela, presi-
dent of Argentina, 126
maskilim, 14
Matamala, Carlos, 248
Mateluna, Eva, 155–56
Matta, Roberto, 110, 113, 269n38
Matus, Carlos, 195–96
Max Nordau Instruction and Benefi-
cence Society of Valparaíso, 23
Megacausa No. 14, 270n54
Meiser, Otto, 145
Melo, Rolando, 90
Memoria Viva Foundation, 178, 184
memory, as foundation of Jewish tradi-
tion, 77–78
memory stones, Jewish ritual of, 174–75.
See also remembrance, practices of
Mendoza, Alicia de, 45
Mendoza, César, 45
Mercaz (synagogue). *See* Círculo Israelita
de Santiago
Merino, Marcia, 119
Meschkat, Klaus, 106
Metropolitan University of Educational
Sciences ("El Pedagógico"), 266n39
Meyer, Rabbi Marshall, 52–53
"military pronouncement," use of term,
181–82
military service, for Jews in czarist
Russia, 11–12